Breaking Out
of the Box

Related books of interest

Social Work Field Directors: Foundations for Excellence
Cindy A. Hunter, Julia K. Moen, and Miriam Raskin

Navigating Human Service Organizations, Third Edition
Rich Furman and Margaret Gibelman

Modern Social Work Theory, Fourth Edition
Malcolm Payne

Essential Skills of Social Work Practice: Assessment, Intervention, Evaluation, Second Edition
Thomas O'Hare

Straight Talk about Professional Ethics, Second Edition
Kim Strom-Gottfried

An Experimental Approach to Group Work, Second Edition
Rich Furman, Kimberly Bender, and Diana Rowan

A Hands-On Manual for Social Work Research
Amy Catherine Russell

Writing Clearly for Clients and Colleagues: The Human Service Practitioner's Guide
Natalie Ames and Katy FitzGerald

Social Service Workplace Bullying: A Betrayal of Good Intentions
Kathryn Brohl

Rural Social Work in the 21st Century
Michael R. Daley

Breaking Out of the Box

Adventure-Based Field Instruction

Third Edition

Kelly Ward
Robin Sakina Mama
Monmouth University
School of Social Work

OXFORD
UNIVERSITY PRESS

OXFORD
UNIVERSITY PRESS

Oxford University Press is a department of the University of Oxford.
It furthers the University's objective of excellence in research, scholarship,
and education by publishing worldwide.

Oxford   New York
Auckland   Cape Town   Dar es Salaam   Hong Kong   Karachi
Kuala Lumpur   Madrid   Melbourne   Mexico City   Nairobi
New Delhi   Shanghai   Taipei   Toronto

With offices in
Argentina   Austria   Brazil   Chile   Czech Republic   France   Greece
Guatemala   Hungary   Italy   Japan   Poland   Portugal   Singapore
South Korea   Switzerland   Thailand   Turkey   Ukraine   Vietnam

Oxford is a registered trade mark of Oxford University Press
in the UK and certain other countries.

Published in the United States of America by
Oxford University Press
198 Madison Avenue, New York, NY 10016

Library of Congress Cataloging-in-Publication Data

Ward, Kelly, LCSW, 1962–
   Breaking out of the box :
   adventure-based field instruction / Kelly Ward, PhD, MSW, Monmouth
University, Robin Sakina Mama, PhD, MLSP, MSS, Monmouth University.
      —3rd ed.
      p. cm.
   ISBN 978-0-19-061561-0 (pbk. : alk. paper)
   1. Social service–Fieldwork. I. Mama, Robin S. II. Title.
   HV11.W354 2016
   361.3—dc22

                                                            2015006936

Some exercises were originally printed in the books below. Reprinted with permission.
Rohnke, K. (1984). *Silver bullets*. Beverly, MA: Wilkscraft Creative Printing.
Rohnke, K. (1988). *The bottomless bag*.Dubuque, IA: Kendall/Hunt Publishing Company.
Rohnke, K. (1984). *Cowtails and cobras II*.Dubuque, IA: Kendall/Hunt Publishing Company.
Sikes, S. (1995). *Feeding the zircon gorilla*. Tulsa, OK: Learning Unlimited Corporation.

In the spirit of the authors' experiential approach to field practice, noted artist
Richard Hull has created a cover that portrays both the social worker's journey and
the shattering of expectations. With geometric planes in ecstatic colors, Hull illustrates
the ordered chaos of fieldwork using variable textures and an "endless box" motif
that appears frequently in his work.

ISBN 978-0-19-061561-0

9 8 7 6 5 4 3

Printed in Canada.

*To Bob for your time and support around
this project over the years.*

*To Saifuddin, Aziz, and Zahabya for
all your encouragement and support.*

*To our students at Monmouth University
in the BSW program who tested the exercises
and the text for us over the years.*

Contents

Welcome to the Field

This book will probably seem unconventional to you at first. In fact, some of the activities that you will be asked to participate in will not immediately seem relevant and may even seem strange. We have been using these activities in our social work field classes for well over a decade. We have found that students understand the objectives and enjoy learning the points that we try to make in each exercise.

As students, you will find your readings for class will be on a particular topic, such as trust and developing relationships. While you are reading, your teacher is preparing an adventure-based or experiential educational exercise. The exercise relates to your readings, but more importantly relates to events or the process of being in your field internship. The goal of each exercise is to provide you with a different perspective to use in your field placement.

We request that you be open-minded to this teaching method and think "outside the box"—step outside of your comfort zone. If you can do that, most, if not all, of you in this class will have fun using the exercises while learning valuable skills for your practice in social work.

In this 3rd edition, we have added more features. Besides the integration of other curriculum areas, end of chapter exercises, and "thoughts to ponder" boxes, which were already part of the book, we have now made the following changes:

- ✔ suggestions for the 2015 EPAS covered by sections of the chapters
- ✔ macro practice content added to every chapter (as we see macro practice as generalist practice)
- ✔ new human rights and social justice content
- ✔ gender neutral language
- ✔ social media issues addressed
- ✔ information about learning styles
- ✔ guidelines for talking to and writing about clients
- ✔ updated psychosocial and process recording models
- ✔ a home visit checklist
- ✔ updated guidelines for safety while out in the field

2015 Educational Policy and Accreditation Standards (EPAS)

1. Demonstrate ethical and professional behavior.
   1a. Make ethical decisions by applying the standards of the NASW Code of Ethics, relevant laws regulations, models for ethical decision making, ethical conduct of research, and additional codes of ethics as appropriate to context.
   1b. Use reflection and self-regulation to manage personal values and maintain professionalism in practice situations.
   1c. Demonstrate professional demeanor in behavior, appearance, and oral, written, and electronic communication.
   1d. Use technology ethically and appropriately to facilitate practice outcomes.
   1e. Use supervision and consultation to guide professional judgment and behavior.
2. Engage diversity and difference in practice.
   2a. Apply and communicate understanding of the importance of diversity and difference in shaping life experiences in practice at the micro, mezzo, and macro levels.
   2b. Present themselves as learners and engage clients and constituencies as experts of their own experiences
   2c. Apply self-awareness and self-regulation to manage the influence of personal biases and values in working with diverse clients and constituencies.
3. Advance human rights and social, economic, and environmental justice.
   3a. Apply their understanding of social, economic, and environmental justice to advocate for human rights at the individual and system levels.
   3b. Engage in practices that advance social, economic, and environmental justice.
4. Engage in practice-informed research and research-informed practice.
   4a. Use practice experience and theory to inform scientific inquiry and research.
   4b. Apply critical thinking to engage in analysis of quantitative and qualitative methods and research findings.
   4c. Use and translate research evidence to inform and improve practice, policy, and service delivery.
5. Engage in policy practice.
   5a. Identify social policy at the local, state, and federal level that impacts well-being, service delivery, and access to social services.

5b. Assess how social welfare and economic policies impact the delivery of and access to social services.

5c. Apply critical thinking to analyze, formulate, and advocate for policies that advance human rights and social, economic, and environmental justice.

6. Engage with individuals, families, groups, organizations, and communities.

6a. Apply knowledge of human behavior and the social environment, person-in-environment, and other multidisciplinary theoretical frameworks to engage with clients and constituencies.

6b. Use empathy, reflection, and interpersonal skills to effectively engage diverse clients and constituencies.

7. Assess individuals, families, groups, organizations, and communities.

7a. Collect and organize data and apply critical thinking to interpret information from clients and constituencies.

7b. Apply knowledge of human behavior and the social environment, person-in-environment, and other multidisciplinary theoretical frameworks in the analysis of assessment data from clients and constituencies.

7c. Develop mutually agreed-on intervention goals and objectives based on the critical assessment of strengths, needs, and challenges within clients and constituencies.

7d. Select appropriate intervention strategies based on the assessment, research knowledge, and values and preferences of clients and constituencies.

8. Intervene with individuals, families, groups, organizations, and communities.

8a. Critically choose and implement interventions to achieve practice goals and enhance capacities of clients and constituencies.

8b. Apply knowledge of human behavior and the social environment, person-in-environment, and other multidisciplinary theoretical frameworks in interventions with clients and constituencies.

8c. Use interprofessional collaboration as appropriate to achieve beneficial practice outcomes.

8d. Negotiate, mediate, and advocate with and on behalf of clients and constituencies.

8e. Facilitate effective transitions and endings that advance mutually agreed-on goals.

9. Evaluate practice with individuals, families, groups, organizations, and communities.

9a. Select and use appropriate methods for evaluation of outcomes.

9b. Apply knowledge of human behavior and the social environment, person-in-environment, and other multidisciplinary theoretical frameworks in the evaluation of outcomes.

9c. Critically analyze, monitor, and evaluate intervention and program processes and outcomes.

9d. Apply evaluation findings to improve practice effectiveness at the micro, mezzo, and macro levels.

EPAS by Chapter

Chapter 1
Getting Started

Orientation to the Field and to the Profession of Social Work

When first entering any field internship, you are certainly hesitant. You know what you would like to happen—a positive and fun learning experience where you finally get to practice your social work skills and knowledge. However, you are nervous and apprehensive about what will really happen. You have probably already interviewed with your supervisor and have some idea of which population the agency serves and what services it provides. Nevertheless, your role and the development of relationships are unknown entities at this point. Please note we will use the word agency throughout the book to refer to this as the place of your internship. Some of you will be in hospital settings, schools, or NGOs. This was the best "generic" term we could ascribe here. Also the words internship, placement, and practicum are used interchangeably.

Before you begin, take a look at the National Association of Social Workers (NASW) Code of Ethics, specifically the preamble. (The code appears in appendix A.) The preamble provides a foundation for social work practice. It speaks about the mission of social work and our belief in social justice and social change, and it clearly describes our core values in social work practice. Each core value has an ethical principle that enhances our understanding of that value.

Value: Service
Ethical Principle: Social workers' primary goal is to help people in need and to address social problems.

Value: Social Justice
Ethical Principle: Social workers challenge social injustice.

Value: Dignity and Worth of the Person
Ethical Principle: Social workers respect the inherent dignity and worth of the person.

Value: Importance of Human Relationships
Ethical Principle: Social workers recognize the central importance of human relationships.

Value: Integrity
Ethical Principle: Social workers behave in a trustworthy manner.

Value: Competence
Ethical Principle: Social workers practice within their areas of competence and develop and enhance their professional expertise.

These core values and ethical principles will guide you over the course of your social work career. They will also help you tremendously as you begin to engage in your field internship. Throughout this book the NASW Code of Ethics will be highlighted and discussed. This is your time to get to know your Code of Ethics well.

For those of you in Canada, our friendly neighbor to the north, there is a Code of Ethics written by the Canadian Association of Social Workers (CASW) designed to be consistent with the International Federation of Social Workers' Declaration of Ethical Principles of Social Work. Along with that document CASW has also created the Guidelines for Ethical Practice. Both of these documents are available online and in appendixes B and C, respectively. The Code with the Guidelines and the NASW Code of Ethics are similar and we will delineate the differences and reference the appropriate documents when we discuss ethics throughout the book.

The Canadian Code of Ethics also has six values. In the Canadian Code, each value has multiple principles, unlike the NASW code, which lists just one. It is most important to recognize the similarities between the two. The only difference is that CASW's values include confidentiality and NASW's code includes the importance of human relationships. This does not mean that either code is right or wrong or that either country does not value confidentiality or human relationships. Rather you should begin to see how similar the profession is no matter where you decide to establish your career. The values for the CASW are (1) respect for the inherent dignity and worth of persons, (2) pursuit of social justice, (3) service to humanity, (4) integrity of professional practice, (5) confidentiality in professional practice, and (6) competence in professional practice.

The Canadian Code of Ethics ends after the values, and the second document, the Guidelines for Ethical Practice, mirrors the section in the NASW Code of Ethics called "Ethical Practice."

Orientation to Your Internship

You have your work cut out for you in the first few weeks, which is primarily your orientation time. Orientation includes time to adjust to the agency, your role, your colleagues, and your clients. Give yourself time to get oriented to the agency and your assignments. Often your supervisor will have you read the agency policy handbook. It may seem boring and a waste of time, but it will be useful later and is a standard and usual practice for any new employee. Any additional training required of new employees is useful as well. Although the odds are that you are not getting paid for your internship, you are expected to perform like an employee. Use the first few weeks of supervision to discuss questions about the agency and your role while an intern. At this point, you are developing a *relationship* with your agency and your supervisor.

In this time of orientation, your goal is to get familiar with your agency's general mission, who it serves, and how it functions. This includes getting to know your supervisor, other employees, and clients. At the same time, you are beginning a new semester at school, getting familiar with the expectations of your professors, and working with fellow students to complete the objectives of this class. It is a challenge to start and develop so many relationships. So how will you approach the task? What will you do first?

For those of you who have worked in the field of social work already, but without the actual degree, you have some advantages. You understand the community resources and know much of the terminology, and this can be a huge advantage. It also can bring some challenges both in the classroom and in the field. Be open to learning different techniques and ways of achieving the same goal than you already think you know. It is important for all students to be open to the feedback they will get from their supervisors and instructors. This is even more true for the experienced students. Stay open, don't get defensive. For those of you doing your internship at your place of employment, be sure to advocate that you are doing different tasks and skills to really benefit from the experience. Try to keep those two roles separate. Finally, as students you will have multiple internships. For everyone, but especially for those of you doing your internship at a place of employment, try to change to a different internship for the next placement you have. The more varied your placements and supervisors, the more well rounded you become as a social worker and the better your résumé looks.

Finally, be sure that if your school has a student handbook for the social work program, you read it and adhere to the policies developed by your program. Rarely if ever will they conflict with your agency. If they do, bring that to the attention of your field director as soon as possible. Following those expectations will allow you to have a more positive experience as a student.

The Agency Routine

Early on in your internship you will need to become familiar with the agency's daily routine. How do people speak to each other—do they use first names? How does the day begin—with a team meeting, with coffee? Are there agency rituals you need to be aware of? For example, are birthdays or holidays celebrated? Do they socialize together? If so, do you join in or not? More later.

Why is this important? First, you want to be able to observe how the agency is structured and administered. The atmosphere of the agency envelops its clients, consumers, board members, and staff and affects the provision of services. Second, you want to become part of the team and find your fit quickly while you are an intern.

Getting Involved in Office Politics

You should observe and be part of the agency routine. Having said that, be cautious about office politics. What are office politics? It is the behind the scene background noise that interrupts the workflow. This includes gossiping, commenting unofficially, critiquing a coworker's performance, or making snide comments about the supervisor. Every office has it, and all too often student interns get pulled into them. For the sake of your professional development, you must avoid getting involved in office politics. How do you do this?

Make it a point to talk to everyone. Don't listen to and certainly don't participate in gossip. Be careful about giving advice or opinions regarding staff issues (unless asked specifically by your supervisor). Do your best to stay neutral. Another way to avoid office politics is to keep your professional and personal life separate. Try not to be friends with coworkers and by all means avoid dating someone at your internship. At the beginning of the internship, if asked to socialize with your colleagues outside of a work function, it is safer to say no for now. Once you get the lay of the land it may become clear to you that it may be OK to consider socializing much later on in your internship.

Do observe the office politics and learn from them. You can discover many good and bad ways to administer and/or to be a positive colleague and run an agency just by watching.

Safety in the Field

Safety in the workplace is a topic of serious concern and is one that you need to think about also in your field internship. The Bureau of Labor Statistics in 2007 estimated that 61 percent of all nonfatal injuries from assaults involving violent acts occurred in health care and in social services. We have all heard or read stories in the media of social workers who have been fatally wounded on their job by their clients. While we do not want to stereotype clients as dangerous, we would be remiss if we did not cover this topic.

Violence in the workplace has increased over the years, and social workers are not immune to it. There are a number of external, environmental factors that have increased the risk of violence to social workers as they attempt to carry out their work. Some of these include:

- The prevalence of handguns and other weapons among the general public, and hence sometimes in the hands of clients, their family, or their friends

- The increasing use of hospital emergency rooms for the care of individuals who may be in acure distress or who may have violent tendencies

- The increasing presence of gangs

- Low staffing levels and the increasing use of the home visit

- Poor economic stability for the individuals and families with no realistic alternatives that can be sought

Taking safeguards does not mean that you disrespect your clients or that you are judging them. Rather, you are taking precautions and helping prevent potential harm from occurring for all concerned. The key is to be aware and to be pre-pared to ensure your safety and, in the end, your client's safety as well.

A number of recommendations are going to be made here. In addition, you should check the following:

1. NASW Guidelines on Social Worker Safety in the Workplace, https://www .socialworkers.org/practice/naswstandards/safetystandards2013.pdf

2. Guidelines for Preventing Workplace Violence for Health Care and Social Service Workers, US Department of Labor, OSHA 3148-01R, 2004

3. Children's Services Practice Notes on "A Look at Safety in Social Work," http://www.practicenotes.org/vol3_no2.htm

Automobiles

When taking your own car into the field, be sure not to leave any confidential material in the car, in case it is stolen. If you are on the way to a home visit, take the file in with you (if it is permitted to leave the office). If your agency is now using electronic means to track clients, you will then bring in your I-pad, tablet, or whatever system is currently being used. Use your trunk for any other mate-rial that does not need to go into the house with you. Anything that you will put in the trunk should be put in the trunk prior to going out in the field. Preferably, what you should be taking into the house is the file, note paper, a pen (or your computer or tablet if your agency allows those out of the office), your cell phone (if you have one), and nothing else, including your purse, if applicable, and coat.

Find out what your agency expects about driving clients in your personal car. Larger agencies will have agency vehicles and will tell you not to drive clients in your car and then should cover insurance for students to drive agency vehicles. Other agencies will have policies that permit taking clients in your car. Read your student handbook or ask your field instructor what your program's policy is before committing to the agency about driving any vehicle with a client in it. Find out from the agency about liability insurance (both for accidents and personal injury) when your passenger is a client in your car or in the agency vehicle. Using your car for professional use can add enormous premiums to your personal insurance. Always check with your own automobile insurance company as well. However, sometimes the agency policy will cover you during work. Find out and make a decision based on your situation and your individual driving record. Hopefully your supervisor asked you some of these questions in your preplace-ment interview.

When you are going out in your car for an appointment, with or without a client, make sure someone in your agency knows where you are going and your approx-imate return time. Keep in touch as plans change, so that someone besides you knows where you are. Carry a fully charged cell phone with you if you have one and activate your GPS chip in your cell phone so they can find you if you are out of contact too long. If you don't have your own cell phone, perhaps the agency has one to use while you're out of the office on agency business. Even if you carry a phone, take change or a calling card with you. You never know when you may run out of batteries or are in an area where you can't get a signal. Although pay phones are becoming obsolete, they are not impossible to find. Rural social workers may need to use a client's or a neighbor's phone; a calling card will come in very handy. Discuss with your supervisor issues with cell phone coverage. Develop a plan for how to handle travel to areas where your cell phone does not have good reception. You can always seek a local police or fire deparment as well, should you need a place to make a phone call. Always park in a well-lit area, and check the back of the car before getting in it just in case. Of course it goes without saying to follow all traffic laws in the areas that you are traveling.

Home Visits

There are many practice areas in social work that would have you making appointments or dropping in unannounced at your client's home. Child welfare, adult protective services, hospice, home therapy, and school social work are all examples of social work that is frequently done in the client's residence.

Home visits are designed to see the client in their own environment and assess their living conditions as well as their safety—these are two of the more important aspects of the visit. You want to make the visit as easy as possible for the people who live in the home. The less your clients need to worry about you, the easier it is for you to do your job. As you don't know what condition the house is in, the less you carry in, the less likely you are to carry out insects or stains from furniture. Before we go any further, while we are about to talk about more safety issues, we want to remind you again not to overreact and be fearful of home visits or the people who live in the homes. We just point out precautions so that you are aware of basic personal safety skills. Also remember this is not a social visit, though you are a guest in your client's home and should act as such. However, it is best to get in and get out as quickly as possible. Declining any food or drink is advisable, but in some cultures it would be an insult to refuse. Be sure to bring this up in class if you will be doing home visits.

Before arriving at a house discuss the neighborhood with your supervisor. Pay attention to traffic patterns and be aware of the exits and entrances to the buildings you enter. View your surroundings and observe exits. Night visits should be avoided; if they are necessary, please use a buddy system.

When you arrive at a client's house be sure to identify yourself by name and agency. Show ID if you have one. Ask the client if you can enter their home to complete your task. Tell them what your task is and how long you expect it to take. Find out who else is currently in the home and have the client lead you into the home, with you following them on any stairs and in hallways. Following them allows you to make a quick exit or assures you they cannot use a weapon that you don't see coming. Suggest to the client that you meet in a common living area such as a dining room or a living room. Try to avoid meeting in a bedroom as that is the most common area where people keep guns; similarly, avoiding meetings in the bedroom limits any allegations of sexual impropriety. Conducting lengthy interviews in the bedroom ought to be avoided, but a question or two about the room or who sleeps there is acceptable. Another room to avoid is the kitchen because of the access to knives or other weapons.

If you work for a child protective services department, you may be required to view all rooms in the house including where children sleep. You should always follow the protocol set forth by your agency and purpose surrounding which rooms in the home need to be observed. A sample checklist for home visits is in appendix G. Many agencies will require you to go on home visits with a coworker. If there is a policy like that, follow the policy and find out the reason it is in place. It could be a very sobering experience to find out why that policy exists.

Wherever you are when working with clients, make sure that you know where your exit is and that no one and/or nothing is blocking it. This is particularly important when working with decompensating psychiatric patients or those with violent criminal records when they are irritable or agitated. Dress professionally yet comfortably. If you need to move quickly, professional clothes are not as easy to move in, and you don't want to be worrying about running in high heels and a tight skirt, or a suit jacket that you put over a chair that you need to quickly grab when you are trying to be safe.

When in the home there are items you want to check for sure. Are the utilities working? That includes water, electricity, and heat. Is there adequate and appropriate food? Is there a place to sleep for everyone in the house and appropriate bedding for children? If your agency is sending you on a home visit they most likely have a checklist of other items to check to make sure that the house is safe like the one in appendix G. You should always follow your agency's protocol exactly when conducting a home visit.

Agency Safety

Just because you are in your work building does not mean you are completely safe. Know the neighborhood and the neighbors. Let them know who you are. Communication is very critical to your safety, both on and off the job.

If your agency has installed some kind of emergency system (e.g., intercoms, panic buttons), find out how and when to use them. The emergency system was installed at great expense for a reason. Hopefully, you will never have to use it, but it would be good to know. Likewise, if the agency offers a nonviolent physical-restraint class, take it. The techniques, especially verbal de-escalation, will come in extremely handy sometime in your career as a social worker or even as a parent!

Like CPR training, safety is a life-saving technique. When you learn it, you say to yourself, I hope I never have to use this. Staying alert is critical to your safety in the field. Beyond what is listed in this section please know that NASW also has safety information provided for members. Please find the link below.

Working at Night

When you have to work after dark in your agency there are a number of things to consider. The first is, do you really have to work at night? Other than group homes, hospitals, nursing homes, and places similar to this that naturally stay open 24 hours, offices do not usually stay open past 5 or 6 p.m. unless there is an event taking place. We all need to catch up with our work from point to point, and if need be it is safer often to come in to work a bit early than to stay late in an office by yourself.

That being said, there are times when this does happen. So, if you have to stay past dark in the office by yourself, consider the following:

- Let someone else in the building know that you are staying late. Many buildings have evening staff or supervisors. It is helpful for someone else to know you are actually working in your office and give them a concrete time that you will be there and then be done (and then stick to this).

- If you have done the above, then also let that person know when you leave. Not only are you developing a trusted relationship, you are also relieving that person of some stress of not having to worry about you.

- Always lock the main office door and also your office door, depending on how the office is configured.

- Let someone else outside of the building (a friend, colleague, or parent) know that you are in your office and then again let them know when you have left and are safely in your car.

- Always keep your phone on with the GPS device on.

- Don't blast music just to keep yourself company; you need to be able to hear what is going on around you.

- Try to see if a fellow worker needs to stay late and plan to stay on the same day and walk out together.

- Drive with the doors locked, windows up, and nothing on the passenger seat that entices a carjacking incident.

When Your Client Is the Community

Social workers who work in a community setting do not always see clients on an individual basis. Their work tends to be more "mezzo" or "macro" in nature, meaning that they are either working with groups (mezzo) or organizing in the community (macro). When a social worker is involved in community organizing, we often say that their client is the whole community they are working with. This is very different from having an individual client. Suddenly, you are thinking about the dynamics and relationships among large numbers of people rather than those between you and one person, or between you and a family.

There are some special considerations to think about when your client is the community:

1. As an organizer in the community, you might know more people than you would if you were just seeing individual clients. The boundaries between your organizing and your personal life therefore can get blurred and you need to be able to keep good boundaries as much as possible.

2. Many people think that when you work in the community you don't need good people skills. This is not true. You will use all your social work skills in working in the community just like you would with clients.

3. Working in the community is also not a 9–5 job. Organizing often requires people to come out early in the morning or late at night to be able to meet people in the community at places where they are most likely to be congregating, such as train stations, bus stations, shift changes at factories, etc. Many organizers work on weekends as well, so the five-day workweek is not always the typical workweek for a community organizer or community developer.

4. Community organizing also requires different strategies and tactics than working with individual clients. A wonderful resource on this is the Midwest Academy's book *Organizing for Social Change* by Bobo, Max, and Kendall.

5. Dual relationships when you work in the community are much harder to avoid, especially when you work in a small community, neighborhood, or rural area. The same people you may be working with in a coalition that is working for better schools may also be some of the same people you do business with (they could be your grocer, your roofer, or your car repair person). It is in these relationships that you draw on all your professional skills as a social worker to keep clear boundaries between your work and your personal life, but you have to realize that the two will be much more closely aligned than when you are in clinical work.

Community Meetings When Topics Are Volatile

If you are working as a macro social worker in the community, there will come a time when you are holding a meeting where not everyone in the room agrees on what should be accomplished. Community organizing, planning, or development are areas of social work practice that require us to often walk a fine line between all the issues (and actors) that are at play on any given topic. In order for a community to fully address their concerns on an issue—let's say on an increase of drug use in their neighborhood—there will be many opinions on what is the cause, whose fault it is, and what should be done about this issue.

If you, as a social work intern with a community agency that is working on this issue, are going to organize a community meeting, you have to realize from the beginning that the meeting will not be just a regular meeting where everyone is nice and polite. Of course, you make every effort to start off that way and make sure that everyone is respected and their voices and opinions heard, but you have to plan ahead for the volatility. How do you do that?

Let's continue with the example of neighborhood drug use for a minute. Every community meeting begins with the where, when, why, and who questions.

Where—Where do you hold the event? Is there a neutral space that everyone has the ability to get to, that has parking, good lighting, and is not culturally, racially or ethnically biased? If the neighborhood in question is a lower socio-economic neighborhood that is racially mixed, we would not hold this meeting in a middle class, white neighborhood that is 15 miles away, for example.

When—When do you hold the event? Late afternoon? Week nights? Weekend? Do you need to think about childcare? Do you need to think about when people in this neighborhood generally work? If they are shift workers, is there a better time than others? You don't want to pick a day and time that basically says to people: We are excluding you from this conversation. You may need to consider holding multiple meetings on a variety of days and times to meet the needs of the community.

Why—Why are you holding the meeting? What do you hope to get out of it? There is nothing worse than to come to a meeting where people end up getting angry and have nowhere to go with their emotions and thoughts. Have a clear purpose and state it in your advertisement of the meeting and then at the beginning of the meeting. Be consistent with your purpose from beginning to end. Always have some action item to take away from the meeting. What will you do next? What are the next steps? Where do you go from here?

Who—Who gets invited to the meeting? This is the place that organizers often make their biggest mistakes. Who gets invited and who gets left out? Who gets to speak? Who gets a role? Be very careful and think this through, as it will determine how your meeting will go even before anyone opens their mouth.

After you have worked on these questions, there are other pieces of holding a community meeting that are very important. Do you need refreshments? Are you going to allow the press to come? If yes, you absolutely need "press packets" (materials to provide to members of the media about what you are doing) or at least you need to designate someone from the organization to be the person to talk to for all press questions. How long will you let questions and answers come from the audience? Who will chair the meeting? This is also an important question because without a strong chair, the meeting could get out of hand quickly.

You need someone who is not afraid of volatility and who will not take resentment from the audience PERSONALLY (this is key—the chair cannot lose their temper). They need to be able to steer the discussion and make everyone feel that they have been heard. The chair of the meeting also needs to be able to get everyone to move to the action that you desire toward the end of the meeting.

If there is a real question of violence occurring, you need to think about having someone like a bouncer who can help restrain people or a police presence at your meeting. Uniformed police at a meeting will change the tone of the meeting, but there are times when it is necessary to have them there.

As an intern you will not be holding this meeting by yourself nor making any of these decisions. Your supervisor will be the person making sure the evening is safe, directing the conversation flow, and giving you direction. Talk with your supervisor about what is expected before, during, and after the event to assure everyone's safety as well as the success of the meeting.

Liability Insurance

Although it's an uncomfortable topic, we have to discuss the possibility that an accident in judgment regarding a client, coworker, or the agency or an error may occur while you are practicing social work. Even pricklier is the fact that someone might try to sue you or report you to your state licensing board for your actions while you are working as an intern or as a social worker. The incidence of litigation or licensing board hearings is rare but a real possibility that cannot be ignored. Following the code of ethics, reading and understanding the law in your area of practice, and the use of supervision are your best options to minimize the opportunity for dereliction or misconduct. To protect yourself, your agency, and your college or university there is liability insurance (also sometimes called malpractice insurance). Like car insurance, homeowners insurance, or any of the several other insurances that offer us protection, the policy is essential to have for the "just in case" incident and something we hope not to ever use. Liability insurance is used to cover situations due to negligent acts, errors, and omissions that can arise from your professional practice.

Your college or university may carry insurance for you as student interns, or at minimum will be able to tell you where to get it if you need to carry it yourself. Once you start working as a social worker the agency will carry liability insurance for you. If you ever opt to be self-employed (private practice, consulting work, home therapy, teaching a class at your alma mater or at your own agency) you will need to purchase your own malpractice insurance. You also have the option of course to carry your own insurance while a student or working at an agency. Luckily, this insurance is relatively inexpensive for the safety it provides you for those "just in case" incidents. There are multiple places to purchase this insurance. Although not endorsing one insurance company over another, the National Association of Social Workers (NASW), our professional organization, does have a branch where social workers may purchase liability insurance. You do not have to be a member of NASW to take advantage of this benefit.

Other Safety Issues

✔ Can you think of areas of concern for you that have not been covered?

✔ Is there information you should know, based on your geographical region, that has not been addressed here?

✔ Can you share other safety hints with the people in your class?

✔ Discuss this issue in supervision and see what safety policies your agency has.

Developing Job Descriptions and Learning Agreements

One of the first things you will need to do with your supervisor is to establish a learning agreement for your time in the field internship. This time in field is yours to learn, understand, and integrate ideas into your professional life as a social worker. These ideas about what is expected from you come from your vision, the agency needs, and your professor's assessment of your growth areas. Considering all these factors, establish your goals for the semester. The format for this is usually a job description or learning agreement, so that you can be accurately assessed on your progress. For instance, if you have always wanted to conduct an individual counseling session with a client, that would go in your agreement. At the same time, your agency has a real need for case management, so that too will go into the agreement. Finally, your professor happens to know that you have a real fear of facilitating a group; that too goes into the agreement. The agreement gives you an understanding of what is expected of you and becomes a working document for supervision and for wise use of your time as an intern. The earlier in the semester you settle your learning agreement, the clearer you will be about how to plan your week.

It is a good idea to read through your field evaluation *before* completing your learning agreement, because you can tailor your agreement to what you will be evaluated on at the end of the semester (or year). This agreement can usually be revised, especially before going into a second semester. Take the learning agreement seriously. Spend time thinking and working on this important document. The more you experience now as an intern, the more competent you will be, and competence will give you confidence when you start out as a paid social worker. Finally, self evaluation is an ongoing process. Don't wait until the end of the semester to reflect on what you are doing, how you are doing, and what you are learning. Use the worksheets at the end of the chapter to help you think about your learning agreement.

Work Ethic

For most of you, your entry into the profession of social work will also be your first professional job. Throughout the book we will be providing suggestions on how to prepare for a meeting or the proper way to discuss an issue with your supervisor. We give you this information because we think it is possible no one else has ever given you an idea of what to expect regarding work ethic and work habits. If you know this information, that is great, but it bears repeating. Often in social work a crisis will occur and you may not be able to leave work right on time, or you may need to come in earlier than usual to address an important issue. Realize that the social service field is a very small world and many people know each other because they have either gone to school together or worked together in other agencies. You always want to put your best foot forward when you first meet people, being on time, being prepared, meeting deadlines, and communicating clearly, because information about you as a professional (good and bad) will travel fast, and you are building your reputation. You will be the new person on the block, so be flexible and show willingness as well as initiative. This might mean occasionally volunteering to come in on a weekend for a major program that is being offered, or even moving chairs and tables for a meeting. Ask when you don't have enough work to do or don't understand what has been given to you. Be sure to keep busy with agency- or other job-related work. Supervisors do not want to see us checking the latest news on our social networking page or texting friends about plans for later that night!

Another note of caution: We all have very busy lives, as do you. You might have a job (or two) and beyond being a student you belong to student organizations or have responsibilities in the community in which you live. While we are sure that your supervisor may be sensitive to these commitments, they don't necessarily want to hear that your sorority or the PTA bake sale is more important than your internship. It gives the impression that the internship and learning how to be a good social worker is not important to you. Make every effort to follow through on your commitment to the agency and let them know you're learning and their agency is important to you.

We recognize that most of the internships and placements at your school (and ours) are volunteer, or nonpaying jobs, free labor. Although it is for free it still is very important that you make the internship and the work you do there a priority. This is for the sake of your career as well as the reputation of your school and most importantly for the well-being and care of the clients the agency serves. When we mention for your benefit it may mean a good reference but it also could mean a job and the beginning of your professional career.

While we are discussing work ethic let's talk about a value near and dear to our hearts, that is, how we talk about our clients. We would like to suggest some guidelines to be used in classrooms, staff meetings, case conferences, or any other location whether clients are mentioned orally or in writing.

Guidelines for Talking about Clients

1. Be respectful. Keep in mind the social work value of human dignity.

2. No derogatory terminology, such as "crazy" or "weird."

3. No minimizing a client by applying adjectives such as "cute" or "adorable."

4. No mimicking the client's voice, language, or nonverbals.

5. No "blaming the victim." Seek to understand how and when "the system" may have created or exacerbated the area of concern.

6. No discussing a diagnosis unless someone qualified has told you the diagnosis. Likewise, do not diagnose if you are not qualified to do so.

7. You can use their real first names as the classroom is an extension of your field; avoid using last names. When writing, never use the real names of the clients.

8. Avoid negative judgments in your head or out loud.

9. People-first language should always be used—someone is not an addict, they are a person addicted to drugs. Someone is not borderline—they are a person with a borderline personality disorder.

10. Be succinct and clear; everyone who needs to talk should have time.

11. Be attentive to your assumptions and your stereotypes based upon personal and professional experiences.

12. Everything that is talked about stays within this course and section and is not explained to other sections or other students including roommates, partners, and parents.

Guidelines for Writing about Individuals in Client Status
by Barbara Arrington, MSW

1. Be careful of descriptive language and adjectives both in talking and in writing of individuals in client status.

2. Do not write a diagnosis—instead write exactly what you observe. Instead of writing that the person was "depressed" write that the person was tearful and articulated statements of low self-worth.

3. Don't be afraid to quote a person directly. Don't change their words.

   a. Write what you see and what they told you.

   b. Don't write your assumptions, your thoughts, or your judgments. Only write the facts.

4. Keep in mind that anything you write will be read potentially by the person in client status, your supervisor, doctors, and other colleagues. Your

writing should be clear, concise, and to the point. You are representing and advocating for the person with your writing.

Thoughts to ponder

How do you want to present yourself?

- ✔ What is the work ethic you want to present?
- ✔ What is expected in terms of hours and times you need to be present?
- ✔ Is lateness accepted or never tolerated?
- ✔ What is acceptable clothing to wear at the agency?
- ✔ Are tattoos and piercings allowed to be exposed?
- ✔ If they are allowed, do you want to reveal your tattoos and wear your piercings in a professional setting?
- ✔ Is there an official dress code?

How does your field internship handle breaks and lunches?

- ✔ Does the agency have them?
- ✔ Are they informal?
- ✔ Do you count the time for lunches into your field hours or not?
- ✔ Do you bring a skill or prior experience that may help the agency?

Work Attire

Your work attire should be professional. Now is the time to start developing a new wardrobe. A few pairs of pants, a few blouses/shirts, a blazer/jacket, and a sweater that all match allow you to create a variety of mix-and-match outfits when you are on a budget. You need to save tight or revealing clothing for socializing with family and friends. For those of you who have been wearing your pajamas to class, that time has come to an end! Clothing should be loose and comfortable, but conservative. If your agency allows you to wear jeans, this is not the time to wear your favorite pair that is getting worn and has rips and holes. Nor is it the time to wear a T-shirt with a saying on it that could be construed as insulting or sexually explicit. Sneakers/tennis shoes/athletic shoes are not appropriate workwear either. Although, at some agencies, your work will include playing with children or adolescents so they may want you to wear athletic shoes. When you can dress casually, choose a nice blouse/shirt an/or sweater to match your jeans instead of a sweatshirt or football jersey. Some agencies have very detailed dress codes, for instance no open-toed shoes. Talk with your supervisor and read your policy manual regarding the dress code. Other no-no's we have heard from supervisors include flip-flops, yoga pants, labels/brands blatantly displayed (creates barriers between clients and students/staff because of socioeconomic status), expensive or excessive jewelry, and hats. Also ask about situations where it is important to be dressed in a certain way, for instance a court appearance. Judges determine the dress codes in their courtrooms.

Chapter Exercises

At the end of every chapter there is a short exercise that will help you to reflect on your field placement. Use your imagination to negotiate the twists and bumps in the road of your internship!

We will also ask a question from the other curriculum areas that you have already had or have currently with this course. HBSE is the abbreviation for Human Behavior and the Social Environment. These questions are geared toward helping you link your other course work with and apply it to your internship.

You may want to consult Internet resources that can provide information related to this chapter. For example, the Massachusetts Chapter of NASW has specific recommendations for safety at work, safety guidelines for social workers, and techniques for defusing or talking down explosive situations.

Integration of other course material	
HBSE	After meeting your first client, can you say what stage of development they are at, according to the theories you learned in human behavior?
Policy	When learning about agency policy, did you find a policy that is beneficial to the client? What about detrimental?
Practice	What social work skills do you use when having your first conversation with a client or supervisor?
Research	Do you have a question about your agency that could be a research project?

Resources

US Occupational Health and Safety Administration
http://www.osha.gov

European Agency on Health and Safety
http://osha.europa.eu/en

International Labor Organization
http://www.ilo.org/global/lang--en/index.htm

Massachusetts Chapter of NASW
http://www.naswma.org/displaycommon.cfm?an=1&subarticlenbr=51

Political Savvy
http://www.politicalsavvy.com

Office Politics
http://nptimes.blogspot.com/2012/01/dealing-with-office-politics.html

University of Michigan Safety Webinar
https://www.youtube.com/watch?v=Ox6SMyDaPjE

NASW Safety Checklist
https://www.socialworkers.org/practice/naswstandards/safetystandards2013.pdf

 **Begin to develop your learning contract. Answer these questions. Take notes with you when you sit down with your supervisor to discuss your contract.**

What do I want to learn from my internship experience?

What specific knowledge do I want to develop?

What specific skills or techniques do I want to learn or sharpen (e.g., interviewing, assessment, referral, group work)?

Is there an area of social work that I feel I don't have a grasp on or feel that I can't fully integrate (e.g., why policy or research are important to my daily social work practice)?

Do I want to work independently?

Can I have flexibility in hours, or are my days and times set?

Are there other agency activities I want to be exposed to (e.g., budgeting, team meetings, administration, board meetings, grant writing)?

What kind of a relationship do I want with my supervisor? My coworkers?

Add other thoughts you have about your internship.

Chapter 2
Building Professional Relationships

For many of you, this may be the first time you are developing a professional relationship. Relationship building takes time, commitment, and work on both ends. In a professional setting such as your field placement, you must develop multilevel relationships with the agency, your colleagues, your supervisor, and your clients.

Now is the time for some self-reflection. Take time to decide how to develop a reputation for yourself. It is too early to determine what theory you will prefer to work from, and possibly what population you will want to work with, once you have your degree. However, it is not too early to think about your professional reputation. From the beginning of your fieldwork, others begin to assess you as a professional and watch to see if you are capable of becoming a competent, caring, professional social worker.

Your Relationship with the Agency

Developing a relationship with an entity may seem a little strange. However, it is extremely important. When you applied to be an intern, chances are your application was reviewed by people other than your supervisor. Perhaps a board had to approve your internship, or a volunteer coordinator, or the director of personnel. Individuals within the agency have already begun to form a relationship with you. The longer you stay there, the more your relationships will continue to develop. Other people in the agency will be important for you to know and meet with, in order for you to understand their roles within the agency. These might include the agency president or CEO, active board members, and your supervisor's immediate superior. The more people that know of you and the more you understand their roles, the stronger your relationship with the agency grows.

Never underestimate administrative assistants and secretaries. They often are aware of most of the agency's ongoing projects and know who is in what meeting and where and why the meeting is taking place. An administrative assistant who has been at the agency a long time is an invaluable asset. Administrators, including your supervisor, will rely on their assistants for information and assessments regarding interactions with you. You will be able to rely on the administrative assistant for your day-to-day support, like supplies, keys, maintenance reports, and messages. Get to know the assistant quickly!

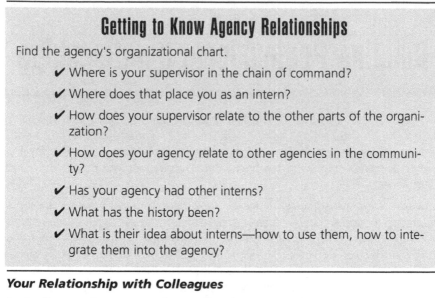

Getting to Know Agency Relationships

Find the agency's organizational chart.

✔ Where is your supervisor in the chain of command?

✔ Where does that place you as an intern?

✔ How does your supervisor relate to the other parts of the organization?

✔ How does your agency relate to other agencies in the community?

✔ Has your agency had other interns?

✔ What has the history been?

✔ What is their idea about interns—how to use them, how to integrate them into the agency?

Your Relationship with Colleagues

By "colleagues," we mean the people who are in your immediate department (i.e., those who you come in contact with regularly). For example, you are an intern in the psychiatric unit at a large hospital. Colleagues would be those people on the unit who share cases with you and work day-to-day cofacilitating groups, or meeting as a treatment team. These would be your peers if you were hired as a social worker. Although you already have a supervisor, each of these people has a great deal of information about the particular department, and specific skills they were hired for. Watch them interact with clients, and talk to them about their job and why they do it.

These relationships are resources you are developing during your internship; use them to get answers to your questions or advice regarding a particular client or policy. If you develop the relationships properly, you may get hired at your internship. At the very least, you could use your colleagues as references and resources after you leave your internship and start working as a professional in the field.

Thoughts to ponder

What do you need to build a professional reputation?

✔ What is your foundation?

✔ What are the building blocks?

✔ When and how do you add to your reputation?

How much of your reputation comes from your classroom learning?
How much comes from you?

One of the challenges to this relationship with colleagues and the one with your supervisor is determining how to keep these relationships professional. In past jobs, you may have become friendly with your coworkers, going out together after work and sharing intimate details about your life. Although it is tempting, we caution you *not* to start your professional relationships with that type of information. The longer you are at the field placement, the more likely that personal relationships may develop, but remember this is a professional setting and professional relationships are crucial. Learn what you can from your colleagues and keep in mind the professional reputation you are trying to develop. To do this, stick to questions and comments about work, not about music preferences or the latest episode of your favorite television show. Questions and comments about the day's schedule, about clients, and about agency procedure are great places to start. When in doubt, comments about the traffic on the way in or the weather are always safe. Think and wait a bit before adding your colleagues to Facebook, Twitter, or any other social media venue, as you want to keep your professional and personal relationships separate, especially as an intern.

The NASW Code of Ethics specifically addresses relationships with colleagues in several sections of the code. Section 2 is devoted entirely to social workers' ethical responsibilities to colleagues, and covers issues like respect, confidentiality, collaboration, disputes with colleagues, referral for services, sexual relationships, sexual harassment, impairment of colleagues, incompetence of colleagues, and unethical conduct of colleagues.

CASW also addresses work with colleagues in section 7.1, highlighting how important those relationships are and how important it is to respect those people as professionals and handle these relationships the same way that NASW suggests in section 2.

Your Relationship with Coworkers

Your relationship with coworkers is just as important as other relationships. Coworkers are the other people at your agency who are not directly working with your team. This could include administrative staff, finance/accounting office/maintenance/custodial staff. If you are in an agency where space is at a premium, you may be sharing an office with one or more people. In this situation, clients' confidentiality becomes an issue, as well as negotiating space, having private telephone time to make calls to or about your clients, and giving and receiving feedback from your peers. In order to do this, you need to develop solid relationships with your coworkers. Developing a relationship with your coworkers does not mean your coworkers need to be your best friends, nor does it mean you have to socialize with them outside of work. What it does mean is that you form a working relationship that allows for space, respect, and support. Each of your colleagues may well have something to offer you in terms of insight and experience, expecially if you are just starting in the field.

The NASW Code of Ethics section on ethical responsibilities to colleagues is operable here as well. Review the Code of Ethics regarding your responsibility to coworkers, as well as to the agency and your clients. It very clearly lays out a set of expectations that could safely guide a solid working relationship for you and your colleagues.

Your Relationship with Your Supervisor

Your supervisor at the agency can be utilized like your instructor for this course. Supervisors agree to accept an intern for several reasons. Maybe they would like to train and guide someone new in the field or believe that they should give supervision because someone in the field helped them as a student. Perhaps your supervisor believes that, once you are trained, you will be able to provide more social work services to the agency's clients.

It is your responsibility to come to your supervisor prepared with questions regarding the agency, how integration of classroom material will apply to your clients, and referrals and networking. This includes discussing information you need for class assignments, clarity about how to practice a specific skill that needs work, or a request to work on a project or a specific task because of the potential benefit you see in being involved. Supervision is also a time to discuss any issues that you consider roadblocks to successfully completing your field placement. These issues may include transference issues, personal knowledge of the client, or even car trouble or a family illness. As with your colleagues, remember that this is a professional relationship. Questions like "What did you do this weekend?" will not develop that relationship and in fact may harm the professional reputation you are trying to develop.

It is your supervisor's responsibility to assign you tasks and projects as well as to give you feedback on the work you produce. Sometimes you will not like the tasks you have been assigned, or will believe them to be busywork. Remember that there is a great deal of paperwork in social work, and ask yourself, if you were not doing this work, who would be? If the answer to the question is your supervisor or another social worker, then it is a social work task that must be completed. If you feel you are not getting the learning experience you expected or that is required for class, you must advocate for yourself. Go back to your learning agreement and use it in supervision to discuss your tasks and the commitments made by the agency to your learning. Assertiveness works very well in these situations, not aggressive or passive-aggressive behavior. Assertiveness will be covered in the next chapter.

Be prepared to speak with your supervisor every week. Use an agenda to help you organize your thoughts for supervision. We will also discuss this in chapter 3. Find out from your supervisor if you are able to call them after work and on the weekends (i.e., in case you are sick). Discuss with your supervisor how to discuss clients if you are texting to ensure client's confidentiality.

Be sure to follow the chain of command that is established in your agency. Do not go over your supervisor's head or around them if you didn't like the answer you were given. To give an example of this let us share a very large mistake made by one of us in our first job with an MSW. One of us was responsible for all the HIV programming and medical care of all the residents who had HIV and AIDS in a drug treatment program. A resident who did not have HIV or AIDS contracted chicken pox. Alhtough he was sent home to recover, he had exposed all the residents with HIV/AIDS to a potentially deadly illness for them. Simultaneously the CDC (Center for Disease Control) was in the city and when they heard about the situation there was a sense of panic and they suggested that the residents with HIV/AIDS needed to have a shot of gamma globulin as soon as possible to boost their immune systems. The author didn't hesitate and ordered overnight shipment of the product and arranged for the nurse to come on a Saturday morning to administer the gamma globulin. Whe she saw the executive director later he asked a few questions. Did I consult with my supervisor? Who approved the overtime for the nurse? How much was the item? Well, the author didn't do any of the above. I thought I was going to be praised for my efficiency and acting to save the lives of the residents. My Immediate supervisor was more than angry. I low dare I tell the executive director first? How dare I spend money out of his budget without asking and how dare I ask a nurse under his supervision to come in for overtime? The meeting with the executive director, supervisor, and author was long, heated, and difficult. In the end it was agreed that what I did was correct but that I had gone about it all wrong. I learned a very valuable and lasting lesson that day. Also the gamma golbulin was thousands of dollars. Agencies don't have that kind of reserve, so budgets were revised and none of the residents with HIV/AIDS caught the chicken pox!

The Faculty Liaison

Most social work programs have faculty who serve as a liaison between you and your field agency. Sometimes these people are the same faculty who teach your field seminar class; sometimes they are other faculty in the department. Whoever your faculty liaison is, he or she is an important person to discuss field issues with, especially if you think you are not developing a proper relationship with your agency supervisor, or if you are not being given the opportunities to practice your skills that were agreed upon in the learning agreement.

Do not expect that the faculty liaison will solve all your problems for you—you must learn how to do this yourself. Think of your internship as work—if the situation you are concerned about happened when you were employed, what would you do? If you have an issue with a colleague or coworker you may want to try to address it with them before involving your supervisor. As an intern if you are unsure of how to handle the situation it would be appropriate to receive advice from your faculty liaison. If the use is programatic or policy related the first approach is to talk to your supervisor, even if you are having issues with the supervisor! All agencies expect you to follow certain procedures or protocols when you have a problem. The first in line is the supervisor—do not go over his or her head to someone higher in the organizational chart or to the director of the agency until you have spoken with the supervisor. If you and the supervisor cannot resolve your problem, speak with your faculty liaison. At times the faculty liaison might have to mediate between you and your supervisor. This role is part of being a liaison, so be sure to use this resource when the need arises.

The NASW Code of Ethics contains several sections that relate directly to situations involving supervisors and student interns. Section 2.07 prohibits sexual activities with supervisees, students, trainees, or other colleagues. Section 3.01a states that social workers who supervise or consult need to have the necessary knowledge, skill, and competence to do this work. Section 3.01b states that supervisors must be responsible for setting clear, appropriate, and culturally sensitive boundaries, while section 3.01c prohibits dual or multiple relationships with supervisees. Finally, section 3.01d requires that supervision should always be provided in a fair and respectful manner.

CASW Guidelines for Ethical Practice in section 3.5 contains a number of provisions for social work educators and supervisors on their responsibilities to students and students' responsibilities to their clients. Among those are educators and supervisors instructing only in their areas of competence. Students are not to represent themselves in an inappropriate manner to their clients (e.g., say they are social workers when they are still interns).

Your Relationship with Clients

Client relationships are a little different than the relationship with your supervisor and your colleagues. In this relationship, the client needs your skills and networking abilities, similar to what you need from your supervisor. The client depends on you. This places a client in a vulnerable position, which social workers must respect and protect until the client is no longer dependent. One of your major goals with clients is to help them become more independent. Then they can move on in their lives, utilizing the skills you have helped them learn.

You have probably heard many times that if you show warmth, empathy, and genuineness, you will usually be successful in the client's eyes. It is very true and bears repeating here. Take time to consider how to approach your clients and how you can assist them. Be as forthcoming as possible about what you are able to help with (e.g., you cannot provide housing through your agency, but you can refer them somewhere that can). Most people can sense whether you are respectful and will trust you in return. Know when to say, "I don't know the answer to that question." You never want to give the impression that you know more than you do—clients will respect the fact that you can say you don't know. They will want an answer, however, and you must be able to get back to them quickly after you research what they need to know.

Also remember that your role with clients never changes—you are always their social worker, even if they are no longer a client with your agency. We always tell our students, "Once a client, always a client." You and your client cannot be friends, you cannot use their services (e.g., your client is a roofer and you need a new roof on your house), and most of all, you cannot be involved intimately or in a sexual way.

The NASW and CASW Code of Ethics both begin with our ethical responsibilities to clients, and both include very detailed requirements. These include our commitment to clients, self-determination, informed consent, competence, cultural competence and social diversity, conflicts of interest, privacy and confidentiality, access to records, sexual relationships, physical contact, sexual harassment, derogatory language, payment for services, clients who lack decision-making capacity, interruption of services, and termination of services. CASW also includes a section specifically for the protection of vulnerable members of society (implied in NASW code) and CASW is much more detailed in the maintenance and handling of client records. We also have commitments to the broader society, which by default includes our clients. Our ethical commitments here include social welfare, public participation, public emergencies, and social and political action. Go to the code in the appendix and look at all these sections. Professional social workers must be well-versed in the Code of Ethics of their country and know how to use it.

Socializing and Work

Confidentiality is easy to break, even unintentionally. Be very careful of socializing and talking about work with your colleagues. You never know what a small world it is until you have broken a client's confidentiality outside of work and find out that the waitress is your client's cousin!

Community Resources

Take time to get to know your work environment and the community. The kid who hangs out on the street knows everyone, and one day it may be useful that he knows you or even that you know him. Buy from local merchants, so that they are familiar with your face; it helps reinforce or improve the agency relationships in the community. What resources are in place in the community and what deficits exist? Agency resources are like your neighbors at home. Hopefully you know them, like them, and can offer some mutual support and aid sometime.

How do you develop these relationships? What are the important elements that one needs for these professional relationships? At the end of this chapter are sample worksheets for you to use in recording contact information or community resources. Use them as you get to know your community.

Elements of Relationship Building

Being Culturally Sensitive in Relationship Building

While you work on developing your relationships at your internship, keep in mind the importance of being culturally sensitive. Cultural sensitivity requires you to both have an awareness of other cultures and know how to integrate that awareness into your work as a social work professional. You will be meeting people of different genders, ethnicity, ages, religions, sexual orientations, and professions. It is important to get to know them without disrespecting them or insulting them. Most likely you will never intentionally insult them, but a form of nonverbal communication or a comment may be understood differently from how you meant for it to be. For instance, in Orthodox Judaism, men do not touch women. If you are a woman and you hold out your hand to shake the hand of an Orthodox Jewish man, it would not be accepted and the atmosphere could become uncomfortable. Or you are talking to someone who speaks a different language than you and you decide to repeat what you just said but say it very slowly and loudly so the person you are talking to will understand. One final example would be to assume that a Hispanic woman from Chile would know what food is part of the Mexican culture. This becomes crucial to undersand and address, especially as we continue to have more and more refugees and immigrants coming into this country. Take time to learn about the cultures you will be working with at your agency. Take time to talk to members of those cultures and develop relationships; that way, if you do offend people, hopefully the rapport you have developed will allow you to talk about what happened, learn from it, and continue to work together.

Trust

A basic foundation of developing all these relationships is trust. The agency will not trust you if you do not complete projects on time; your coworkers will not trust you if you talk about them behind their backs; your supervisor will not trust you if you forget to facilitate a group; and your clients will not trust you if you breach their confidentiality. These examples illustrate how trust is diminished, rather than developed. How is it built?

This question brings us back to the professional reputation you would like to develop. Do you want to learn to be a competent social worker and develop the skills you have been taught? When asked to do something, are you so afraid of doing it incorrectly that you express your concerns inappropriately or refuse to complete the task? Your agency, coworkers, supervisor, and clients will be able to sense from your words and actions if they can trust you. Your supervisor will not assign you to a task that you cannot complete. Remember, as you are developing relationships with others, they are doing the same with you. As you are observing them, they are watching you. If you take time to develop the relationship, follow through on all tasks, and communicate clearly and openly, trust will build and the relationship will grow. As the relationships build, so too will the confidence level of everyone (you, your supervisor, and your clients), providing you with more opportunities to develop your skills and be assigned more challenging responsibilities.

Dependability

Dependability is another important part of building relationships. Your supervisor and your clients expect that you will do what you tell them you will do. Supervisors expect you to be on time, to be dressed appropriately for your agency, and to call the office if you are going to be late or out sick. If you say you will take on a project or a task, you need to complete it in a timely manner, or ask for help to complete it on time.

Your clients expect you to be on time for home visits and office hours or to call if you cannot keep an appointment. Your clients also expect you to return phone calls in a timely manner. Remember, it is legitimate to tell a client that you do not know the answer to something. You can give them the requested information when you research it—but you must remember to follow through with this information. You quickly lose your legitimacy when you do not answer clients' questions, and when you call and cancel their appointments too many times.

Integration of other course material	
HBSE	What aspect of community work are you doing when you are getting to know the people and the businesses around your agency?
Policy	What is the agency policy about relationships at work? What are the consequences of infractions of the policy?
Practice	What is the best way to approach your supervisor about an issue regarding a client?
Research	How could doing research for classes impact your relationship with your clients?

Resources

Social Work Code of Ethics
http://www.socialworkers.org/pubs/code/code.asp

National Occupational Standards
http://nos.ukces.org.uk/Pages/index.aspx

International Federation of Social Workers, Ethical Standards
http://www.ifsw.org/policies/statement-of-ethical-principles/

Keep a record of all community and agency resources used and contacts made.

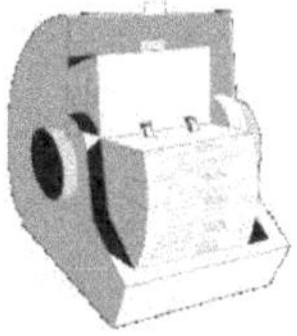

Community Resources Portfolio Template

Agency name:

Contact person and title:

Agency address:

Phone:

Fax:

Web page address:

E-mail address:

Facebook page:

Twitter account:

Agency services:

Eligibility requirements:

Fees:

Handicap accessibility:

Cultural resources (including languages spoken at agency):

Chapter 3
Teamwork:
Your Supervisor and You

At this point in your field experience, we expect that you are now clear about your role within the agency and that you are settling in to the agency routine. Your responsibilities may include case management, group facilitation, developing a resource guide, and other functions of a social worker. You should also be getting ongoing supervision with your field supervisor. Each social work program has a standard requirement for supervision for students in the field. This standard is usually an hour per week with a qualified supervisor, preferably an MSW. Exceptions are rare and usually handled on an individual basis.

Supervisors' Function

Supervision sessions cements the cornerstone of your relationship with your supervisor. You began this relationship at the interview where you received a good understanding of the mission of the agency and about what you would do while an intern. This chapter focuses on what that relationship entails and how it is significant to you. What follows are some general tips that may help you understand how to use your supervisor for supervision and what to expect from that process.

One of the things you have probably figured out by now is that social work agencies are very busy and there is never a dull moment. This means that your supervisor is busy as well. Rarely in today's world do supervisors have a single role in the agency. They may carry a caseload, write grants, serve on several committees, and maintain a relationship with other agencies. Again, supervisors generally agree to take a student intern for a few reasons. First, someone was willing to supervise them when they were an intern, and taking an intern is a way to give back to the profession or to a specific social work program (maybe the one they graduated from). Second, supervisors see supervision as a way of providing more services to their clients in a financially responsible and clinically appropriate way. Third, supervisors like to keep their skills fresh, and having an intern keeps them abreast of the current professional landscape in social work. Finally, they may enjoy training new social workers and helping them develop into professionals. In rare instances, the supervisor's supervisor has agreed to take an intern and has not told your supervisor about you until right before or at your arrival. Regardless of why you are there, supervisors are very busy people, yet they are responsible for providing you with a good experience and exposure to the realities of social work.

For most of you, this is probably not your first job, but it might be your first professional job. If you have worked outside of the social work field, you had a supervisor; in a broad sense, every boss you ever had was a supervisor. However, a manager at a restaurant or fast-food chain is not as concerned about developing your professional skills and your personal development. Your field supervisor is concerned with both. Your supervisor at the agency is concerned about the well-being and safety of the clients. To address that dual role, supervision entails three components: administrative, educational, and supportive.

Details of Supervision

Administrative supervision deals with enforcing agency policy and scheduling work load and everyone's working hours. Your supervisor will give you an understanding of agency policy, work duties, your schedule, and how you will be evaluated. Administrative supervision takes a great deal of time, since supervisors have to administer the work of the unit they are responsible for. They not only schedule work hours, enforce agency policy, and distribute cases but also know about what every worker under their supervision is doing, including what they are doing with each client case. You will come to understand the importance of team meetings as well as individual supervision as you watch your supervisor engage in administrative supervision.

The second role of a supervisor is educational supervision. In this role, the supervisor reinforces what you have learned in the classroom, enhancing and elaborating information as needed for that particular agency, and discusses cases with you. The supervisor will explore your theoretical framework and how you are applying it to your cases. As your supervisor is providing educational supervision, you will finally connect all that you have been learning directly to your work with clients. The supervisor also looks at the educational needs of the entire staff and works to ensure that they receive the educational experiences that they need or want. This could take the form of scheduling in-service training at the agency, sending staff to continuing-education workshops, developing a resource library at the agency for anyone to use, and even developing policy that reimburses employees for tuition spent on furthering their education.

The third role is supportive supervision. It means offering understanding when you have a difficult case, or suggesting how to proceed. Supportive supervision is given every time your supervisor helps you understand your feelings about how the internship is going. Supportive supervision occurs on a regular basis at the agency when employees need to change their work schedule because of a personal problem, or when they need time off to deal with a death in the family, or when they need to seek outside counseling for a drug or alcohol problem. Supportive supervision is not therapy—its focus is to enable the employee (or intern) to cope effectively with their work. These details of supervision are delineated in depth in Kadushin and Harkness (2014), *Supervision in Social Work*.

Very often you will be able to analyze a supervision session after the fact, to fully understand which type of supervision your supervisor has given you.

How should supervision be formatted and scheduled? Supervision can be ongoing before and after your task (talking to a client, facilitating a meeting, establishing a discharge plan, etc.), can be a preestablished hour set aside each week, or can be group supervision with other social workers or interns that your supervisor is responsible for overseeing.

The NASW Code of Ethics offers some clear guidance on the issue of supervision and consultation, in section 3.01:

(a) Social workers who provide supervision or consultation should have the necessary knowledge and skill to supervise or consult appropriately and should do so only within their areas of knowledge and competence.

(b) Social workers who provide supervision or consultation are responsible for setting clear, appropriate, and culturally sensitive boundaries.

(c) Social workers should not engage in any dual or multiple relationships with supervisees in which there is a risk of exploitation of or potential harm to the supervisee.

(d) Social workers who provide supervision should evaluate supervisees' performance in a manner that is fair and respectful.

The CASW ethical principles also discuss supervision in section 3.4. In addition to the general provisions of the code, social workers in supervisory or consultation roles are guided by the following specific ethical responsibilities.

3.4.1 Social workers who have the necessary knowledge and skill to supervise or consult do so only within their areas of knowledge and competence.

3.4.2 Social workers do not engage in any dual or multiple relationships with supervisees when there is a risk of exploitation of, or potential harm to, the supervisee. If questioned, it is the responsibility of the supervisor to demonstrate that any dual or multiple relationship is not exploitative or harmful to the supervisee.

3.4.3 Social workers evaluate supervisees' performance in a manner that is fair and respectful and consistent with the expectations of the place of employment.

CASW specifically also lays out the guidelines for responsibilities to students in section 3.5.

Generally speaking, once you are an MSW for a few years you will probably be asked to be a supervisor. Frequently, supervision in social work is an elective course when you get your MSW. Think about taking that course if the idea of being a supervisor appeals to you. If you don't take an elective on supervision, you can probably pick up a course on supervision post-MSW while getting your continuing-education units (CEUs). Some states require a postgraduate course in supervision in order for one social worker to supervise other certain levels of social workers to advance to the next level. In other areas of the country, such as rural areas, the supervisors may be BSW or even one of your faculty members depending on how many supervisors are available at the time.

How to Prepare for Supervision

Our first suggestion for how to prepare for your supervision session is to think ahead and develop an agenda for your supervisor. At the end of this chapter is a sample form that you can use to develop your agenda. If you have a particular question, write it down or bring the material with you. If you are going to discuss a client's case, have the entire file with you, organized so that you can readily find the information you need. That may mean writing some notes and questions, so that you can find what you need during your allotted supervision time.

We realize that you may not know exactly how to prepare for a meeting. And we mean no disrespect by the next comment, but it is our experience that many students who have only babysat or waited tables prior to their internship don't know what sounds obvious. Always come to any meeting with a pen, your calendar, and a pad of paper. You can assume that at the meeting you will always set another meeting date and time, and that you will always have action items to take care of after the meeting, which is why you bring your calndar and a note pad. You should know the topic for the meeting—read any material sent about the topic of the meeting—and be prepared to share information that you have on the subject. It is a good idea to write down any questions that you have about the topic. If you need to travel for the meeting, be sure to leave enought time to get there and not be late. You want to be on time for the meeting, whether everyone else is on time or not. Being on time includes getting something to drink, going to the restroom, and being in your seat and ready no later than the start of the meeting. If you have a cell phone, leave it off during your internship time. These helpful hints should allow you to look quite professional and motivated to learn the profession.

Sometimes your supervisor will not know the answer to your questions. That is OK. Although they are a more experienced social worker than you, your supervisor is still human and not perfect! He or she may need to consult someone, or may refer you to another source to get the information. Both ways will help you get the information and teach you at the same time, so it matters not which approach is used.

Make sure that you are clear both in asking your questions and in what you hear when listening to the answers. Your questions and the answers will impact how you service your clients, and everyone wants to be sure that client care is safe and accurate. You need to remember the answers to all of your questions for your supervisor. That is how you will build your knowledge of the field and the services your agency offers. Most likely similar issues will continue to come up throughout your internship. Show your competence and intelligence to your clients and your supervisors by not having to ask the same questions over and over. That is one reason why it is a good idea to take notes to refer back to from sessions with your supervisor.

Regularly check the agreement that you and your supervisor negotiated. When you developed the agreement, it should have been inclusive enough to expose you to every aspect of social work your agency provides, especially the components on your evaluation for your specific program. If you have a second semester of internship in your school, you might want to renegotiate the learning agreement based upon your knowledge of the agency and your skills as they have developed by midyear.

Your internship is an extension of the classroom, and your supervisor is there to guide you through the "real" social work cases. You can think of your supervisor as another one of your professors—guiding you and helping you grow, both personally and professionally.

Negotiating What You Need

What happens when your supervision does not go as planned? In spite of all the effort you make to develop and maintain a good relationship with your supervisor, things go wrong. Sometimes the easy flowing dialogue/teaching described above does not work out exactly as planned. It could be your supervisor is overcommitted and doesn't have enough time, it could be lack of work and you are bored, it could be a personality clash that is hard to cope with, or it could be your skills and work ethic are not what the agency expected and are causing difficulty. It could also be a myriad of other reasons. You and your supervisor will need to work out these difficulties.

As two people in the same profession striving for the same goal, which is the care and treatment of your clients, you need some confluence of ideas and a comfortable working relationship. Any difficulty you are experiencing has to be addressed. Yet you are concerned about bringing up the issue because this person, your supervisor, is responsible for your evaluation and you would like a good grade for class. You might also wonder if you are right about certain things, and you don't want to confront your supervisor—after all, he or she has more experience than you and has worked at the agency longer. Who are you to be second-guessing or guiding your supervisor and the process? This is a perfect time for you to understand that you need to address uncomfortable issues. Concerns should be remedied as they come up. That way the concerns don't fester and result in a mess. We encourage all students to try to address problems with their supervisors. If they are unsuccessful, we as faculty will intervene. Faculty and liason don't get involved right away, so that students can develop the ability to advocate for themselves and clients.

Chances are, though, that you don't like confrontation and get very anxious about having to approach your supervisor about anything remotely challenging or questioning. Besides, you may even get uncomfortable about fighting with family or friends. However, what we are talking about doesn't have to end up in a fight and isn't exactly confrontation. It is being assertive and standing up for your rights. Or it is advocacy and standing up for the rights of your clients. Either way, advocacy or asserting yourself are essential skills you will need in both your personal and professional life, so it is worth spending time learning how to discuss uncomfortable issues with your supervisor.

Thoughts to ponder

✔ How do you let your supervisor know that you don't understand or that you feel as though you lack knowledge and/or experience to do what he or she has asked?

✔ Which type of supervision (supportive, educational, or administrative) does your supervisor use most often with you? Is that what you need?

Assertiveness

Being assertive, whether you are advocating for yourself or for a client, is really about being able to communicate what you are trying to say without violating the rights of others, humiliating them, or being aggressive. Aggressiveness comes when you are selfish and destructive to others, maybe being demanding or inconsiderate in the process. If you are not assertive or aggressive, you are usually passive, which comes across to others as weak, self-sacrificing, and compliant. When we look at these traits, it is sometimes easier to view them as a continuum, with assertiveness in the middle and the ultimate professional goal.

Passive   Assertive   Aggressive

It is not easy to be assertive. Finding the right balance of saying what needs to be said without going overboard into aggressiveness, especially in a new situation and with a supervisor, is very important. It is a skill that social workers need to master so they can successfully advocate for their clients and themselves.

So how do you have an assertive conversation? Great question, and the fast answer is practice. If you are traditionally not someone who lets people know what you want or need, this will be very important for you. The steps are simple but take practice. As you practice, it will get easier. Sometimes you may sound too aggressive, sometimes you may feel that things didn't go well or got worse; when that occurs, you have ended up closer to being passive on the continuum. There are four basic steps to being assertive.

1. Be clear and specific about what you are looking for in the conversation. Start with "I" statements and own what you are saying. "I want," "I need," "I feel," and "I think" are all great ways to start your conversation. Continue being clear and state details about what you want and why. Avoid accusing statements like "you didn't tell me " or "you said." Better is "I didn't know" or "I thought I heard you say."

2. Always be direct, open, and honest. Although it is easy to talk to people who aren't involved in a particular issue, you will avoid gossip and office politics if you direct your comments to the person you have concerns about and only that person. Sometimes we catch ourselves talking to others, "because you were wondering if this was just a problem for you or if others were experiencing this." But if you talk about others, especially your supervisor, don't expect to be respected or considered professional.

3. Own your message all the way through; continue with "I" statements. Don't bring anyone else into the discussion unless you have been appointed spokesperson for a particular group of people and have been clear from the beginning that you speak for them all. (Right: I feel I have too many cases to handle. Wrong: I feel I have too many cases and everybody else thinks so, too.)

4. Ask for feedback about how you sounded and communicated. Be sure to carry out the dialogue about the issue first. Sometimes, depending on how the encounter goes, you may ask for feedback at a later time.

If you think you will be really anxious about being an advocate or being assertive, write down key points and keep the rules with you during the discussion. Try really hard to stay on topic and cover everything. You don't want to revisit the topic again if you don't have to. If you successfully assert yourself, you should feel more confident, build respect with your supervisor, develop a sense of control, and learn how to compromise without feeling as though you lost completely or are helpless.

Timing can be very important when you are discussing issues or trying to be assertive or advocate about an issue. Don't pop your head in the door five minutes before the end of the work day. If a crisis is occurring at work, that is probably a poor time as well. We suggest making an appointment and letting the person know this is an important topic to you. That way, you can hope to have his or her undivided attention.

Mastering the technique of being assertive will be beneficial for both your professional and personal life. A critical part of it is your nonverbal communication.

If you say all the right things but accompany them with body language or facial expressions that are not congruent with your message, then you will defeat your purpose. Keep control of your voice tone, volume, and speed and your body motions. We will cover more about nonverbal communication in chapter 6. Ensure that the message received is assertive.

Classroom exercise

Pair off with a person in the class and role-play an instance where you wish that you could be more assertive. Preferably select an issue at your field placement, but if you don't have a field placement issue, a personal issue will also work. Play yourself and have your partner be your supervisor (or the person you have the issue with). Follow the four steps and practice the situation. Have your partner give you feedback about how he or she felt while you made your points, and then have him or her critique what you did and said. Then reverse the roles.

Shared Meaning

The result of your conversations should be shared meaning. You and your supervisor should be developing a mutual understanding and agreement. Gender and cultural issues are worth a mention here. Don't let culture or gender get in the way. Sometimes different cultures or the opposite sex communicates differently. Spend time making sure those differences do not cause a misunderstanding.

Age and what area of the country you come from can also constitute issues of cultural sensitivity. Think, for instance, about the different words we use for the same items, depending on our age or where we grew up. Older people may call their couch a davenport. One of the authors has a friend who calls her jeans dungarees and goes to the market instead of the grocery store. In New Jersey you buy soda; in Ohio you buy pop. In Philadelphia you buy a grinder, in New Jersey you buy a sub, and in New Orleans you buy a po'boy. With so many words for the same items, it is easy to see why it may be so confusing. Learn about not just word choice but the traditions and rituals of other cultures so that when you are conversing with your supervisor you both understand what the other person is saying and culture enhances the conversation rather than impedes it.

Thoughts to ponder

✔ Perhaps cultural sensitivity and assertiveness would be interesting topics for supervision this week!

Integration of other course material	
HBSE	How did your supervisor assess your skills when you came to interview? What HBSE content did they use in making a decision about you?
Policy	What are the policies at your agency about how people become supervisors? Is specific training in supervision required?
Practice	How does developing a good supervisory relationship help your practice with clients? What does your practice class teach you about supervision?
Research	Are there any good research studies on the use of supervision in social work?

Resources

Assertiveness Training
Humboldt University Counseling Center
http://www.humboldt.edu/counseling/assertiveness.html

Psychology Information Online
http://www.psychologyinfo.com/treatment/assertiveness.html

The Mental Health Directory
http://mentalhelp.net/psyhelp/chap13/chap13e.htm

Kieran's Home Page, a tremendous site on supervision, from a social worker from New Zealand
http://www.geocities.ws/kieranodsw/personal.htm

Supervision is a very important part of the field internship. Make sure you have a regular time for supervision every week with your field supervisor. Take time to make a brief agenda for each supervisory session, from asking questions to getting help on a particular case.

Date of supervision session _____

My agenda for supervision

Questions I have

Resources I think I need

Chapter 4
Developing the Professional Persona

Professional Use of Self

Your classes and field experience have exposed you to a variety of skills and tools. Your knowledge base of social work issues has broadened in school. And hopefully you have seen other social workers in action and have seen how they have developed their own unique styles. It is that style and its development that we would like to address here. That style is known in the field as professional use of self. Professional use of self involves how you integrate several components to develop your own style. Those components that make up your professional self include what you know (the tools, knowledge, techniques, and theories of social work), your personality, your belief system, your life experience, your use of relational dynamics, your use of anxiety, and finally the use of self-disclosure (Dewane, 2006). Through the rest of this chapter, we hope to explain more about these different components so that you can begin to think about your journey developing your own professional use of self.

Before explaining the professional use of self, we want to add that your professional self will affect your work no matter what kind/level of social work you choose to do. Many people mistakenly believe that professional use of self is appropriate only for those who decide to do micro work, or clinical social work. This is not accurate. Although relevant in micro work, professional use of self is relevant to all levels and types of social work, from micro to macro, with individuals, families, groups, organizations, and communities.

Professional Tools

Everyone who enters the field of social work is taught the same tools and skills: active listening, paraphrasing, the use of open-ended questions, and reflection of feelings are some examples. You will be better at some of these skills than at others. You might think that a colleague does some skills much better. How each of us develops these skills is the way we differentiate ourselves from others. You may be able to ask a lot of open-ended questions and get a good portion of the client's story, whereas someone else is able to reflect feelings and then explore a specific problem more in depth. Neither of these skills is better than the other, but one may be more useful for one type of a client than another. Honing your skills and deciding which skills you are best at is the first component of professional use of self.

Personality

The next component is your personality. In the exercise in this chapter we will look at personality a little more specifically and hopefully in an enjoyable way. You have already developed your personality and matured, especially if you are a nontraditional student. You know by now if you are not a morning person, or if you need to go to bed early because you don't function well in the evening. You know if you are a procrastinator or are task oriented, and you know if you have a good sense of humor or sometimes don't tell jokes well or don't always understand what is so funny. Each of your personality traits, good or bad, enters the room with you when you go to work as a social worker. While we are working, we are human beings as well; we continue to interact with other human beings in an engaging and authentic way. Try to identify with what your clients are experiencing. How you view the issue being faced is affected by your personality and by your view of the world, and it is important that you understand that your client's experience is mediated by his or her perspective and personality as well. If you are someone who considers him- or herself to be funny, be cautious about how and when you use your sense of humor in your professional life. Be sure that it is well received and that the timing is appropriate and that it is not sexually inappropriate or insulting to any vulnerable population, culture, or religion.

Belief System

Along with your personality, your belief system and your life experience also affect your work as a social worker. Your belief system develops along with your personality, formed by, for example, your gender, ethnicity, religion, and family. How we understand life is based on our belief system and life experience. This life experience will help us clarify what issues we are able to work with, what we do not like to do, or what we are not able to do. Life experience includes touching. Some cultures are known for touching and some families touch (i.e., hug or kiss) more than others. In social work, touching is an art and can be used only for the benefit of the client. The nonverbal messages that come with touch and lack of touch are extremely important. Knowing how you feel about touch and your willingness to touch clients is part of the personal exploration you need to undertake. Perhaps the section on nonverbal communication later in chapter 6 will help you understand the use of touch in your life. Belief system is not just about touch, but about how we think and feel about issues, our viewpoints on certain actions and behaviors, and so many more topics. Be sure to check with your supervisor about the agency policy on touching. You may not be able to touch the clients (or other staff), and you need to be aware of the policy and the reason for it.

Life Experiences

Life experiences help and hinder how we approach issues. It is important to get to know yourself and understand who you are. If we have had traumatic events happen in our life, we must heal from those events before we are able to ask others to do the same. An excellent example of this is if your parents had a particularly bad divorce and since then you have had difficulty trusting any potential boyfriends or girlfriends and cannot maintain a relationship. Until you deal with this issue, you will not be able to help clients develop and maintain healthy relationships. You may need therapy yourself, and certainly supervision, and then reflection and observation of yourself, when interacting with clients in these situations, to monitor how you affect the situation.

Questions to ponder

Some questions to ask of yourself to learn about who you are could include:

- ✔ Why did I choose social work?
- ✔ What do I bring to the profession that will help?
- ✔ What do I bring to the profession that will hurt me?
- ✔ What issues will make me feel uncomfortable?

Relational Dynamics

As we continue to look at the components of professional use of self, the use of relational dynamics is next. This concerns how we relate to others. Some of you may be concerned with appearing nonjudgmental when you are working with your clients. You may be so careful that you act unnatural and your facial expression and emotions are stunted in your effort not to hurt clients' feelings or jeopardize the relationship. Being nonjudgmental does not mean being nonreactive; sometimes you cannot be prepared for the stories that you will hear. Be empathetic, be yourself, and engage in a relationship with your clients. This relationship has a different set of boundaries than other relationships in your life, which we will address later in the semester, but make no mistake—it is a relationship.

Internal Reactions

While you are not able to stop yourself from changing as you continue to learn and grow, you should recognize that some of that growth will cause anxiety. This anxiety is normal and is expected. You want to do a good job and prove that you are competent to yourself and your supervisor. Your anxiety is natural and will decrease as you become more skilled. An example of this is the anxiety that you feel the first time your supervisor says it is time to facilitate a group by yourself or when you have to present a case for the first time to your supervisor.

Transference and Countertransference

We would be remiss not to mention transference and countertransference here. Although this is discussed further in chapter 13, a large part of professional use of self involves the importance of understanding how we respond to each other within our professional relationships. Transference is a client's response to a social worker when they are treating you like someone else in their life. Countertransference occurs when a client reminds you of a person in your life and you react to the client with that in mind. Always being aware of these issues in the social work process helps the client though the issues and helps you develop a stronger professional self. When self-disclosing, countertransference could be more likely to occur. People's life stories have parallels and you will experience connnections when self-disclosing that you may not expect.

Self-Disclosure

The final component of professional use of self is self-disclosure. When a client asks you what you would do, and you have actually experienced a similar situation in your life, you have to make a decision whether to share what you have done. The clear and easy answer is to say, "Don't disclose," but this becomes an increasingly gray area as we try to develop relationships. Sometimes self-disclosure—maybe sharing what movies you have watched recently, what music you listen to, or even whether you are married—is useful for building rapport with a client. It is not useful to go into detail. Self-disclosure should only benefit the client and should not take the focus off the client. Let's say that you have been or are on an antidepressant and the client is just beginning a new regimen of the same antidepressant. You can share that you know there are possible side effects—but not say how you know—and still be helpful. You probably don't want to open up that you were or are on the meds or why. That may take the focus off of the client, which is not a good idea.

Self-Disclosure in Community Work

Self-disclosure in community work can also be a little different than when working with individual clients. As a community organizer, one is expected to be a little more up front about who one is and why you are working in a community to be able to gain the respect of the community. People need to get to know who you are, and this sometimes requires you to talk about yourself more. This does not mean that you are sharing a lot of personal details about yourself, especially if you have mental health issues. Community members will be looking, however, to see how you "mesh" with them, and what makes you similar to them. Try to keep your conversations about the community and the work you will accomplish. Sharing in a community meeting means your personal information will be shared everywhere in the neighborhood before you even know what happened.

One last piece of professional use of self is self-awareness. Later in the book we will discuss stereotypes.

Chapter Exercise

While you start to think about professional use of self you may be wondering what some of your personality traits are. Which traits will benefit you in social work and which ones could be a challenge as you enter the professional workforce? The exercise for this class is called the Color Workshop and will be given to you by your professor who will request it from the book publisher. The Color Workshop is designed to let you see your areas of strengths and your areas of growth. You will also see that there are other personalities that are perhaps not as complementary to your personality. This will present challenges as well, including working with your supervisor and clients. After you have determined your color, look at the chart in Table 4.1 to see how your personality compares to others.

Table 4.1 Color Personality Chart

	Gold	Green	Blue	Orange
% of the world	33–50	10–13	12–15	12–33
Good career choices	Business, administrators	Academics	Social work, engineers, organizers	Artists, entrepreneurs
Strengths	Traditional, fulfills expectations	Seeks to understand everything, independent	Morale boosters, imaginative	Learns quickly, troubleshooters
Troublesome areas	Rigid, boring, system-bound	Can appear arrogant or too intellectual	Bleeding heart and too sensitive	Unpredictable, not very serious
Famous people	George Washington, Mother Teresa	Oprah Winfrey, Eleanor Roosevelt	Albert Einstein, Margaret Thatcher	Steven Spielberg, Donald Trump

Source: Adapted from www.Keirsey.com.

As you enter into your first professional job, you will be exposed to many different personalities that are working toward the same goal. Conflict arises between people because their different personalities work in incompatible ways. Learning to compromise and use every person's developed or mature traits will help your team work better together. When working with others, including your supervisor, it is useful to know how you approach the goals of the agency and what you can offer. You can also ask for assistance from your supervisor to help you with the underdeveloped traits of your personality. Look at your color and be aware of when and how your developed traits can work toward the goals of your agency. Just because your supervisor is your manager doesn't mean that you won't have personality differences. You may be orange and willing to try new techniques with a client, but your supervisor is more cautious. He or she may want to role-play with you to be sure you have all the aspects of the technique, and may want you to be very selective as to which clients you use it with and when you use it.

Your color can give you an *estimated* idea of both your learning style and your Myers-Briggs© personality. The charts on the next page provide those approximations.

Remember, we all have secondary colors that we need to enhance. These are the parts of our personality and temperament that need to be more developed—we have these traits, but they are just not as strong as our primary color.

How can you use your color with clients? As you develop rapport with your clients, you will be able to determine what areas the client wants to work on and then develop the treatment plan. Based upon what you know about yourself, you will know in what areas you can easily help clients and where you will need support. For instance, say you are a gold personality. If your clients want to be more organized because they can never get a project done on time, you are the perfect person to help strategize options for them. However, if your clients want to be more spontaneous and live on the edge without being anxious about it, you won't be able to help them without support, because you don't see a reason to be spontaneous.

Thoughts to ponder

Look at the characteristics that apply to your color.

- ✔ What are your developed or mature areas?
- ✔ What are your underdeveloped or immature areas?
- ✔ Are any areas overdeveloped or dominant?
- ✔ Are there totally untapped areas that you need to develop?

Kolb's Learning Style by Color	
Orange Accomodating—The accommodator's learning style has the opposite strengths from the assimilator, emphasizing concrete experience and active experimentation. The greatest strength of this orientation lies in doing things, in carrying out plans and tasks, and in getting involved in new experiences. The adaptive emphasis of this orientation is on opportunity seeking, risk taking, and action. This style is called accommodating because it is best suited for those situations where one must adapt oneself to changing immediate curcumstances. In situations where the theory or plans do not fit the facts, those with an activist style will most likely discard the plan or theory.	*Blue* Diverger—The diverger's learning style has the opposite learning strengths from the accommodator. It emphasizes concrete experience and reflective observation. Its greatest strength lies in imaginative ability and awareness of meaning and values. The primary adaptive ability of divergence is to view concrete situations from many perspectives and to organize many relationships into a meaningful "gestalt." The emphasis in this orientation is on adaptation by observation rather than action. It is called diverger because it works best in situations that call for the generation of alternative ideas and implications, such as a "brainstorming" idea session. The style suggests a preference for socio-emotional experiences over task accomplishment.
Gold Converging—The converging learning style relies primarily on the dominant learning abilities of abstract conceptualization and active experimentation. The greatest strength of this approach lies in problem solving, decision making, and the practical application of ideas. The style works best in situations where there is a single correct answer or solution to a question or problem. The style suggests a preference for task accomplishment or productivity rather than for more socio-emotional experiences.	*Green* Assimilating—The assimilating dominant learning abilities are abstract conceptualization and reflective observation. The greatest strength of this orientation lies in inductive reasoning and the ability to create theoretical models, in assimilating disparate observations into an integrated explanation. As in pragmatist, this orientation is focused less on socio-emotional interactions and more on ideas and abstract concepts. Ideas are valued more for being logically sound and precise than for their practical values. It is more important that the theory be logically sound and precise.
Adapted from: Honey, P. & Mumford, A. (2000). *The learning styles helper's guide*. Maidenhead: Peter Honey Publications Ltd. *Kolb, D. A. (1983). Experiential Learning: Experience as the source of learning and development. Prentice Hall.*	

Personality Colors and Myers-Briggs©

Introversion vs. Extroversion (I or E)	Sensing vs. Intuition (S or N)	Thinking vs. Feeling (T or F)	Judging vs. Perceiving (J or P)
Gold	Green	Orange	Blue
ISTJ	ISTP	INFJ	INTJ
ISFJ	ISFP	INFP	INTP
ESFJ	ESFP	ENFP	ENTP
ESTJ	ESTP	ENFJ	ENTJ

Adapted from: Myers-Briggs, I. (1995). *Gifts differing: Understanding personality style*. Mountain View, CA: Davies Black.

These examples are a tiny fraction of the many interactions that can occur with your coworkers, supervisor, and clients, but we think you can understand the issues that may arise and how they need to be addressed as they come into focus during your internship. Working with people of opposite personalities may take extra time because at first you probably won't be talking the same language, but the time you spend figuring out how to work with one another is well worth the effort. The end result of any project you are working on will be more fulfilling if multiple personalities can see a project through to completion. As this happens, trust develops and relationships grow.

The NASW Code of Ethics contains a section on social workers' ethical responsibilities to colleagues. Section 2.01 deals specifically with the issues of respect.

(a) Social workers should treat colleagues with respect and should represent accurately and fairly the qualifications, views, and obligations of colleagues.

(b) Social workers should avoid unwarranted negative criticism of colleagues in communications with clients or with other professionals. Unwarranted negative criticism may include demeaning comments that refer to colleagues' level of competence or to individuals' attributes such as race, ethnicity, national origin, color, sex, sexual orientation, age, marital status, political belief, religion, and mental or physical disability.

(c) Social workers should cooperate with social work colleagues and with colleagues of other professions when such cooperation serves the well-being of clients.

Of course, CASW has similar standards and expectations on how to work with colleagues as NASW.

Developing Your Personality and Professionalism

Now that you know more about your personality and know what is more developed or mature and what is underdeveloped or immature, it is your responsibility to select areas that you need to improve in.

Developing yourself as a professional is an important part of your personality. Your internship is your entrée into the field of social work. You have a unique opportunity to determine how you want to be viewed and what you want your reputation to be as a professional social worker. Are there traits you developed as a student or employee elsewhere that you want to take into your new profession? Conversely, are there traits or habits you want to leave behind? Be aware of what you believe are the characteristics of a good social worker. Which of them do you have? Which do you need to develop?

Your professional self starts to develop here and now, and follows you through graduate work and each and every job. It is your reputation as a professional that will take you from job to job and will develop your career. What do you want people to say about you as a social worker? How do you want to be remembered by former clients?

The History of Social Work

But what is a profession? Why is social work considered a profession? To answer this, let's look at some history. In the *Encyclopedia of Social Work*, Goldstein and Bebe (2010) explain the historical context for the formation of NASW. They talk about the early disagreements among social workers and discuss how each segment of social work wanted to have its own organization. These segments eventually agreed on a set of standards and became one organization in 1955.

Part of the process of developing NASW was knowing what creates a profession. A variety of concepts encompass a profession. The first is the ability to appropriately use the knowledge and skills (techniques and tools) of the profession. A second concept is of the qualifications (degree, license, experience) of that profession. The third is establishing and adhering to common values and ethics.

What does that mean to you? Well, as you passed each class toward your degree, you proved that you have the ability to appropriately use the knowledge and skills of social work. You will continue to perfect your tools and techniques and to learn more, but you have met the first criterion. When you graduate, you will have a degree and will need to figure out what license you need in your state. Finally, you have to agree to follow the values and ethics for social work delineated in the Code of Ethics.

Goldstein and Bebe (2010) refer to five other criteria that make a profession a profession, not just a job. These criteria include a theory that is common to everyone in the profession, the authority to act, power to give public sanctions, a code of ethics, and a common culture. The profession of social work meets all these criteria.

Knowing all of that, are you willing to commit to the profession? Do you have concerns about your ability to be a professional social worker?

Integration of other course material	
HBSE	Where do you think personality develops in terms of someone's physical and emotional growth?
Policy	How is policy influenced by the personalities of those constructing it?
Practice	How does your personality reflect and influence how you work with clients and coworkers?
Research	Could your color influence your ability to do research? If so, how?

Resources

National Association of Social Workers (NASW)
http://www.socialworkers.org

Association of Social Work Boards (ASWB)
http://www.aswb.org

Inroads Consulting Group LLC, creator of the Color Workshop
http://www.inroadconsulting.com

David Keirsey on temperament
http://www.keirsey.com

Matrixx System, National Curriculum and Training Institute
http://www.ncti.org/business/ws_realcolors.php

 Have you ever come to this sign in your field internship? When, and under what circumstances? Describe what happened and what you did.

Chapter 5
Expectations and Stereotypes

This chapter will help you clarify what perceptions you are carrying around with you, as well as what perceptions people may have about you. Before we can proceed, we need to define some essential terms: expectation, perception, stereotype, and generalization.

Expectation: to look for with reason or justification (i.e., we expect college students to have good writing skills), to suppose or surmise, anticipate the occurrence or coming of (*Random House College Dictionary,* 1984).

Perception: the psychic impression made by the five senses (sight, sound, smell, taste, and touch), and the way these impressions are interpreted cognitively and emotionally, based on one's life experiences (*Social Work Dictionary,* 6th edition).

Stereotype: preconceived and relatively fixed idea about an individual, group, or social status. These ideas are usually based on superficial characteristics or overgeneralizations of traits observed in some members of the group (*Social Work Dictionary,* 6th edition).

Generalization: the process of forming an idea, judgment, or abstraction about a class of people, things, or events based on limited or particular experiences (*Social Work Dictionary,* 6th edition).

Your Expectations

Let's begin with your expectations. You may not even be aware of how many expectations you have until you start thinking about them. For instance, what are your expectations for this class and your teacher? Spend a few moments jotting these down.

My expectations

1. _____
2. _____
3. _____
4. _____
5. _____
6. _____
7. _____

8. _____

9. _____

10. _____

Does your list include how quickly you expect a response to e-mail or a phone call? What about expectations that you will get an A for the final grade? Do you expect your teacher to be available during office hours?

Are your expectations reasonable? Are they realistic? It is reasonable for your teacher to be available during posted office hours. It may be not reasonable for you to be upset that you e-mailed your teacher Thursday night and had not received a response by Friday morning. If you are a B student, is it reasonable or realistic that you get an A in this class?

What happens when these expectations are not met? How do your perceptions of the class and of the teacher change? Go back to your list of expectations and think about whether they are reasonable and realistic. Do you need to change any of these expectations? Remember, expectations are not goals. They are what we impose on people and/or events. Our perceptions are often what cause the feelings we have when a situation or event is past.

Let's say that you heard from other students that your American history teacher is as old as America and has a monotone voice. What is your expectation? Perhaps that the class will be boring? Are you dreading it? But when you get to class, your teacher has added jokes to the lecture, dresses in costume for the time period that is being taught, and has rewritten the outline for the entire class, making it thoroughly enjoyable. Your expectations of the class made it even better, because your expectations were originally so low.

Another situation is your graduation day (which should be happening soon after finishing this class!). What are your expectations—sunshine, good weather for picture taking, and lots of space for you to bring your significant other, your parents, maybe your children, or other members of your extended family? But, since nature is in charge of the weather, your graduation day is cold, windy, and rainy. Your grandparents are sick and don't want to come out in the rain. Your expectations were high, so the day may have been ruined. You still graduated, you still received your diploma, but you felt let down and disappointed after graduation.

These two situations exemplify why expectations are so important. Spend some time thinking about what your expectations are for your field placement. What are your expectations of your supervisor? What are your expectations of your clients? Are they reasonable? Are they realistic? Spend a few minutes to answer these questions. These are important questions to answer about your field placement because your expectations will affect your relationships in the field.

Thoughts to ponder

✔ What are your expectations of your agency?

✔ What are your expectations of your supervisor?

✔ What do you expect of your clients?

✔ Are these expectations realistic?

✔ Are these expectations reasonable?

Field Placement and School Expectations

While you are forming your expectations of the agency, your supervisor and your clients are doing the same of you. Just as your expectations need to be reasonable and realistic, their expectations need to be reasonable and realistic. Some of their expectations will come from their previous experiences with interns, their personnel policies, and the application or résumé you wrote to apply for the internship.

It is reasonable for your supervisor to expect you to follow the agency policies. However, it may not be reasonable for your supervisor to suddenly change your hours or require more hours than what is expected for your internship. The agency may have had interns before, and their experiences with these previous interns may have helped them determine what they want from you, or what you will be doing. They may expect you to want the same experience as the previous intern, which may or may not be true. Your supervisor has the right to expect you to come prepared to supervision meetings and the right to expect you will be honest about what you want to learn and how your experience has been thus far. It is unreasonable for him or her to expect you to know everything there is to know about social work and about the specific types of clientele the agency serves, since you are there to learn.

Sharing expectations openly and honestly at this juncture in your field placement is an excellent place to continue building rapport with your supervisor. Let him or her know your expectations of them, the agency, and the clients they serve. Ask if your expectations are reasonable and realistic. Ask your supervisor to share his or her expectations of you. Are those expectations reasonable and realistic, based upon your knowledge and experience? Tell your supervisor about your confidence level or concerns about meeting the expectations discussed.

To prepare for this discussion with your supervisor, think about expectations he or she may have about your abilities. Be prepared to explain your knowledge and skills in social work, and with the particular client base the agency serves.

Let's use the same thought process about expectations the school may have about you. By this time the faculty have had many classes with you, providing you with a solid foundation of generalist social work practice. What do they expect from you? As field teachers for many years, we expect that our students represent the university in a professional and mature manner. We don't expect perfection, and we do expect students to make mistakes. We don't expect those mistakes will permanently harm a client or the school's relationship with the agency. We expect knowledge of ethical social work practice, but we don't expect a student to sit around and observe for the entire internship. In the classroom, we expect all our students to come prepared to talk about their internships and bring in cases and questions that have confronted them in the field. We don't expect to answer all the questions, but we do expect effort on the part of our students to listen and to research a topic that they need to have more information on.

Does your teacher have similar expectations? Are these expectations reasonable and realistic? Spend some time with the syllabus from the class and with your teacher to find out what his or her expectations are of you.

These questions may seem trivial to you, and you may think, "Why do I need to even think about who expects what from whom?" We urge you to remember the examples in the beginning of the section. It was expectations that caused the difficulties on graduation day and the opinion you had about the American history teacher. It is important that expectations be clear in all directions and with all parties. Your internship can get unnecessarily convoluted if expectations are not clear, reasonable, and realistic. We urge you to be sure that expectations are addressed in some detail among you, your agency, and your teacher.

Expectations from Clients and the Community

Many of our clients who seek services are completely unaware of what agencies can provide, and more importantly what a social worker is and what their responsibilities entail. In their study, Winston and LeCroy (2004) asked the general public, "What does a social worker do?" The majority (90%) answered that social workers are responsible for child protection; specifically, taking children away from their homes. Nearly one-fourth of the respondents knew of no other jobs that social workers do. As a soon-to-be graduate, you could come up with at least twenty other jobs social workers do. This is where stereotypes begin to take shape. All over the country in the past few years, social workers have taken criticism for some decisions made by child protective services in various states. (This is a good time to point out that not all state protective services offices require a social work degree when hiring their front-line workers.) Social workers are seen not only as the people who take away children but also as incompetent at doing that job. Stories in almost every state in America report that children have been harmed by a parent or guardian when a child protective services agency was allegedly supervising the home.

Many social workers, especially those who are in child protective services work, are stigmatized as doing a poor job of protecting children. Those stereotypes lead to prejudices that may impact your ability to work with your clients. If your clients have preconceived ideas about you because of news reports, or if their own experiences with other social workers have not been rewarding, you may need to spend a great deal of time building new relationships and breaking down those stereotypes. Hopefully this will not happen frequently, and your clients will look at you as an individual who can help with their situation. You may even be able to develop positive ideas about what social workers do and how they can assist their clients.

If you are a social worker going to work in the community as an organizer, planner or in another macro role, chances are most people will not know why you are there or what your role is all about. This is another opportunity to educate people about social work and our history as community workers and about the skills we bring to helping the community. Just as with any client system, you will need to establish your relationship and credibility with the community you are working with, and this will take time. You need to establish trust, build a relationship, and show that you have knowledge and expertise to offer and share.

Working with communities and community groups allows you to work in collaboration with others who are often directly affected by a particular problem or social issue. You have to remember that they will know more about the issue from a visceral level (living with this) than you do—unless you live in the same community and are experiencing the same issues. Your relationship with the community as a social worker is then one where you are working in partnership to help bring about the needed change.

Your Intern Status

This is a good time to talk about how to handle the fact that you are a social work intern and not yet a licensed, degreed social worker. It is against the NASW Code of Ethics and probably against the law in your state for you to misrepresent yourself as a social worker, and it was probably never your intention to do so. Section 1.04a of the Code of Ethics addresses this:

> Social workers should provide services and represent themselves as competent only within the boundaries of their education, training, license, certification, consultation received, supervised experience, or other relevant professional experience.

CASW Guidelines for Ethical Practice addresses competence in several locations, but specifically in section 7.1, "Maintain and Enhance Reputation of Profession."

7.1.3 Social workers cite an educational degree only after it has been conferred by the educational institution.

7.1.4 Social workers do not claim formal social work education in an area of expertise or training solely by attending a lecture, demonstration, conference, workshop or similar teaching presentation.

7.1.6 Social workers do not make false, misleading or exaggerated claims of efficacy regarding past or anticipated achievements regarding their professional services.

Some clients may be uncomfortable working with someone who is not yet a social worker. It is important to be honest with your clients. Assure them you are completing your degree, obtaining valuable training by being an intern, and being supervised by a licensed, degreed professional. Let your clients know that you may not know everything they need off the top of your head, but you will get all the answers for them. Remember, be empathetic. How would you feel if you were receiving care from a trainee? How do you feel when you are in a store and get the new clerk who doesn't know what they are doing? Some of us are patient with trainees; others wonder what we did to deserve the new person who is so very slow. Be sensitive and patient if clients are uncomfortable about your status—help them process their concerns with you. Do not conceal your intern status. At the same time, do not belittle your status. You are not JUST an intern. You have had many classes and training and have developed good skills just to get to this point. Don't diminish your skills by saying your are "just" an intern.

Stereotypes and Generalizations

Stereotypes are negative responses to someone, based on our previous experience or knowledge base. Generalizations are a sweeping characterization of an entire group of people based on usually a few traits—some of which could be true, but most of which don't apply, especially as you look closely at everyone in the group. For example, a common generalization is that all Latino men favor a "macho" image. However, Latino men are made up of Mexicans, Cubans, Colombians, Ecuadorians, Spaniards, Peruvians, etc. Their cultures each differ and not all may even consider machismo as a part. Another example of a stereotype would be that all alcoholics don't seek treatment when their lives have become unmanageable—for some that means a lot of fighting with significant people in their lives, the loss of jobs, or loss of all their money and consequent legal trouble. Do you see the difference?

Think of the specific population your internship serves. Give a generalization and a stereotype for them. Compare your answers with others'.

Stereotype or generalization?

Generalization	Stereotype

We all have stereotypes taught to us through our families, the media, and our personal experiences. Be conscious of your stereotypes and make sure that they don't interfere with the services you provide your clients. Conversely, do try to discover the generalizations that exist about a specific population that you have not had experience with in your life. Generalizations can provide very useful information that will make your work with clients faster and more focused for their needs.

Just as you have stereotypes, your clients will have stereotypes about you because of your age, sex, race, ethnicity, and marital status, and because you are a social worker. Take time to answer their questions about you (without revealing too much personal information). Those conversations may make the social work process easier for them and you.

Microaggressions

Stereotypes do everyone a disservice. Some are blatant and obvious. Others are said or thought and the person who says or thinks them doesn't believe that they are racist or in any way offensive. These comments have been identified as microaggressions. There are five types of microaggressions: (1) microassualts, (2) microinsults, (3) microinvalidations, (4) colorblindness, and (5) dyconscious racism. Microassualts are explicit racial slights that are primarily characterized by verbal or nonverbal attacks meant to hurt the intended victim. For example, blacks are born with lower IQ's. Microinsults are communications that convey rudeness and insensitivity and demean a person's racial heritage; usually a subtle snub unknown to the perpetrator that has an insulting message for the receiver of the communication. For example, "I'm not prejudiced, I have black friends." Microinvalidations are communications that exclude, negate, or nullify the thoughts of a person of color; such as, "Joe told me he was American, but I always thought he was Asian." Colorblindness is an attempt to minimize or distort the existence of racism by saying such things as "we are all the same" or "I don't see color, I wasn't raised that way." The last of the microaggressions is dyconscious racism, that comes from a person accepting that this is just how it is and blames the victim, with comments such as "being white has nothing to do with my success; I have worked hard to get what I have."

We introduce these ideas here because all of us have to constantly assess and critique ourselves to determine if we need to educate and regulate ourselves when it comes to stereotypes about racism. More can be read about this in the article by Malott et al. at the end of the chapter, which also contains an exercise to help you identify microaggressions even better.

In summary, working with clients is an ongoing process that involves time, continuous effort, and good communication skills, along with good social work technique. Be aware of your expectations, and determine if they are realistic and reasonable. Also be sure that there is open dialogue with your clients about your intern status at the agency. Make sure you are clear about the difference between stereotypes and generalizations, and try to disregard and eliminate stereotypes. Make use only of generalizations that apply to the client in front of you.

Integration of other course material

HBSE What generalizations and stereotypes do you know about the opposite sex? Label them as stereotypes or generalizations.

Policy What laws have been passed in America to make sure we don't act on our stereotypes and treat someone unfairly?

Practice What does a client expect you to do when meeting him or her?

Research What question could you study to determine what stereotypes clients have about social workers? Or, how would you make generalizations about social workers?

Resources

Public Broadcasting System Global Connections (PBS)
http://www.pbs.org/wgbh/globalconnections/mideast/educators/types/lesson1.html

International Online Training Program on Intractable Conflict
http://www.colorado.edu/conflict/peace/problem/stereoty.htm

Malott, K. M., Paone, T. R., Schaefle, S., & Gao, J. (in press). Is it racist? Addressing racial microaggressions in counselor education. *Journal for Creativity in Mental Health.*

When did this sign best describe a day in field or in your educational program? What did you do to slow down?

Chapter 6
Communication: Building Bridges, Not Walls

What Is Communication?

Communication comes in various forms: verbal (tone, speed, and words) and nonverbal (gestures, postures, facial expressions, and body movements). All communication takes place in a context (the reason for the communication) and in an environment (a room, an office, the street, a subway station, the hospital, etc.). Communication also includes the written word.

When people communicate with each other (other than in writing), they are listening to the words, observing the gestures and other nonverbal behavior, and perceiving the message through the context and environment. All of these factors influence how the message is received, how it is interpreted, and the meaning that is assigned to it. In written communication, the words we choose set a tone (harsh, appreciative, informative, etc.) and lead the reader either to understand our message or to become more confused.

It is very important in social work to be clear in our communications with clients and to think about how to communicate appropriately with them. It is also very important to also make sure that our communication to others about clients is clear and succinct. Next to accessing resources (housing, food, etc.) communication is one of the main problems that our clients come to see us about. It is at the core of almost every relationship problem that enters our doors.

You have chosen to enter a profession that is very valuable to society. Social work provides services and fulfills a variety of roles within any community. In fact, we provide the majority of frontline mental health in the country. In order to satisfy the roles and understand what we are doing, we have to be able to communicate effectively. Who do we need to communicate with? Our peers in the social work major, the faculty in the classroom, and now our supervisor, coworkers, and most importantly our clients. You will most likely speak differently to each of these groups. Even when topics are similar, the level of communication will be different for each group. So how do you learn to develop a new style of communication with your clients?

First, think again about the type of relationship you would like to develop with your clients. Some of the important concepts include developing trust, making clients feel welcome, using your active listening skills to engage them in conversation, and assisting them with the issue that brought them to your agency.

Examples of communication skills
social workers use in interviewing clients

✔ *Reflection of feeling*: Clarify the client's feelings and encourage further expression of those feelings. "You seem to be angry about the fact that you failed the test even though you studied hard."

✔ *Paraphrasing*: Express the ideas of the client by putting together the main points and emphasizing what you think the client is saying. "So you are saying that you are overwhelmed by the health issues that your doctor is unsure about, and the fact that your job is not stable due to the economy."

✔ *Open-ended questions*: Ask a question that can be answered by more than one word. "So how was your vacation? Tell me all about it."

✔ *Eye contact*: Use your eyes to show clients that you are listening and understanding what they are saying.

✔ *Furthering the response*: Encourage clients to continue expressing themselves, sometimes with a voice sound like "umm" or "uh-huh" and sometimes with a body gesture that says "go ahead").

Know with Whom You Are Communicating

Our relationships with people around us are very dependent on how we communicate with them. Every time we prepare to communicate with another person, whether orally or in written form, we have to first think about who it is we are trying to communicate with. Is it a colleague? Is that colleague a paraprofessional? Is that person new to the field, or someone who is a seasoned professional? Why does this even matter? It matters because you want to engage in a conversation that joins you with people, not one where either party feels intimidated, belittled, or revered in such a way that you can't develop a relationship with them as a human being.

Many professions use specialized language that allows professionals to communicate with each other in an easier and sometimes more efficient way. "Jargon" is the term for this specialized language. A good deal of jargon consists of acronyms, like TANF (Temporary Aid for Needy Families). Some jargon that social workers use you are already aware of, such as "biopsychosocial," "intervention planning," and "summarizing statements." These terms would not come up in conversation with a client but are perfectly acceptable to use with your colleagues. Depending on what agency or population you are working with, there could be agency-specific jargon or population-specific jargon as shown in the box on p. 69.

Some jargon social workers can expect to hear

In drug and alcohol rehabilitation

The rooms	A 12-step meeting like Alcoholics Anonymous
Dirty urine	A urine sample that has traces of drugs or alcohol in it
The hot seat	When someone is the focus of a group session

Hospital work

PRN	As needed
HTN	Hypertension
Dx	Discharge
BID	Twice a day

Board of social services

Section 8	A type of housing that is subsidized through the government
WIC	Women and Infant Children, a program for giving essential foods with appropriate nutritional value to mothers of newborns

Educational settings

IEP	Individual educational plan, similar to a treatment plan and given to every student who has been classified as needing special education (or having a learning disability) and who will receive special services
504 Plan	Result of public law 93–112, section 794, part 504, which provides for special accommodations for a student who has no learning disability but still needs additional services to be successful in school

It will take you a while to learn all of the jargon used in your agency. When you don't understand it, it is completely acceptable to ask what it means. It is the only way to learn. Once you know the jargon, it may take a while to feel comfortable using it, and even longer to use it properly. The common language allows you to communicate across disciplines with colleagues in other professions like nursing, criminal justice, and education.

As you use this common language, your communication with your colleagues will improve. It is important to have clear communications with your clients, and so it is *not* a good idea to use jargon with them. The NASW Code of Ethics, section 1.03, provides specific rules on informed consent and how to communicate with clients. These rules cover clients who are not literate, who do not have the capacity to provide informed consent, who receive services involuntarily, and who receive services via electronic media. "Informed consent" is another example of jargon. It means that the client needs to understand what it means to receive social work services and to agree to them, including assessment, intervention, follow-up, and research. In order to obtain informed consent you must provide clients with full disclosure about who is doing the treatment, risks, alternatives, supervision, and expenses.

Another form of communication is cursing or swearing. It is very commonplace and commonly tolerated (in some places even acceptable). In your professional relationships it is not acceptable to curse or swear. If you curse and swear even occasionally, you must try to refrain from using these words. You may have other colleagues who swear and curse, but it is never, ever acceptable in your work setting. Neither is it acceptable to throw a temper tantrum, act out, or become the office bully. Once again, the NASW Code of Ethics is very clear on this matter. Section 1.12 states,

> Social workers should not use derogatory language in their written or verbal communications to or about clients. Social workers should use accurate and respectful language in all communications to and about clients.

The CASW Code of Ethics is not as specific with regard to derogatory language but it is specific about respecting the individual (Value 1) and being culturally sensitive about the language (see Section1.2.5).

Communicating with Your Clients

So far we have focused on communicating with your colleagues. You must also know your audience when communicating with your clients. What is their age, their cultural background, their gender, and their religion? These factors all affect how you might communicate with your clients, what they will tell you, and how they will talk to you. If you are a traditional-age student and are working with adolescents, you may know their slang or street terms, which will prove useful to you in the long run. It will give you credibility and make conversation easier. However, you may need to ask the adolescent what a word or phrase means if you do not know, just as you ask about jargon. That is OK. The same is true when speaking to elderly people. They may choose words that are no longer used regularly, and you may need to clarify what they mean. You should not use the client's terminology when it is culturally insensitive or rude.

A great deal of information is available on cultural communication. As social workers, we need to be cognizant of the words we use with clients or colleagues and the meaning behind them. Words take on different meanings in many cultures.

We also need to be aware of how communication is carried out with people in a culture that is different from ours. Do you make eye contact? Is it appropriate to shake hands when greeting the client? Who do you speak with first—the father or mother? Under what conditions do you speak with the children? These are all issues to explore with your field teacher and your agency supervisor.

If you are not clear about what you want to say to a client, wait for a moment and gather your thoughts, so you are sure of what to say. Use standard English when you speak. Just as your writing is judged, your speech is judged by others. When you use incorrect tense or an inappropriate word, people think of you as dumb, ignorant, or uneducated. Most people are reluctant to trust people who appear to not know what they are talking about. You want to sound competent. It is perfectly acceptable to not know an answer or a resource. This does not make you appear ignorant as long as you find out the answer and let the client know the same.

That being said, you will use your social work skills to communicate clearly and build relationships with both your colleagues and clients. These skills include active listening, summarizing, clarifying, paraphrasing, open-ended questions, interpretation, and information giving. You will also pay attention to nonverbal behavior, voice tone, voice speed, and eye contact. Practicing all these skills with coworkers, roommates, and family members often will help you get more comfortable with them.

Active listening encompasses all these skills and means that you need to be present in the interview. You can't be thinking about your significant other, what you are going to have for lunch, or the group you need to facilitate later on in the day. Active listening means that you keep your focus on your communication, which will develop your relationship with that specific person.

Communicating When Your Client Is a Community or Social Issue

Communication as a community worker is just as important as it is when you are working with individual clients and families. You will never be effective in a community if you do not communicate well. Communication here is not only implied as your skills as an individual, but also how you use communication systems in working with a community. Technology has helped to change how we can effectively communicate with our community groups, and there are numerouse ways to use technology in our communications plans. However, here are a few general points to keep in mind:

1. Communication to a community must be thought about from all levels of who is in the community: age level, education level, language level—and materials need to be developed that can reach all of these memebers, if necessary.

2. Communication to a community must come in several different ways since everyone responds differently to how they get "news." So take into consideration: radio, television, print, e-mail, and now all forms of social media on how to reach the community members. This could be posters, signs, tables in high volume traffic areas, or posting and inviting people on Twitter or Facebook.

3. Find out if your community has access to such things as cell phones or computers with Internet access. There are still communities we serve

who use dial-up phones and have no computers, Internet access, or cell phones and cell towers in their area.

4. Communication must be planned. You cannot do one e-mail blast and expect it to do all your work. Over the months that you are working on a campaign in a community, you will need several types of communication with the community.

5. You must think about "who" is delivering your messages. Is there a member of the community who is trusted? Would that be a good person for television ads, or radio interviews, or newspaper interviews? Do your print materials look biased in any way? These are all important questions to think about.

6. Is there a good social media platform to use? Should social media be used?

People-First Language

One other thing to consider when communicating with others is the use of people-first language. This simply means that when talking with and about other human beings, we remember they are people with a diagnosis, not simply a diagnosis (Snow, 2008). This concept developed from work with people who have disabilities. If you talk about a human being with a diagnosis, it really sounds very different from talking about the diagnosis. Examples of this include saying "a person with a disability" rather than "a handicapped person" or "she has autism" rather than "she is autistic." The second phrase, "she's autistic," tends to be heard as "all she is is her diagnosis," and really all people are more than their diagnosis. The language here is vitally important, as the word choice forms impressions in people's minds that can be very limiting in our approaches with people, and by using people-first language, we can open up conversations and relationships. A person who has a disability will respect you more for being careful and conscious of your word choices. Even if the group of clients you are working with calls themselves a name, that doesn't mean you should too. As an example, often you hear people say "I am a drug addict." You do not need to use those words.

Nonverbal Communication

Now that we have spent so much time on your verbal communication and word choice, we would like to switch gears to a very important topic. Nonverbal communication just may be the primary way we communicate with others. Nonverbal communication has entire volumes written about it, and many universities offer electives in nonverbal communication that could be worth taking. Some researchers have said that up to 93 percent of our communication is nonverbal, with facial expressions, hand and body gestures, and posture making up

55 percent of that communication, and voice tone making up the other 38 percent. Clearly, if nonverbal communication constitutes that much of how we communicate, we need to spend a little time discussing it.

Experts in the field of communication break up our nonverbal communications into several different categories: proxemics, kinesics, haptics (tactile) and olfatics communication, paralanguage, occulesics (looking/eyes), environment, silence, and time. Unfortunately, we cannot go in depth here on all these features, but we would like to define them a bit and get you to start thinking about observing your clients—as well as your own communication—a little bit differently.

Proxemics involves how physically close we get to people. In the United States we generally have four different ranges that we prefer to keep people within when near our person. The first is 0–18 inches, which we reserve for our close family and friends, those we are most intimate with; females in general will get closer to one another than males. The second range is 18 inches–4 feet where we distance friends, social range (4–12 feet) where acquaintances would be placed, and finally public, over twelve feet, like when you are sitting listening to a presentation or a religious leader speaking to a congregation.

Kinesics is about the human body, how you carry yourself, appearance, posture, and orientation of your body (sitting, standing, lying, facial expression, hand and body movement, and gesture). Tactile communication (haptics) is about feeling, how often touch occurs or what the touch says when it occurs. Olfatics is about smelling things like body odor, perfume, or alcohol. Paralanguage is more about the tone and pitch of your voice, including the speed and volume in which you speak. Eyes have always been important in nonverbal communication, known as occulesics. The last three are about your environment (your office, your agency setting); how well you keep time tells people a lot; and finally, when you use silence to your benefit within communication.

Let us paint you a picture. You have a new client you are meeting at 3:00. Your supervision time is running late and you still have to go and check messages because you are expecting information about your new client from the referral source. It is now 3:10. You run down the hall very quickly, mumble hello to the client in a hurried voice as you look toward your office, and tell him or her to go that way while you stand at the corner of the reception area opposite where he or she is sitting.

What might the client feel about how his or her first session is going to go?

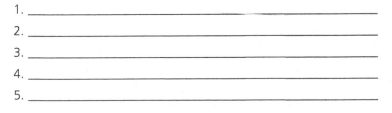

1. _____

2. _____

3. _____

4. _____

5. _____

What do you know about the client?

1. _____

2. _____

3. _____

How would you handle this situation differently and what would the nonverbal communication tell you?

1. _____

2. _____

3. _____

The Written Word

Earlier we mentioned that written communication is also very important in our work with clients. Later on in this book we will review documentation, but for right now you need to know that how you write has an impact on clients. Choosing the correct words, writing in a logical and clear manner, making sure that your meaning and intent are clear, and of course having good grammar and spelling are essential when you write about or to clients. Because we now rely on fax machines and e-mail for some of our correspondence, we also need to take measures to ensure confidentiality of client information. We must ensure we reply and forward messages correctly and, of course, spell and write in a grammatically correct manner. It is important to note here that e-mailing and more importantly text messaging are creating a new set of rules about communication. The abbreviated phrasing and incorrect sentence structure is causing people to forget when and how to use capitalization, punctuation, and full sentences. When you are contacting anyone in your professional life, it is important to follow conventional rules of English grammer. Along the same lines, although e-mail is a time saver, if there is a controversial topic or opinion it is still preferable to have those conversations in person or by phone since sometimes e-mails are misconstrued, and sometimes relationships are also damaged.

Thoughts to ponder

✔ Who will be the hardest person for you to communicate with? Why? What can you do to resolve this issue for yourself?

✔ What is the skill you are having trouble showing competence in? Who can you practice with? What is the best way to practice?

✔ How do you ensure that your agency uses fax machines and e-mail correctly?

Integration of other course material	
HBSE	What questions can you ask to determine what stage of Erikson's development your client is in?
Policy	How can we minimize jargon to make the social service system more accessible to clients?
Research	What has research shown to be the traits a social worker needs to have in order to engage with a client?
Practice	What practice skills do you feel you are already competent in?

Resources

Mind Tools, General Business/Professional Development Site
http://www.mindtools.com

Nonverbal Behavior/Nonverbal Communication Links
http://nonverbal.ucsc.edu/

United Kingdom Jargon List
http://www.socialworkeducation.org.uk/help/jargon-buster/

University of Montana Social Work Dictionary
http://socialwork.health.umt.edu/Master%20of%20Social%20Work/Curriculum /SocialWorkDictionary_updated_2012_Oct23.pdf

 When did you have to "give way" to a supervisor, colleague, client, or fellow student? Without using names, describe each incident, why you "gave way," and whether it was beneficial to you or to the other person.

Supervisor:

Colleague:

Client:

Fellow student:

Other:

Chapter 7

Insight into Your Clients' Perceptions

When working with clients, we use our own skill sets to understand where they are coming from and what their perception of the problem is. To demonstrate that, we offer you a case scenario and explain some terms that will help you understand what the client is trying to express to you.

Empathy

Try to go back a few years in your history. Whether you are a traditional student or a nontraditional student, you had to decide what college you wanted to attend and what major and career you wanted. What process did you go through to choose a school and a major? Did it mean going to look at schools, attending open houses, searching the Web, receiving e-mail and regular mail from many schools? Maybe it included conversations with faculty and staff from a variety of majors, conversations with coaches, and of course the admissions office and financial aid. During the application process, you have to write essays, take exams like SATs/ACTs, send records, and get letters of recommendation. Then you have to wait for the acceptance letter. When you are accepted, you go through preplacement testing and scheduling of classes. Just when you think you're done, there is housing, buying books, and finding all of your classrooms. Although it's an exciting time, it's also stressful and frustrating. Trying to get answers, calling people, playing phone tag, and waiting and waiting and waiting are very frustrating.

We remind you of that time because sometimes we forget the details of an experience when it's over. But when you can recall that time of stress, you will more likely treat a freshman wandering around campus with kindness rather than with frustration.

When you treat that freshman with kindness and understanding because you remember your experience, you are treating that freshman with *empathy*. Empathy is putting yourself in someone else's shoes, or as defined by *The Social Work Dictionary* (Barker, 2013) it is "the act of perceiving, understanding, experiencing, and responding to the emotional state and ideas of another person." In the case of the freshman, empathy is easy because you actually were one at one time in your life. With clients, empathy may not always be as natural because you may not have experienced what they are going through.

Empathy is different from sympathy. Sympathy is the ability to share and feel the same emotions as your clients. Most often you won't feel the same emotions that your clients do about their situations, but you can always be empathetic. It is important that you understand the difference between empathy and sympathy. Sympathy is when you "feel sorry" for your client. Empathy is when you can say you understand them and what they are going through. For instance if someone tells you that they were just diagnosed with an inoperable brain tumor, you will have multiple emotions. When you "feel sorry" or "feel bad," that is sympathy. When you listen intently to someone and you understand their thought process and feelings, that is empathy. Sympathy can get in the way of your ability to be fully available to the client; therefore, it is important that you discuss your feelings about your clients in supervision or in your journals for field class.

Let's look at a case and see if you can think of things that this client may be going through, at which time empathy could be an effective tool.

Alice is a twenty-one-year-old single mother of two children, who are ages four and one. Her significant other is the father of the second child and is currently unemployed. Alice is referred to you by her psychiatrist, who is treating her for depression. Alice is also stressed by her financial situation. She tells you that she is working for a retail store as a cashier/stock clerk, making minimum wage and averaging ten hours a week. She lives at her parents' house, but her mother is requesting she leave as soon as possible due to lack of space. Alice has no health insurance, an unreliable car, and a high school diploma. Alice's significant other has been emotionally and physically abusive to her, but she believes he will change.

Based on this scenario, list some issues that the client is going through during which she would benefit from the use of empathy.

Issues that you can show empathy about

1. _____
2. _____
3. _____
4. _____
5. _____
6. _____
7. _____
8. _____

Does your list include:
fear of significant other?

worry about her living situation?

concern about her financial situation, including paying for her counseling and medication?

resentment toward her mother for asking her to look for another place to live?

frustration about being a single mom of two children?

anxiety about lack of hours and stability at her job?

concern about child care for work and counseling?

What else did you see? All of these issues give you the opportunity to express empathy and give you the ability to develop your relationship. Look at your list again. What are some empathetic responses to some of the emotions you expect your client to have?

Empathetic responses to issues

1. _____
2. _____
3. _____
4. _____
5. _____
6. _____
7. _____
8. _____

Empathy does not imply that you agree or disagree with how the client is managing his or her life. Nor does it mean that you have experienced the same type of situation in your personal life. Rather, it shows the client that you have the capacity to hear and understand his or her feelings. In fact, it is not our job as social workers to agree or disagree with clients' decisions about their lives. Agreeing or disagreeing is judgmental and power-laden behavior.

Even if you have been in a similar situation, you may have handled the issues differently because of who you are. Often, clients will ask you what you would you do if you were in their situation. What you would do in a similar situation is not relevant here, because this is not about you. Remember, it is a completely different person who is coping to the best of his or her ability. When a client asks you what you would do, it is an unintentional trap. Be careful not to go there.

When you answer the question "What would you do if," you answer based on *who you are*, not who the clients are. Since your life experiences and your support systems are your own, you will answer this question differently than your clients will. But, it is their lives and how they perceive their choices that matter.

Empathy involves staying with clients and supporting them while they make choices and carry them through.

This is a good time to discuss cultural sensitivity again. Some nonverbal communication, such as a wave hello or good-bye or pointing with your finger, transcends culture. Some nonverbal communication is not the same; for example, some cultures do not touch as much as others. Be sure that there is no miscommunication because of culture; as the social worker, this responsibility falls mainly on you.

Also recognize that there will be many instances when, because of culture, people are unable to see as many options as you do for them. For example, one of the authors once worked with a Hispanic woman whose mother died and in her will the client was given the family home. The client was laid off from her job, subsequently having serious financial difficulty. While trying to help the client brainstorm her options the author (then the social worker for this woman) kept suggesting to her to sell her house. This was not an option for her because it had been the family home for four generations. She felt obligated to find a way to keep the house, but the author did not understand that. The social worker was culturally insensitive and didn't understand the responsibility bestowed on her client by her mother to keep the house as a sense of pride of the family achieving "the American Dream." Understand what the cultural responsibilities and obligations are, as well as what boundaries an individual's cultures establish for them.

Let us look again at Alice's situation. You may see very clear decisions for her that will help her resolve some of her problems. Alice could break off the relationship with her abusive significant other, get a job that pays more and guarantees more hours, and force the significant other to pay child support. But what if Alice views the situation differently?

What if Alice thinks she should get a place with her significant other and have him provide child care while she gets more hours at her current job? You are there to assist her, not to answer questions for her. Ultimately, the decision is hers to make, and she has to implement it and live with what she decides. Your job is to ask questions that help her to feel clear and certain about her decision, and then provide resources and support to make that decision happen.

Your perception of the issues presented and Alice's perception are clearly different. When you are using your reflective listening skills, you should be hearing how the client perceives the situation. When you hear ambiguity and uncertainty, you should ask clarifying questions. If her answers worry you, state that concern in a way that confronts her belief. However, remember that your job as a social worker is to get her to be sure she is OK with her decision and has thought out her options. It is *not* to get her to do what you think is best. Dealing with the client's perception, not your own, makes this process possible.

Letting clients make their own decision makes them responsible for the outcomes and empowers them to be independent. We, as social workers, want both of these elements for our clients. When Alice makes the decision to move in with the abusive significant other, keep the same job, and have her abuser watch the children, you may cringe inside. However, she is exercising her right to self-determination. You may need to talk with your supervisor about the abuser watching Alice's children. There may be a need to call your child welfare or protection office if there is concern about the abuser hurting the children. If that is the case, you or your supervisor may want to inform Alice of your need to call.

Self-Determination

Self-determination is one of the ethical concepts of social work. According to *The Social Work Dictionary* (Barker, 2003, p. 387), self-determination is

> an ethical principle in social work that recognizes the rights and needs of clients to be free to make their own choices and decisions. Inherent in the principle is the requirement for the social worker to help the client know what the resources and choices are and what the consequences of selecting them will be. Usually self-determination also includes helping the client implement the decision made. Self-determination is one of the major factors in the helping relationship.

In the NASW Code of Ethics, client self-determination is an important part of section 1 (section 1.02), "Social Workers' Ethical Responsibilities to Clients."

> Social workers respect and promote the right of clients to self-determination and assist clients in their efforts to identify and clarify their goals. Social workers may limit clients' right to self-determination when, in the social workers' professional judgment, clients' actions or potential actions pose a serious, foreseeable, and imminent risk to themselves or others.

The CASW Guidelines for Ethical Practice dedicate an entire section (1.3) to self-determination. Sections 1.3.1–1.3.6 give details about respecting the client's right to self-determination. For example, according to section 1.3.1, "Social Workers promote the self-determination and autonomy of clients, actively encouraging them to make informed decisions on their own belief."

In order to successfully allow Alice self-determination in her case, you have a responsibility to make her aware of her choices and the consequences of those choices. You also have to assist her in finding the resources she needs. In Alice's case, what are the potential consequences of her choices?

Consequences of Alice's choices

Positives	Negatives

What are ways that you, as a social worker, can make Alice aware of the positive and negative consequences of her choices?

Skills and tools used to assist clients to see consequences

1. _____

2. _____

3. _____

4. _____

5. _____

6. _____

7. _____

8. _____

What are the resources you want to link Alice with in order to assist her in making these decisions?

Resources to help clients make decisions

1. _____

2. _____

3. _____

4. _____

5. _____

6. _____

7. _____

8. _____

How would you go about finding other resources for Alice as she implements her choices?

How to find resources and access to resources

1. _____

2. _____

3. _____

4. _____

5. _____

6. _____

7. _____

8. _____

Allowing clients the right to self-determination can sometimes be very difficult. Certainly you don't want to see Alice abused again. However, the best you can do is make sure that she is aware of possible consequences and give her resources to assist her: you cannot stop her from moving in with her significant other. Sometimes, the client will decide that he or she has made the wrong decision. Hopefully, you will have the opportunity to assist the client in making a new decision and implementing that. We say "hopefully" because sometimes the decisions clients make have consequences that prevent them from working on other alternatives. In Alice's case, what if her significant other seriously injures her during a fight? Clearly, that was one of your fears when she told you she wanted to stay with him. But even if you discussed that, you cannot stop it from happening. Other clients' situations could result in homelessness, jail time, or perhaps moving, and you can't help them make a different set of decisions.

How do you handle your client's choice when you think he or she is making the wrong decision? That is a tough question. You must be careful not to pressure the client or degrade his or her choice in any way. "I'll help you get resources," or "I'm there for you if this doesn't work out," or "This will be tough, but we will give it our best shot," are all appropriate things to say. Avoid comments like "I think you are making a poor decision," "You are on your own since you made that choice," or "I never would have chosen that." To learn how to handle this situation, seek supervision about the matter, be sure you have provided all the resources, and wait for the client to make the situation work, or for him or her to come back to you, admit it was a bad decision, and try to change the decision.

Another issue to consider regarding clients' right to self-determination is that often your sessions with clients are limited by outside sources (HMOs or mandated treatment for court-ordered clients). Although you still need to honor the client's right to self-determination, you may need to be more directive and bring up issues in a different manner to assist in the therapeutic process. You still need to build rapport and give clients the right to choose what actions to take, but in a shorter time frame than may be ideal.

Self-Determination from a Human Rights Perspective

Self-determination is a concept that has international implications and is one of the many links between social work and human rights. The concept is present in two major international documents: the International Covenant on Civil and Political Rights (ICCPR; United Nations, 1997) and the African Charter on Human and Peoples' Rights (African Charter; CIAD, 1981).

In the ICCPR, self-determination is found in part 1, article I, which states:

1. All peoples have the right of self-determination. By virtue of that right they freely determine their political status and freely pursue their economic, social, and cultural development.

2. All peoples may, for their own ends, freely dispose of their natural wealth and resources without prejudice to any obligations arising out of international economic cooperation, based upon the principle of mutual benefit, and international law. In no case may a people be deprived of its own means of subsistence.

3. The States Parties to the present Covenant, including those having responsibility for the administration of Non-Self-Governing and Trust Territories, shall promote the realization of the right of self-determination, and shall respect that right, in conformity with the provisions of the Charter of the United Nations.

In the African Charter, the right to self-determination is found in chapter 1, article 20:

1. All peoples shall have the right to existence. They shall have the unques-tionable and inalienable right to self-determination. They shall freely determine their political status and shall pursue their economic and social development according to the policy they have freely chosen.

2. Colonized or oppressed peoples shall have the right to free themselves from the bonds of domination by resorting to any means recognized by the international community.

3. All peoples shall have the right to the assistance of the States parties of the present Charter in their liberation struggle against foreign domina-tion, be it political, economic, or cultural.

Clearly, both of these documents refer to self-determination in regard to the political status of individuals and peoples. However, also contained here is the provision of self-determination in economic, social, and cultural rights, which can include the right to social services, among other basic human rights.

The UN Declaration of Human Rights in Comparison to the NASW Code of Ethics
by Rosemary Barbera

Along with these documents there is also the UN Declaration of Human Rights, which was adopted by the UN General Assembly in 1948. The UN Declaration of Human Rights has some similarities to the NASW Code of Ethics, as seen in the chart below.

Comparison of the United Nations Declaration of Human Rights with the National Association of Social Workers Code of Ethics

UN Declaration of Human Rights	NASW Code of Ethics
• Recognition of the inherent dignity and of the equal and inalienable rights of all members of the human family is the foundation of freedom, justice, and peace in the world	• Primary mission of social work is to enhance human well-being and help meet the basic human needs of all people
• All humans are born free and equal in dignity and rights • Right to life, liberty, and security of person • No slavery or servitude	• Mission is rooted in a set of core values • Service to others above self-interest
• No torture or cruel, inhuman treatment • Right to recognition as a person before the law • All equal before law and entitled to protection without discrimination • The right to an effective remedy when rights have been violated	• Primary goal is to help people in need and to address social problems • Social Justice • Challenge social injustice • Pursue social change
• No one shall be subjected to arbitrary interference with privacy, family, home, or correspondence • Right to marry and end marriage	• Promote sensitivity to and knowledge about oppression and cultural and ethnic diversity • Dignity and worth of the person • Respect the inherent dignity and worth of the person • Self-determination • Importance of human relationships
• Right to choose whom to marry • Peaceful assembly and association	• People are an important vehicle for change • Integrity • Trustworthy • Honest • Competence • Continue to learn and enhance knowledge • Contribute to knowledge base

Although not every social worker knows about the Universal Declaration of Human Rights (UDHR), it is a very significant document in history that outlines for us the basic human rights that everyone in every country should expect. As Eroles articulates, "Social work and human rights have a very close relationship" (1997, p. 56), which calls on us to be active in the construction of a new state where the human rights of all are respected. Social work in the United States articulates a close relationship between social justice and social work in the NASW Code of Ethics. Since respect for human rights is a vehicle toward the construction of a just society, the relationship between the UN Declaration of Human Rights and the NASW Code of Ethics is significant. To that end international social work organizations such as "the IFSW and IASSW consider it imperative that social workers clearly commit themselves to the promotion and protection of human rights without reservation" (Eroles, 1997, p. 119).

It is likewise important to consider that social work from a human rights perspective helps us attain the very basis of our professional principles: the preoccupation for serving, for being useful, more than anything, to the weakest members of society; to intervene specifically confronting social problems until we are able to assure that the necessary conditions that guarantee all basic necessities are met (Sánchez, 1989, p. 21).

The UDHR, the NASW Code of Ethics, and the IFSW Statement of Ethical Principles contribute to a social work practice that advances human rights and confronts injustice and oppression.

The UN Universal Declaration of Human Rights contains provisions for civil, political, economic, social, and cultural rights. Oftentimes these are described as negative and positive rights. A negative right forbids others from acting against the right holder, while a positive right obligates others to act with respect to the right holder. Positive rights do not exist until they are acknowledged in a contract. While these rights are often thought of in an individualistic way, they are really about bettering the community of humanity. Unless these rights are respected for all, no one is safe. As such, human rights needed to be contextualized beyond the individual level. Given social work's commitment to improving the quality of life for all, this fits nicely with the profession's commitment and obligation to working for change at multiple levels. Later human rights documents also discuss issues of collective rights. These would include rights that affect the quality of life of all living beings, such as the right to live in a clean, safe, sustainable environment. The UN Universal Declaration of Human Rights is an excellent tool to use as a guide to social work practice. It is found in appendix F for your reference.

Cultural Sensitivity and Client Perception

There is a growing body of literature in social work on cultural competence or cultural sensitivity with clients. A social worker who works with clients from other racial, ethnic, or religious groups needs to have a special sensitivity to their clients' perceptions of social service provision.

A few issues to consider and discuss are

- ✔ the importance of establishing relationships,

- ✔ the importance of knowing your own cultural values, ethics, and norms,

- ✔ the importance of learning about other groups, and

- ✔ the importance of learning how to sensitively frame questions to clients. Can you think of other issues?

Using Clients' Strengths

When linking your clients with resources, don't forget one critical resource, the clients themselves. Ask the client what he or she considers personal strengths. Then point out strengths that you see that the client has not pointed out. Strengths can be internal or external to the client. Sometimes a strength is a personality characteristic like creativity, or being strong-willed or organized. Sometimes it is an external strength like strong family support or financial resources. Don't forget about tangible strengths as well, like a job, a house, health insurance, or a car. Using a strengths-based approach helps the client develop the ability to confront weaknesses they would otherwise not be able to deal with without assistance. The client's strengths are a valuable asset for solving the issues at hand.

Two theories that you will be exposed to in your social work practice rely heavily on the client's strengths: resiliency theory and the strengths perspective. Building on a strong foundation (the client's strengths) gives the social worker time and support to minimize the weaknesses that may never go away. When completing the assessment and when receiving information about the client, remember that you can start working only where the client is, not where you expect him or her to be. This point, starting where the client is, is easier to explain in mathematics. You would not try to teach a first grader algebra when the student has not learned the concept of two-digit addition. With a social work client, you don't want to be numerous steps ahead either.

You may also think in terms of Maslow's hierarchy of needs: from bottom to top, Maslow (1970) lists a human's needs as physiological needs, safety, love, esteem, and self-actualization. Maslow says the needs at the bottom need to be met before you can get to the next level. Therefore, if you have a homeless client, you don't want to be working on self-actualizing. Instead, you want to be providing food and shelter for that client. Find out where clients are, what their thoughts and emotions are about the issue, and be there with them in that spot.

Alice may only be wanting to move in with her significant other to make him happy, so he won't abuse her again. Hear that statement and empathize with her about the situation; don't rush to tell her there is nothing to be afraid of, and to break up with her significant other. Don't jump steps. Stay with clients and let them go through the process at their own speed.

Using a Community's Strengths

The best way to talk about using a community's strengths in working with a community is to talk about Asset-Based Community Development, a movement that has been pioneered by John McKnight and his colleagues at the School of Education and Social Policy at Northwestern University. http://www.abcdinstitute.org/.

This method looks at each neighborhood or community and takes a practical approach to assessing and cataloguing the community's strengths and assets, often diagramming this on a map or other pictorial design. Once this is done, gaps often reveal themselves, which can then be worked on by the community using the same strengths and assets of the community, so that it is the community itself that is helping to solve its own problems and issues, rather than having others from the outside coming in to "fix" the community. Remember this is the community's initiative, not yours, and you have to use very good listening skills and always keep their goals at the forefront of all activities. Respecting their right to own the initiative shows respect, helps develop relationships, and creates a better chance of the initiative becoming self-sustaining and something the community will be proud of once you leave.

Johari Window

Named after its inventors Joseph Luft and Harry Ingham, the Johari Window is a way for you to visualize different components of the person who is sitting in front of you and may help you understand his or her perception a little more clearly. Luft and Ingham's model has four quadrants (windows) that divide people's awareness about themselves into categories.

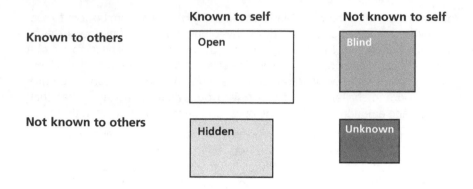

Luft and Ingham believed that we all have information about ourselves that is known to everyone (open), like our names or maybe where we work (Luft, 1970). Then they claimed that there are things that we do not know about ourselves but others see (blind), like that when we first meet people they think we are mean. The third quadrant is what we know about ourselves but is hidden to others (hidden), for example, we have a medical problem, and the fourth quadrant is what we have not learned about ourselves and others do not know either, like what our lives will look like in twenty years. The examples here are broad but what we know about ourselves and don't know can also include personal characteristics and abilities.

Every person will have different-size quadrants because of who they are and what they share. But those quadrants help every person decide what his or her perception is of a certain problem. When we are working with clients, they know two of the four quadrants (open and hidden) about themselves, and you, as the social worker, know two quadrants (open and blind). However, they are not exactly the same quadrants. Depending on how open clients have been and how self-aware they are, they may know substantially more about themselves than you do. They may have a better perception about what they can do or what to act upon. As a social worker, you are working on getting the client to have a large open quadrant and very small blind and unknown quadrants.

Pick someone else in the class who knows you fairly well. Spend some time filling out your own Johari window in the open area and then spend some time thinking about the blind area of your partner. Compare notes on those two areas. Did your partner know what you considered to be open information? Did your partner know the things you considered blind?

Comparing quadrants

Your open area	Your partner's blind area

Thoughts to ponder

✔ How would you go about creating a larger open area in your Johari window?

✔ Is having a large open area appealing to you?

✔ How do you figure out what is in your unknown area?

Integration of other course material

HBSE   What does stage of development have to do with how clients perceive the world?

Policy   When is a client's right to self-determination not the priority?

Practice   Do you have suggestions on what social work techniques can help someone decide what is known to others and not known to self?

Research   How does your client's perception impact the single system design research model?

Resources

Johari Window
http://www.mindtools.com/CommSkll/JohariWindow.htm

Mental Health Network on Empathy
http://www.mentalhelp.net/poc/view_doc.php?type=doc&id=52423&cn=298

Self-Determination
http://www.centerforself-determination.com/

African Charter on Human and Peoples' Rights
Asset-Based Community Mapping
http://www.hrcr.org/docs/Banjul/afrhr.html

International Covenant on Civil and Political Rights
http://www.hrweb.org/legal/cpr.html

What can you do independently at your internship and what do you have to ask permission to do? Describe both situations and how they make you feel.

Chapter 8
Put It in Writing!

When we talked to social work students about why they want to be social workers, no one ever told us that it was because they love to write or that they heard social work documentation is fun. Believe it or not, social work documentation doesn't even rank in the top ten reasons to become a social worker☺! Yet documentation is a vital component of every social work job. Social work documentation comes in a variety of styles and has many purposes. Each agency that employs you will have its unique form of documentation, which depends on the state regulations and accrediting bodies that oversee the services that the agency provides.

What we want to discuss here are the most common types of social work writing—what they are, what context you might use them in—and how to improve your writing skills. We will cover progress notes, psychosocials, process recordings, treatment plans, quarterly reports, discharge summary, written referrals, grant writing, business letters, administrative, statistical reports, and writing for publication. In covering these areas we will discuss good writing skills, writing styles, and plagiarism.

Progress Notes

One important lesson about documentation that you will hear over and over again in your career is this: *if it isn't written, it never happened.*

If a client of yours who was laid off from his job goes to his old place of employment, kills his former boss and coworkers, and then kills himself, there is bound to be an investigation. Who has access to those records during the investigation is another subject, but definitely your supervisor, the agency director, and perhaps an agency lawyer are going to look at those files. If you did not write in your notes that your client denied suicidal and homicidal ideation, you and your agency could be held responsible for all the deaths, because the proper documentation is not in place. That is not something you want to go through, so remember: **document . . . document . . . document**! *If it is not in writing, it did not happen!*

You need to keep accurate records of any action about a client that occurred when you were involved. This includes phone conversations, any correspondence about or with the client, and notes from contacts and sessions with your client. If you called to cancel a meeting with a client, you should write the date, time, and what happened (e.g., talked to the client, no answer, busy, left message on an answering machine or with a person). Nowadays you may also be leaving e-mails or texts. If your agency allows these electronic notifications be sure that the e-mail and or text are professional and in a proper English, not text language. If you receive messages from a client, through a receptionist, in writing, or on voicemail, you may transfer that information into a case file or keep the message in a separate section of the file. Believe it or not, most times it's easier to do both, because little notes get lost, but it is always helpful to have the original. Just an added note about documentation in the era of the electronic world. Your notes will be time and date stamped as well as be integrated into other person's notes depending on how your agency completes documentation. You must document and must learn the best way to document. Is it at the end of each session (this is ideal), the end of the day, or the end of the week? Be sure to discuss documentation strategy with your supervisor.

Progress notes come in many different formats, and you should determine what format your agency uses. During the course of your career you may learn many formats. Some formats that the authors are familiar with include

SOAP: subjective information, objective information, assessment and conclusion, plan

DAP: data, assessment, plan

POT: problem, orientation, treatment plan

POR: problem-oriented record

Now there are jargon and acronyms for you, as discussed in chapter 6!

Each of these types of documentation captures similar content. Find out as soon as you start at an agency what format the agency uses. The same information documented two different ways, in SOAP and in DAP, might look like this:

July 20, 2015

S: Client came in for initial session appearing disheveled and tired.

O: Social worker completed intake and addressed appearance, finding that the client has been living in his car since being evicted from his house for not paying rent.

A: Client is in need of housing.

P: Refer client to local emergency housing after confirming eligibility and availability; provide client with transportation.

Kelly Ward, PhD, LCSW, LCADC (actual signature)

July 20, 2015

D: Client states he has been evicted and is now homeless when he enters the agency for his intake assessment.

A: Client feels worried that he has no place to live as well as embarrassed that he is seeking assistance.

P: Refer client to local emergency housing after confirming eligibility and availability; provide client with transportation. Help client feel comfortable with needing to accept assistance.

Kelly Ward, PhD, LCSW, LCADC (actual signature)

Observe that basically the same information is in both types of documentation. Notice that the plan is exactly the same at first, but because you know the client's feelings, you can add a piece that assists the client with his feelings about needing help.

Larger institutions and agencies will have a documentation preference. If you go to a smaller agency or a place that is just adding a social work component to a program, they may not have a procedure in place. At that point, you should discuss the options with your supervisor and check with funding sources and your licensing bodies to see what they suggest. In private practice, you may choose the documentation format that works for you—but be sure to document.

Psychosocials

Psychosocials, sometimes called biopsychosocials or initial assessments, are typically created when a new client comes to your office. As in the case of progress notes, most agencies have their own biopsychosocial forms that contain relevant information for that agency.

Our first suggestion when filling out the form is to remember that the initial goal is to get to know the client and make him or her feel comfortable, not to fill out the form. If you can, read any information that the agency has on this client, especially demographics like gender, date of birth (DOB), and address. If the agency has this information, all you need to do is verify it with the client. Implementing this process in the initial session lets the client know that he or she doesn't have to repeat similar information for the umpteenth time, and it allows you to start with simple questions to ease the anxiety you and your client may be experiencing.

The rest of the information on a biopsychosocial assessment is usually grouped by related questions that allow you to get the information in a conversational way, as you would with someone you are simply trying to get to know. In other words, try to group the questions by similar subjects, but ask them in an order that you think will allow the client to feel most comfortable. When asking these questions, you will begin to use all the questioning techniques that you have learned: open-ended questions, probing questions, clarifying questions, and so on. Try to get an accurate picture of a client's life, how history and the current environment have aided or deterred the client in the current situation, and why the client is presenting to your agency for services at this time.

It is wise before you begin the psychosocial to introduce yourself and to let the client know what you are doing, how long it will take, and who will get to see the information. A standard introduction may go something like this:

> Hello. Mrs. Hughes, my name is Robin Mama, and I am a social work intern here at ABC agency. I need to make sure all of the admissions paperwork is completed before we continue. Is that OK with you? It will take us about 45 minutes and will give me a good understanding of how we can best help you. Everything you tell me is confidential unless you tell me you are going to harm yourself or anyone else. Are there any questions? If not, let's begin. If you don't mind, I will take a few brief notes during our conversation.

This helps your client to understand the process. It also lets your client know that you might take some notes during the interview. One word of caution here: Don't get so caught up in taking notes that you do not listen to or keep eye contact with your client! The client might think you are being rude, and you are—note-taking is to be used judiciously, *not* throughout the whole interview. You must attend to the client when he or she is speaking. If the client becomes emotional in any way, you must put down your pen or pencil and stop writing. The longer you are at the agency the more you will remember the form and develop your own style. At that point you will be able to just have a conversation without paper in front of you.

Let's discuss some of the questions that usually appear on psychosocials. Sometimes you will look at the questions and say, "The question is not relevant to this client, I won't talk about that subject." For instance, sexual activity and sexual orientation are often questions on a psychosocial. Perhaps you have a seventy-five-year-old widow sitting in front of you and you think, "Oh, she doesn't have sex." How do you know? Perhaps her next-door neighbor is a widower and they have been having sex regularly. Or her next door neighbor is female and the widow finally acknowledges that she married her husband to hide her sexual orientation.

Often questions about drug and alcohol consumption are on psychosocials. If you are sitting with a child, you might think you don't have to ask these questions. Well, if you talked to drug/alcohol specialists, they could tell you horror stories of children being high or drunk as young as age eight or nine. You could use these questions to widen the scope of the interview by asking if anyone in their family uses drugs or alcohol and to probe for other important information. Don't overlook opportunities to get more information than the question is calling for on the assessment form.

Another often overlooked question is military history. Again, many people will overlook this when interviewing children. However, their parents may have been in the military or have been killed in action. Maybe the child has never lived in one place for long, because the family was reassigned frequently, thereby having difficulty making and keeping friends. As we are now all living in the age or terrorism and most of us know one or more people in the military. We also need to be sensitive to clients who have returned from combat injured or clients who have family members who are injured or did not return from deployment. [Military social work is a new and evolving field that needs specialized knowledge and skills.]

When working with people who have traveled into or have lived in areas that have experienced terrorism, remember to ask your clients if they experienced the terrorism and their feelings about terrorism. Examples of this would include the New York/New Jersey area because of 9/11, Oklahoma City, or someone who was on a plane that was hijacked. Separate but similar in another category are those who live in areas that have experienced natural disasters such as Hurricane Katrina, Superstorm Sandy, earthquakes, tornados, or fires.

We should also not forget to consider the plight of clients who may now be subject to suspicion due to the consequences of worldwide terrorism. For example, radical Islam and the groups that support it are frequently in the news with their terrorist acts of violence in several parts of the world. The consequence for many people of the Muslim faith is that many Muslims have been subjected to various forms of discrimination all the way up to violence, assault, and death due only to the fact that they are deemed by others to be guilty because of their faith. You may have clients who find themselves bullied, or whose families receive threats, merely because of their religion and not because they themselves are linked to radical Islam. Additionally, other ethnic groups that might "look" Islamic can find themselves falling victim to these random acts of suspicion and violence as well.

Work history is another overlooked part of psychosocials. Anyone working in occupational safety and health will tell you that getting a detailed work history is often essential for medical reasons. Many of the substances or chemicals that people work with can cause severe medical problems or diseases. One has only to look at the experiences of workers who were exposed to asbestos to see how devastating this can be. In the case of asbestos exposure, not only did workers develop lung disease, but their wives often developed lung cancer from washing their husbands' clothes.

Two last suggestions about psychosocials—don't assume ethnicity or gender from your observation. You don't want someone who identifies as a transvestite (cross dresser) or someone else who identifies as transgendered (had a gender reassignment surgery) to not tell you his or her true identity because you assumed the person in front of you was female. Also, don't assume that because a person has dark brown skin he or she is African American. Be culturally sensitive and ask for gender, sexual orientation, ethnicity and racial background. Look in appendix B for a psychosocials format created at Monmouth University School of Social Work, recently updated in 2014 to include a focus on Human Rights as well as a clients' strengths by (used by permission).

While discussing the biopsychosocial it is the perfect time to complete a genogram and ecomap of the client's life. Some agencies have separate forms for you to fill out; if not, just take blank paper or the back of the biopsychosocial and start to draw. If you have not yet learned how to do a genogram or ecomap, take time to learn. Both give an excellent one-page view of the client's life history, highlighting family patterns, relationships, and current connections to other areas of his or her system. The genogram is a diagram, similar to a family tree, that shows relationships and family patterns. In 2012 Monica McGoldrick updated the symbols used for genograms to include gay/lesbian relationships as well as other more modern family formations. Her changes are found in Appendix H. Genograms present at least three generations of a family, including all marriages, divorces, children and pregnancies, ethnicity, and religion. Also include physical location(s) of people in the family, and who lives with whom. Ecomaps are a drawing of a person's relationships and resources. Social workers put symbols together to form relationships, to indicate how people are related, and to determine what common issues they share.

Constructing genograms and ecomaps

Figure 8.1 shows the symbols used in making genograms and ecomaps. We put these symbols together to form relationships, to indicate how people are related, and to determine what common issues they share. Present at least three generations of a family, including all marriages, divorces, children and pregnancies, ethnicity, and religion. Also include physical location(s) of people in the family, and who lives with whom.

If you remember that the form in front of you is not the focus, and that developing a relationship with the client in order to assist them is the goal, then you will do fine. Eventually, when you have been working in an agency for a while, you will be able to remember most of the form and what the client says without writing it down until after the interview.

We need to say a word here about client access to records. Every agency has a policy on whether clients can access their records and, if so, how a client can do this. Section 1.08 of the NASW Code of Ethics contains specific information about client access to records, when this should and should not be available, and concerns leading to protection of client confidentiality. Read the code and ask your agency about this policy.

Figure 8.1

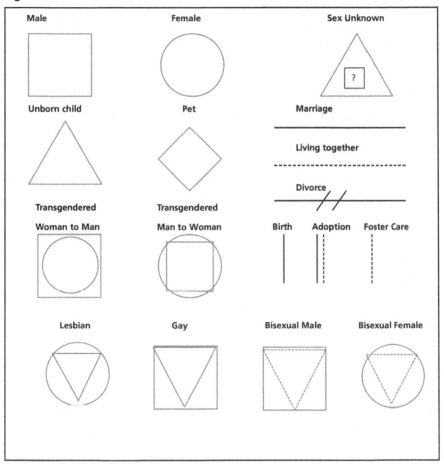

In addition, section 3.04 of the Code of Ethics specifies that documentation should be accurate, meet deadlines, protect clients' privacy rights, and be stored once services are terminated.

Documentation and handling of clients' records is detailed in sections 1.7 through 1.9 in the CASW Guidelines for Ethical Practice. "Maintenance and Handling of Client Records" specifically states:

> Social workers maintain one written record of professional interventions and opinions, with due care to the obligations and standards of their employer and relevant regulatory body. Social workers document information impartially and accurately and with an appreciation that the record

may be revealed to clients or disclosed during court proceedings. Social workers are encouraged to take care to report only essential and relevant details, refrain from using emotive or derogatory language, acknowledge the basis of professional opinions, and protect clients' privacy and that of others involved.

Intervention Plans

Intervention plans (also called treatment plans in most agencies) will be covered in greater depth in a later chapter but need to be mentioned here. Intervention plans are not written as frequently as progress notes, but the intervention plan is the backbone of every progress note you write. The intervention plan is like your road map to get to the end of services. When the client has accomplished all treatment goals, then they have successfully completed treatment. The intervention plan is a living, breathing document that is altered for every positive and negative change that occurs while the client is receiving services. The intervention plan is developed from the initial assessment. Usually the agency will have subareas in the intervention plan for (1) health, (2) education/vocation, (3) employment, (4) relationships, and (5) legal issues. Intervention plans are the legal contract between you and the client. They usually include goals and objectives, names or positions of the responsible parties, target dates, and signatures of all involved in the intervention plan. Be aware that this is a legally binding document and must be adhered to in terms of goals, objectives, and target dates. A sample of an intervention plan appears in chapter 10.

Quarterly Reports

Depending on how long your clients are in your program, you may need to write quarterly reports. If the program is long-term (six months or longer), you will write a report every three months to summarize the quarter, while addressing progress or lack thereof on the client's treatment goals. Quarterly reports may also be requested from referral sources, so that they are kept abreast of the client's status in your program.

Quarterly reports are usually formatted to look like a narrative of each treatment goal in the same order that the treatment plan is written. It is common for the strengths and successes to be noted first, followed by the areas where continued treatment is recommended. Each agency will probably have its own format or form for you to use, so check to see if a format is in place. Here is an example of a quarterly report format.

Quarterly Report for [Client's Name]

Goal one. Client's strengths and completed tasks are written first, followed by areas that need continued work, usually in a second paragraph: Client has a goal to remain drug and alcohol free. During the first quarter of his treatment, the client has submitted urine samples that have tested negative and has received a 90-day key chain from NA (Narcotics Anonymous). Staff continues to see positive changes in his behavior. He has increased insight into how drug use had impacted his life up until entry to the program three months ago.

Goal two. Continue same format, listing positive steps first, followed by areas that need work, such as: Although client remains free of drug and alcohol, he has not yet obtained employment. Client's previous employment was always related to drug dealing (runner, mule, or look out). Due to client's lack of high school diploma and no work experience, the client is struggling. Client has agreed to enroll in adult education to work toward obtaining his GED and test for vocational aptitude.

Goal three. Follow same format.

Summary statement. Summarize how much work has been done, what needs to be done, and recommendations that need to be considered.

Discharge Summary

When the client has completed all of the treatment goals set at admission when you completed the intervention plan, they are ready for discharge. Your documentation should identify the original presenting area of concern, what was done to address this, and what the client needs to do after discharge. An example would be:

Colleen Cannon presented to the hospital with anxiety and depression as a result of the death of her son. Ms. Cannon learned about the grief process, discussed her son and her depression and anxiety in individual and group counseling. Ms. Cannon was also seen by the psychiatrist who prescribed her an antidepressant. Ms. Cannon was encouraged to continue the medication and counseling. An appointment was made for her with a psychiatrist and a social worker at the local mental health center, and she was given a list of support groups. Funding was secured for her medication through the pharmaceutical company.

Referrals

Clients often need more services than what your agency will be able to provide, such as the support groups or medication assistance as listed above. Other referrals could be for rental assistance, food stamps, utility discounts. You will learn these resources once you start in the field, but your client might not know these resources are even available. When you give a referral to a client, you document that information in their file as well as on a separate sheet of paper with the name, address, phone number, web-address, e-mail, contact person, and appointment date and time (if necessary), which is given to the client. You may also have to call and make an appointment for the client, depending on the referral. The documentation in the chart for Ms. Cannon above would say:

> Ms. Cannon has completed her initial treatment. She has an appointment in ABC Mental Health Clinic at 123 Main Street in Old Town with Kelly Ward Social Worker on Monday January 15 at 10:30 a.m. immediately followed with psychiatrist Dr. Sikowitz on the same day. The grief support group is at Our Lady of Angels Church at 3644 Rocky River Drive on Wednesdays at 7:30 p.m. Client was also given the pharmaceutical coupon and the name of XYZ pharmacy who honors the coupons.

Business Letters

As social workers you will be writing many business letters. Official business letters follow a certain format and also have multiple standard components. Knowledge of the correct format will help you look very professional. Grammar and correct punctuation are extremely important. Your letter represents you, and often the person you send it to will never meet you, so the letter reflects on you and your agency. Typos, poor grammar, and sloppy formatting reflect poorly on you, your agency, and the profession. The first page of the business letter should be printed on agency letterhead. The first line of the letter should start six lines down in order to save room for the letterhead logo. Subsequent pages, if there are any, and attachments, are not on letterhead. The first line should be the return address (your address), followed by a line space, then the date of the letter. After another line space, type the name, full title, and full address of the recipient of the letter. Judges are always addressed in this section as "the Honorable" and then their full name. The fourth section is the salutation (for example, "Dear Mr. Black"), followed by a colon. Next comes the body of the letter. The first line of the paragraph should be indented five spaces with one space in-between sentences. The body of the letter is single-spaced, with a double space in between paragraphs. Keep your letter as succinct as possible and be sure to include a way for the person to contact you if they have any questions or need to reply to you. Finally, the closing is usually signed with "Sincerely," then three line spaces (for you to sign your name), and then your name typed, with your title underneath your name. You can ask your supervisor to share with you the format of a letter that has been written by someone at the agency.

Other Documentation

Other forms of documentation for the client are not as common or frequent as progress notes, psychosocials, treatment plans, or quarterly reports, so we just want to make you aware that they exist. When and if you have other direct services documentation, it is best to consult with your supervisor about format, expectations, and appropriate style (e.g., letters to court are always very formal, with proper titles and salutations for judges).

Depending on the type of agency you work in, there is bound to be other direct care documentation. For instance, residential facilities commonly have a journal where staff document the events that occurred during that shift. Although in most places the writing style is very informal (just to bring all staff up-to-date), it is still a legal record and your signature denotes that what you stated is fact. Usually there is also an incident report to document a serious injury or infraction of the program rules, which goes to the agency administration and into the client's files. Incident reports generally are just facts, not observations or opinions. There may also be a medication log if staff dispense medication. Make sure you are trained and feel comfortable dispensing medication if your agency requires it.

Many of the forms and information you process are time-sensitive, so you need to be very aware of reporting deadlines. In some agencies, intakes or initial assessments might need to be completed within 36–48 hours. For child protective services agencies, the turn-around time is much faster. Check deadlines with your supervisor and be sure to allocate time during your day to complete your documentation. There is also special documentation when working with a community. An example of this can be found in appendix H.

Administrative Writings

Thus far, we have dealt with documentation that is primarily related to the client and client services. However, many of you may be working in a macro approach to social work and will have little or no contact with clients; much more writing will be entailed in your job description. Sometimes, even when you prefer direct practice, you are given a supervisory role in which you will be expected to prepare administrative documents.

Many administrators or supervisors prepare quarterly statistical reports. These reports are usually summaries of the entire program that are sent to the program director/president or a funding source. Formatting of this quarterly report is similar to the direct service quarterly report about the client. You will write the report, following the program goals and objectives and listing strengths and weaknesses, and attaching any supporting documentation in an appendix. Sometimes, if you are lucky, the funding agency has a format/form they want you to use, and you can better provide exactly what they want.

Grant Writing

Social work agencies receive funds from various sources. Many agencies rely on grants to fund the services and programs that they provide. Grant money is used to start programs, to fund programs already in place, or to evaluate programs. Some grants are renewable, while others are for a specific time period. Each grant has specific provisions for reporting to the grant source about the program. Sometimes this involves monthly reports, sometimes quarterly or biannual reports, and always a final report. These reports have to be written as specified in the grant. This is not the place to teach you how to write grants. Helpful resources are found at the end of this chapter.

Process Recordings

When you meet your supervisor for supervision, he or she needs to understand what interactions occurred between you and your clients. If your supervisor is present to watch that interaction, you or your client may act unnaturally and your supervisor cannot really observe your skills with much accuracy. In an effort to minimize this problem, process recording was developed. Before audio- and videotaping and one-way mirrors, the only way to observe the interaction was for the social worker to write it down verbatim. In a column next to the conversation, social workers wrote down their thought process. A third column allowed the supervisor to make comments to the social worker. Process recording is an invaluable tool for growth and understanding how you are interacting and communicating with clients. We have heard many social workers who have been in the field for years say that, when they are really stuck, process recording is still the best way for them to understand what is happening in their interaction with the client and what their gut feelings are about that interaction. Appendix E has two examples of process recording sheets. Remember never to video- or audio-tape anyone without written consent, even if you are just sharing the video internally within your agency.

Writing Style

As a student you have been maturing as a writer and may be accustomed to writing in one style. As you can see by what we have discussed, your writing style is about to change. You will need to figure out the appropriate style for what you are writing. As already stated, grants, quarterly reports, and court letters are very professional. Intervention plans are rarely ever narrative and can sound a bit choppy, but they are essentially an outline. Progress notes are short and decisive, whereas logbooks are often fairly informal. Know your audience, and know what is expected with your writing. You may at some point decide that you would like to write for publication. Take a look at articles in your social work journals to see how they are written. Each journal has a particular focus and style—you will need to follow that style if you want your article to be considered for publication.

We have written this book intentionally in a colloquial voice. This is because it is informal and contains fun activities designed for a field class, which is really about discussion. If this book were a policy book or a research book, it would be written in a different style. Hopefully the style encourages you to read it!

You have been writing term papers that require a particular style. The preferred style for social work is usually the American Psychological Association (APA) format. Some disciplines follow the Chicago manuscript style. Please make sure you are aware of the requirements for documenting and completing a bibliography. The styles are very precise and exact. If you ever write for publication, your manuscript will not be read if it is in the wrong format. Spend time learning the correct format because it will benefit you through school and into your professional career. Try hard not to mix formats. This is a common and easy mistake when you are accustomed to one way of writing and then are asked to switch styles.

Regardless of what you are writing, use correct spelling and grammar. When people haven't met you, one of the things they judge you by is the quality of your writing. Don't allow people to think you are unqualified to be a social worker. If your writing skills needs improvement, work on them now while in school. Check to see if your school has a writing center or inexpensive tutors who can proof your work and give you a few pointers. Also, don't rely on spell-check programs in your word-processing programs. Many typing errors won't get picked up by a spell-checker.

Finally, be wary of "auto correct" on your computer, as it can often change the words you are typing into words that you never intended. As an example, one of the authors was e-mailing the other author. We don't remember the actual words that were meant to be typed. But what was sent, without proofreading carefully, was the phrase "rat #@stard." Although we laughed at the phrase when it was pointed out, some of that laughter was out of embarrassment for sending that out and some of the laughter was relief that it was not sent out to someone who would not have appreciated the error.

Writing in social work takes on many dimensions. Find out what is expected and get help if you need it. It can be complicated, confusing, and overwhelming, but stay on top of your documentation and you will be fine.

Creating False Documentation

We would like to caution you at this point about documenting meetings, group sessions, phone calls, or any other work-related issue that has never happened. Under no circumstances should documents be created or falsified. There have been real-life situations that have been sensationalized in television shows and well documented by journalists. Examples such as child protection workers who documented home visits that never occurred or reporting seeing children that were not present at the home at the time of the visit. Falsifying facts that have not occurred is not only unethical but also irresponsible and illegal. Document only what happens and only what you are present for and participate in. Again, documentation is objective reporting of the facts and not trying to slant the facts in any particular way. As an intern, in many agencies you are not permitted by policy or law to document in client records. Or sometimes you are permitted to document but your supervisor needs to cosign your progress notes. Be sure to know what your agency policy is so that you do not violate it because you are unaware. Likewise if you are uncertain about documentation that you have been asked to do and you think it is inappropriate, immediately discuss the request and your concerns with your supervisor. Recently students reported to us that a counselor in a mental health agency had them write progress notes for groups that the student did not attend or observe. The counselor was out of line, had not discussed the task with their supervisor, and put the student at risk as well as the agency. We would hope to never hear that this happens to anyone else. Also, never sign something that you have not read or that you do not agree with. This can put you in jeopardy in much the same way as documenting something that did not happen. Be sure to also sign your appropriate title and your license every time you document. As an intern you will always sign "social work intern." Finally, consequences for false documentation include termination from your job, loss of license, development of a poor reputation, and fines and other legal consequences.

Plagiarism

One last word about writing. Know what plagiarism is and what it is not. Plagiarism is the use of someone else's work without giving them credit for the work. It is illegal and unethical, causing students to fail and ruining careers. Whenever you see an idea in print or on the Internet or hear it in a speech, and you think it will be useful information to your work, give credit to the author/speaker. The APA stylebook gives you an entire chapter on how to cite almost anything. Inadequate referencing is almost as bad as plagiarism, and many consider the two to be equivalent.

The NASW Code of Ethics in section 4.08 spells out your responsibility to give credit.

(a) Social workers should take responsibility and credit, including authorship credit, only for work they have actually performed and to which they have contributed.

(b) Social workers should honestly acknowledge the work of and the contributions made by others.

CASW Guidelines for Ethical Practice addresses this issue as well in section 3.2.4:

Social workers take responsibility and credit, including authorship credit, only for work they have actually preformed and to which they have contributed.

Thoughts to ponder

✔ What are my writing strengths? What areas can I work on now?

✔ What do I feel about process recordings? How can I make it easier for myself to remember the conversation that I will use in a process recording?

✔ What do I understand about plagiarism, and how can I avoid it?

Integration of other course material

HBSE   What is the best way to document history of genetic health problems, mental illness in a family, and substance abuse in order to see patterns developing?

Policy   What are the legal implications if you have documented improperly or have forgotten to document?

Practice   How can your documentation help you enhance your social work practice?

Research   When reading an article on a research study, how can you tell where the authors based their study and why?

Resources

APA Style
Reference Point Software
*http://www.referencepointsoftware.net/order.htm?gclid=CLLu7pPPwL0CFVQV7
AodWB4AzA*

The Purdue Online Writing Lab
https://owl.english.purdue.edu/Writinglab/

Chicago Manual of Style
http://www.chicagomanualofstyle.org

Grant Writing
National Institutes of Health
http://grants.nih.gov/grants/grant_tips.htm

Foundation Center
http://foundationcenter.org/

Nonprofit Guides
http://www.npguides.org

Business letters
The Purdue Online Writing Lab
http://owl.english.purdue.edu/owl/resource/653/01/

Do you ever feel like pulling over
and taking a rest at your internship
or in your field class?

Chapter 9
Pick a Theory, Any Theory

Social work is a profession that you can be proud to be joining. Do you remember learning about Dr. Alexander Flexner in your social welfare history class? Flexner addressed the 1915 conference on charities and corrections and flatly told the social work audience that social work was not a profession. The established professions (law, medicine, and religion) had three criteria for becoming a profession: a body of knowledge used to practice from, specific and defined skills, and ethics. The social work profession meets all three of those criteria now and can be proudly considered a profession even in Dr. Flexner's eyes. The definition of a profession presumes that we are practicing competently as stated in both the NASW and the CASW codes of ethics. One of the tools we must use is a theoretical orientation in our assessment, intervention, and evaluation of the clients we serve. Understanding the variety of theories is important so that you can choose the best theory for the work we will do with the client.

Historically, the counseling profession as a whole (social workers, psychology, and counselors) selected a theory that they focused on, and clients sought them out because they were cognitive behaviorialist or psychoanalytic theory experts. Now the profession has recognized that one-size theories do not fit all people (both clients and social workers), and there should be options to choose from when practicing and doing research. There are so many frameworks to choose from that you will never be expected to know and perfect each one. So we will present the theories in categories, emphasizing what we see as some of the main ideas, goals, techniques, social worker's roles, and how the theoretical framework you choose makes the work you do different for each case.

You probably want to talk to your supervisor about social work theories during your next supervision session. Often agencies like drug and alcohol treatment centers, rehabilitation programs, schools, residential treatment centers, and detention centers choose a theory and model for their entire program. The entire program will be built around that theory, frequently some type of behavioral program. You do not want to be practicing from a theory contrary to what they are using, because it will confuse clients and delay the results you are trying to achieve.

Although some theories work better for some populations (e.g., behavior modification works well with children), one theory is not necessarily better than another. Many theories have their own nuances that you will perfect with training and practice. Based on your personality, values, and skills, you will probably prefer one theoretical framework over the others. That is fine. Just don't limit your practice as a social worker to one theory, because not every client will respond to every theory.

When you discuss theory with experienced social workers, they often do not know what theory they practice, unless of course they work for an agency that has selected a theoretical framework. Sometimes the social worker doesn't know the name of the theory because he or she has adopted an "eclectic style," choosing techniques and ideas from a variety of theories and using what works for the social worker and the client, rather than being a purist and adhering to one theory. Know what skills come from what theory and know why you choose particular skills and techniques.

Neither the NASW Code of Ethics or the CASW Guidelines for Ethical Practice speak directly to the issue of what social work theory you should work from; however, both codes address that you represent yourself accurately, appropriately, and competently.

Before introducing the theory groupings, we present a client case. This case will be used to demonstrate the different theories and how they can be used, in general terms. To go into specifics about the nuances of a case and how to apply the theory would take almost as long as writing about each and every theory. So our plan is to introduce an abbreviated version of the case and show how to apply the basic ideas and techniques to the case.

Case Example—Darlene

Darlene is a sixteen-year-old Caucasian female who is the adopted and only child of an intact family (social work jargon for parents who are still together). She lives in a middle-socioeconomic-class suburb that her parents chose specifically because of the school system's reputation for excellent education and a high college acceptance rate. Mom and Dad are both educated professional people. Darlene has no interest in school, breaks every rule she possibly can, and has done so since eighth grade. The principal of her junior high almost didn't pass her because of excessive detentions and low grades. Darlene is in counseling because she was arrested for shoplifting and her probation requires counseling.

When you meet Darlene, she admits to smoking cigarettes and sneaking alcohol regularly from her parents' extensive liquor cabinet. She has used marijuana and is considering trying ecstasy and sniffing glue. Her first sexual experience was at fifteen when her parents took her on vacation. She sneaked out of the cabin when they were asleep. A "thirty-something"–year-old man bought her alcohol in exchange for sex. She doesn't want to talk about it, but says she is sure he thought she was twenty-one because that is what she told him.

Darlene dislikes school, has mostly Cs and Ds, and has no desire to go to college. She is almost always in trouble for truancy or falling asleep in class. In freshman year, her class went on a field trip to a local drug rehabilitation center to deter drug use. Darlene thought it was "cool" and that it would not be so bad if she had to go there one day.

Darlene's parents are completely at a loss as to how to help her and are currently in marital counseling with a coworker at your agency. Darlene is fairly open and will talk with you about everything but the vacation incident.

The facts above should give us enough information to formulate an idea about Darlene. After we present the theories, we can demonstrate that there is a different approach and focus to Darlene's presenting issues depending on the theory.

We divide the theoretical frameworks into categories that make them easier to understand. These categories are person-centered theories, behavioral theories, cognitive-behavioral theories, psychodynamic theories, and family systems theories. Table 9.1 outlines the major focus and primary features of these categories. We apply the theories to Darlene's case to show how application of a different theory might change the social work intervention with this client.

Table 9.1 Theories Used to Support Social Work Intervention

	Person-Centered Theories
Theories	Existential theory
	Humanistic theory
	Empowerment
	Strengths perspective
	Solution focused
General idea	Client and their environment determines their reality, active participants in the course of their own lives
	Determine behavior through the choices one makes rather than nature or nurture
	Always in the process of developing
Theorists	Carl Rogers
	Kurt Goldstein
	Dennis Saleebey
Human development	Core of each human is trustworthy and positive
	Create an environment of removing barriers to self-actualizing
	Regarded positively by others
Goals	Determined by the client
	Open to new experiences; develop good relationships
	Assume personal and social responsibilities
Helper's role	Be present
	Ability to develop and maintain relationship
	Unconditional positive regard
	Must be in psychological contact with one another
	Must help client experience anxiety for incongruence to motivate change
	Must be yourself
	Accept and appreciate clients as they are
	Empathetic; your values remain at the door
	Empathy and unconditional regard must be felt by the client
Assessment	Person-centered perspective
	Client's assessment more critical than yours
Techniques and process	Experience of being cared for and sense of freedom to express anything
	Slow unfolding of one's attitudes and perceptions
	Gradual movement toward less defensiveness about feelings
	Awareness of incongruities and factors
	A more accurate perception of self, problems, and relationships
	Increase in strength
	Gradual but definite sense of integration of ideal and real self

Behavioral Theories	
Theories	Behavior modification
General idea	Principle of learning and conditioning (shows how behavior is developed, acquired, changed, and eliminated)
	Focus on internal, covert behaviors involved in learning
	Nature versus nurture
	Tabula Rasa (Latin for "blank slate")
Theorists	John B. Watson
	B. F. Skinner
	Ivan Petrovich Pavlov
	Mary Cover Jones
Human development	Behaviors and measures
	Conditioning/response/stimulus
	Extinction/reinforcement
	Shaping vicarious learning
	Socialization
Goals	Assist clients in acquiring new behavior, modifying behaviors, or eliminating undesirable or maladaptive behaviors
Helper's role	Instructor
	Reconditioner
	Coach
	Consultant
	Researcher
	Paraphrase and ask questions
Assessment	Behavioral interview
	Understand clients' behavior problems
	Antecedents and consequences
	Rating scales observations
Techniques and process	Positive and negative consequences
	Actively collaborate
	Instructive model
	Contingency management
	Desensitization
	Counterconditioning, modeling, and assertiveness training

Table 9.1 Theories Used to Support Social Work Intervention (*continued*)

	Cognitive-Behavioral Theories
Theories	Rational-emotive behavior therapy
	Cognitive therapy
	Cognitive-behavioral therapy
	Task-centered theory
	Dialectical Behavioral Therapy (DBT)
	Motivational interviewing
General idea	Looking at thought and how it changes behavior
	Clients' difficulties are result of problems with cognitive process
	Time limited
	Educational approach
Theorists	Albert Ellis
	Aaron Beck
	Donald Meichenbaum
Human development	Active participants in creating their own reality through perceptions and prescribed experience/meaning
	How information is processed in behavior and feeling, which then creates behavior and personality issues
	Cognitive distortions
Goals	Assist client in identifying, challenging, and changing cognitions that negatively affect feelings and behaviors
	Work on self-interest, social interest, tolerance, flexibility, acceptance, commitment, risk taking, higher tolerance of frustration, and taking responsibility for thoughts and feelings and actions
Helper's role	Consultant, trainer, educator, or collaborator
	Differs depending on the theory
Assessment	Assess the thought preceding, during, and following behavior
	Identify dysfunctional thoughts
Techniques and process	Cognitive restructuring

Psychodynamic Theories	
Theories	Drive theories
	Ego psychology
	Interpersonal theories
	Object relations theory
General idea	Nature versus nurture
	Mental activity combined with strength
	View people as energy, health is availability of energy, and issues are static energy, release of energy
Theorists	Sigmund Freud
	Erik Erikson
	Anna Freud
Human development	Stages of development
	Defense mechanisms
	Id, ego, and superego
	Psychosocial involvement in the environment
	Emphasis on relationship and how to relate to others
	Relationships develop
Goals	Create significant change in personality structure and behavior
	Increase awareness of drives
	Strengthen ego and its defenses
Helper's role	Present clients with situation or relationship
	Project feelings, needs, past conflicts, templates, and other issues
Assessment	Indirectly or by inference, behaviorally oriented helper, projective techniques (tests)
Techniques and process	Transference neurosis
	Regress to improve
	Mirroring or idealizing
	Disconnection of self from relationships

Table 9.1 Theories Used to Support Social Work Intervention (*continued*)

	Family Systems Theories
Theories	Communication
	Structural
	Intergenerational
	Strategic and solution focused
	Systems theory
	Attachment
General idea	Consistent arrangement of things related or connected to form unity or to operate as a whole
	Approach equilibrium
	Cannot understand individuals without assessing system in which they are embedded
	Families in context of neighborhood, community, and social system
	Whole system change
	Focus on interpersonal relationships
Theorists	Virginia Satir
	Salvator Minuchin
	Murray Bowen
	Jay Haley
Human development	Subsytems boundaries
	Alignments, disengagement, enmeshment
	Differentiation, triangulation
	Focus on solutions
Goals	Support and enhance the system so as to better serve the individuals
	Change the system
Helper's role	Catalysts for change in families
	Emphasize communication patterns, and teach new communication, practice/rehearse
	Who the helper is is critical, as is the relationship they develop
Assessment	Observe communication, structure, interactions in a family to assess nature of issue
	Ecomaps and genograms
Techniques and process	Family sculpting
	Family roles
	Changing/reclaiming roles
	Manipulations of the system
	Paradoxical interventions
	Ecomaps and genograms

Thoughts to ponder

Look over table 9.1.

- ✔ Do you need more in-depth information?
- ✔ Is there a category of theories that you already feel comfortable with?
- ✔ Is there a category of theories that is hard for you to work with because you don't believe the premise or think it is too complicated?

Application of Theory to a Case

The usual process of working with a client, after taking a full biopsychosocial assessment (including genogram and ecomap), would be to get a good understanding of what the client's goals are for treatment, thus defining what will occur in the social work sessions you will be having with him or her. Once you know the goals, there are two tasks to complete. The first is to choose a theory, and the second is to form an intervention plan. In choosing a theoretical framework, you need to think about what the client wants to accomplish, how much time you have to accomplish the goal, and how comfortable you are with the theory.

Notice the order of those tasks. Often, because of the limited time we are allowed to be with clients, we are rushed to develop an assessment plan. So we may not spend enough time helping clients articulate what they are hoping to accomplish. This step is critical because it is the foundation of the treatment you will provide. If in the process other goals are accomplished, that is good. However, you need to honor the client's ideas as well as any ideas that you may come up with on your own that the client agrees to wanting to address.

The amount of time that is allotted for treatment is determined in a variety of ways. Sometimes it is determined by the client's insurance, and sometimes by the agency or program policy. Agencies determine the time allowed for client intervention either by the way the program was originally designed, or because the agency has received grant money that dictates the length of client treatment. Finally, your level of comfort with the theory depends on how well you paid attention in classes that discussed theory, and how much practice you have had with a specific theory.

Once you have chosen a theory, you can develop your intervention plan. We will discuss the formulation of an intervention plan in the subsequent chapter. At this point we will look at each category of theories presented in table 9.1. We will help you decide what theory to use based on the client's needs and how long you have to work with them.

Application of Humanistic Theories. By choosing to use the humanistic theories, you are looking at Darlene as an individual. What does she want? How does she perceive the issue? What choices has she made in her life that have gotten her to this point? What does she bring to the treatment that will assist her in the treatment process? What areas that she wants to change will she need support in? In order to answer these questions, you will want to develop a strong relationship with the client. The theory has you focus on the process and the relationship, not the issue specifically. During the initial assessment, while you are getting information, you will be exploring and developing the relationship between you and Darlene.

When you are probing for the answers to these questions, Darlene may tell you she likes to take chances and risks. Breaking the rules to her is fun, and she usually gets away with it. She may tell you that the only problem she sees is that she got caught and that she really doesn't want to change, except to be more careful the next time. You know by the way she talks about her escapades not only that she is serious about continuing her behavior, but that she is very smart (since she has been shoplifting for years and has been caught only once). Her goals for treatment would be to make everyone happy so they would get off her back and she can resume her normal activities.

You can certainly work with Darlene on talking about how to develop trust, and how to stay out of trouble so she no longer has a probation officer. But you have other options as well. Using her intelligence as a strength, walk her through her life options, college, jobs, legal records, probation, jail, and parole and see what her plans are for the future. Has she thought far ahead? Does she think her behavior now will interfere with her plans? Is she developmentally mature enough to have the foresight to see how today's behavior will affect her behavior later on? This may seem like a lot of questions to ask, but it helps you and Darlene agree to treatment issues and helps you see what strengths you have to work with while she is in treatment. The focus stays on Darlene. You ask the questions, and the quality of the relationship you have developed with her will allow her to answer in a way that helps her address her goal of getting out of trouble. She may also be helped to gain insight as to what motivates her to be in trouble and how to avoid trouble in the future.

Obviously, because of our space constraints, this is an abbreviated version of the treatment process. But the general idea of humanistic theories is to start where the client is, develop a relationship with him or her, and help the client go where they want to be, hopefully adding other pieces to the treatment to enrich it all the more.

Application of Behavior Theories. When using behavior theories, your role as the social worker is to help extinguish the behavior that is not wanted. This means you need to focus on the issues before you, not so much on the relationship. You would work with Darlene on how to get rid of the unacceptable or inappropriate behavior. You would want to understand what happens before and after the shoplifting that prompts or perpetuates the shoplifting. Your assessment will focus on the motivation behind the shoplifting, the benefits, risks, and consequences. Maybe the good outweighs the bad for shoplifting. Your role then would be to increase the negative consequences so that Darlene would want to stop, or to increase the positives so that she is willing to stop. In this case, shoplifting is an unacceptable behavior because it is against the law. You could develop a system of punishments when the behavior occurs, or you could offer rewards if it does not occur.

Application of Cognitive-Behavioral Theories. Cognitive-behavioral theories differ from behavioral theories in that you want to change the client's thought process, which will then change the behavior. In behavioral theories, you just want to extinguish the behaviors; the thought process is not considered. So when using cognitive-behavioral therapy with Darlene, you would want to understand how she thinks and talks about her behavioral difficulties. Listen carefully to her word choices when she discusses shoplifting. Is it an adventure, is it rewarding, and is it viewed as acceptable behavior to her ("everyone does it")? If so, your goal would be to help change her viewpoint about shoplifting. Restructuring her thoughts, for example, stories, and changing her word choices, will help her see that this is unacceptable behavior that she needs to change. Once the thoughts change, the behavior disappears.

Application of Psychodynamic Theories. Psychodynamic theories look at the unresolved issues of the past that create the current issues. They ask why a problem exists; solve the "why," and the problem will stop. Of all the theories, these take the longest because they involve exploration of the past. Does Darlene steal because she feels unwanted because she is adopted? Does she steal because she has a bad reputation and feels that she has to live up to the reputation? Is she "stuck" in a stage of development? If so, which one and why? Although this theory takes longer, it usually has a longer-lasting effect on the client, because the past issues are resolved and therefore shouldn't cause any other difficulty for the client in the future.

Application of Family Systems Theories. To use family systems theories in the case of Darlene, the social worker would involve the entire family. They would explore with the parents whether their relationship problems have any bearing on the problems that Darlene is having. They would explore how the issues about consistent rule breaking have been dealt with in the family. The social worker would also want to know about other stressors and the current status of all the relationships in the family now. Who talks to whom? Who does Darlene get along with better—Mom or Dad? All of this assessment material would help them figure out what might be altered in their family that would change Darlene's behavior. The assumption here is that if you live within families, they impact you in some way. How are the family relationships manifesting themselves in Darlene's behavior? Once the relationships are changed, "put in homeostasis" or balance, Darlene will act appropriately again.

As you can see by each of the short explanations of the theories, the result is the same. They all address Darlene's behavior of shoplifting. Each theory took a different approach but the outcome is essentially the same. If it were possible for Darlene to go through each theory, and not remember the other, she would express different secondary benefits, such as, she thinks about consequences more (behavioral theory), she is more concerned about how she affects her family and how they affect her (family systems theory), but in each case the shoplifting behavior is gone.

At the beginning of the chapter, we noted that some social workers would use an eclectic viewpoint. They would try a little of everything. They would get the family involved, explore how Darlene feels about her adoption, and look at the relationships with her parents. They might also try offering rewards and punishments and increasing Darlene's strengths so that she doesn't succumb to peer pressure. Sometimes it makes more sense to come at a case from different viewpoints to extract the problem from the person, but it does not always work as well. It is not the purest use of theory, and it is important for you to know what the theory says as well as what works. Depending on the issue, some are better theories to use than others, known as *best practice models.*

Best practice models are theories that have been thoroughly researched on particular social work issues and have been found to work best with a specific issue. For instance through research we know that cognitive behavioral theory works best with those people who are addicted to substances. Ask your supervisor what is the best practice model for the population and area of practice that you are currently interning in. Once you start working, if you change populations, you will need to do some research on the population you will be serving to determine what the best practice model to use is.

When talking to your supervisor about theory, ask about what he or she thinks works best with the client population you have at the agency where you are doing your field placement. Discuss your supervisor's favorite theories and see if you can formulate an idea about what you particularly like about each theory and what you dislike. This discussion may help you decide where you need to focus your time in theory development. After all, you want to choose a theory that is effective for the clients you are currently treating.

Integration of other course material	
HBSE	What theories of development would be useful for you to know about in your field placement?
Policy	How does policy dictate what theory is used in your social work practice?
Practice	Do you feel comfortable with any particular theory now that could guide your practice in social work? What else do you need to know about the theory to use it effectively? What if you are a macro social worker? Could you use these theories? Why or why not? Are there macropractice theories that you need to know?
Research	What theory would you choose to use for a study on the improvement of one of your clients over time?

Resources

Cognitive-Behavioral Therapy
http://www.cognitivetherapyla.com/CognitiveTherapy.php

Cambridge Center for Behavioral Studies
http://www.behavior.org/

Freudian, Lacanian, and Object Relations Theory
http://www.citehr.com/94421-freudian-lacanian-object-relations-theory.html

Allyn and Bacon Family Therapy Web Site
http://www.abacon.com/famtherapy/index.html

Attachment Theory
http://www.personalityresearch.org/attachment.html

Personality Theories
http://www.ship.edu/~cgboeree/rogers.html

Task-Centered Social Work Practice and the Family
http://www.oocities.org/taskcentered/

Have you come across a social work book you want to read in the future? Make your book list here.

Title	Author	Year	Publisher

Chapter 10
Intervention Planning

The further you go into the semester, the more contact you should be having with clients. Whether you are facilitating more groups, or are involved in case management, individual sessions, or community meetings, you can expect that your contact has purpose, which is to assist with one of the goals the client established when the client entered treatment at your agency. To be sure that every contact you have with the client is as profitable as possible, it is important that you be aware of the treatment goals. The intervention plans are in the client file. Every agency has a different format for the intervention plan, but they essentially all want to know the same information. This chapter will let you know what an intervention plan includes, how to determine what the plan should be, and how to word the goals and objectives. We will continue to use Darlene's case, presented in chapter 9.

Developing an Intervention Plan

After completing the biopsychosocial, genogram, and ecomap, it is time to figure out what the client is hoping to accomplish by coming to your agency. Often clients have a vague idea of what they are hoping to achieve but don't know how to get there. Often they are open to other suggestions that you can make, based on what you heard them say in their biopsychosocial. A good way to go about setting up the intervention plan is to start with the client. Ask the client what it is that he or she wants to work on. If you see some obvious thing that you think the client may want to work on, you can ask if that is also of interest. The conversation about things that you want to suggest should be at the end of your session, after the client has told you what he or she wants to work on. At that time, you would schedule the next session with your client.

Take the information you received in the initial assessment (biopsychosocial), and talk to your supervisor. Talk about the important incidents in the client's life and the goals the client wishes to achieve. Give your supervisor your impressions of the client and what goals you thought you would add to the goals the client identified to work toward in treatment. Your supervisor may have suggestions for you based on the information you have gathered and presented.

Choose a theory to use, based upon the client's thoughts and desires, your time frame, and the agency treatment philosophy, if there is one. Once you have selected a theory, you can establish the formal treatment goals and objectives. When the goals for treatment are established, you will need to present them again to your client for approval, clearly indicating what the goals are that he or she wanted to work on, and how to plan to accomplish those goals (the objectives). The form in

Darlene's intervention plan (table 10.1) can be used to develop an intervention plan if your agency does not have a form. Most intervention plans will have the same information in them as the form used here, but it may have a different order or leave out one or two components. For example, we have seen intervention plans that list the strengths but leave out the obstacles and vice versa.

When working on an intervention plan, remember the client is the expert on his or her life. You do not live in the client's shoes twenty-four hours a day, seven days a week. It is your job to help him or her figure out how to avoid and clear the obstacles, but it is the client's responsibility to explain what it is he or she is willing to do and what is realistic to achieve. The clients' right to self-determination is important here. Clients have the right to choose what they will do. Remember the NASW Code of Ethics section on self-determination (section 1.02).

> Social workers respect and promote the right of clients to self-determination and assist clients in their efforts to identify and clarify their goals. Social workers may limit clients' right to self-determination when, in the social workers' professional judgment, clients' actions or potential actions pose a serious, foreseeable, and imminent risk to themselves or others.

Or, if you are from Canada, remember the Guidelines for Ethical Practice, section 1.3.

> 1.3.1 Social Workers promote the self-determination and autonomy of clients, actively encouraging them to make informed decisions on their own belief.

Most times you and your client will be in agreement, but when you think something should be done that the client doesn't want to do, it can be very frustrating and you should be prepared for that. For instance, you may think that Darlene should complete her homework to improve her status in school. She may say that is not important to her, and she is not willing to do her homework or improve her status in school. Your best bet is to really look for the things that will motivate your client to complete treatment. Sometimes this motivation is a reward for finishing, like completing legal obligations. Other times it is just feeling better because the issue is resolved.

What you offer any client is the ability to hear what the issue is and offer suggestions on how to solve the issue. The goal becomes the solution to the issue, and the suggestions on how to solve the issue are the objectives. The easier the objectives, the more likely the client is to complete them and stay motivated. Be sure that the client knows what you are doing every step of the way. But before you can write the goals and objectives, you need to have a good understanding of the theory that you are going to use, because it will make a difference in the intervention plan. After explaining goals and objectives, we will demonstrate two different intervention plans for Darlene, using two different theories from the categories outlined in chapter 9.

Differences between Goals and Objectives

A goal is a very broad and general statement of what the client wants to accomplish, such as "elimination of illegal activities." The goal is usually phrased as a statement, "to eliminate" or "to increase" something that is difficult for your client. The goal is usually not measurable, which means that it is vague, and the objectives are the specifics.

Goals usually fall into five categories: (1) health (mental, physical, emotional), (2) educational/vocational, (3) employment, (4) relationships (family, friends, significant others), and (5) legal affairs. After completing the biopsychosocial you should sort out the goals into those five categories. Prioritize goals based on what the client wants to work on first. If there is an emergency in a particular area, you need to deal with that first (e.g., a medical condition that has to be addressed, like the client has just been diagnosed with cancer and needs to start treatment immediately or maybe they are homeless). If there is no emergency, some of the goals could be worked on at the same time, although some may take longer to complete. For example, someone may need to work on self-esteem, relationships with others, and getting a college degree. All these goals can be worked on at the same time, but the college degree may take longer if the client isn't in school already.

Sometimes goals are clearly evident. If the client has legal or medical problems, you want to get those addressed as quickly as possible. Other treatment goals are not as readily apparent. Examples are improving relationships with friends or decreasing self-deprecating comments because the client thinks that is an increasing problem.

Objectives are the step-by-step actions that will be taken to achieve the goals. In the case of getting a college degree, if you are working with a high school student, objectives include successfully completing high school, taking the SAT or ACT exams, choosing which colleges to visit, visiting colleges, writing applications, making a final decision on which university, attending the school, choosing a major, registering, and successfully completing all courses. You may be thinking that it isn't really a social worker's job to help someone decide what college to go to. However, some people need support and supervision for many of these steps. Helping to make the decision about a school, or really focusing on completing high school, may be something the social worker would help with. Seeing the consequences of their decisions and understanding how to make a decision are skills that lots of people do not have. A social worker can help a client with these skills.

Objectives are concrete changes desired by clients. Objectives are readily measurable and observable because they are detailed and very specific. Objectives are also smaller steps to reach goals. List every step needed to achieve the goals and make sure it is reasonable and attainable. For instance, if someone is having financial difficulty, you would not list winning this week's state lottery as an objective, because it is not attainable and realistic. Objectives need to be time limited, which means that steps get completed in a reasonable time period that will not ruin the client's motivation or discourage him or her because it is so far away. Look at a high school senior's goal of getting a college degree. Graduating from college is at least a five-year goal (senior year and four years at college), which can seem insurmountable, especially when you're in the middle of writing papers and studying for exams!

When we say that objectives are measurable and observable, we are talking about being able to see changes or to measure them through a change in reported behavior by the client or those who see them frequently. Once you have all the objectives written, you need to determine four things:

How will you measure the change?

How will you prioritize the objectives (which ones need to be completed first)?

Who will complete the tasks?

When will the objectives be completed?

Finally, to complete an intervention plan like the one for Darlene, you need to think about what strengths the client has to successfully accomplish the goals. These strengths include systemwide strengths like family and friends as well as personal characteristics that the client may have. After listing the strengths that will assist the client, list the obstacles for the client. What in the client's system will impede his or her ability to attain the goal? Is there any way you can help activate the strengths and eliminate the obstacles?

Displayed next is a way to think about intervention planning that may be helpful to some:

Area of concern:	**What** is the overall issue?
Short-term goals:	**How** do you want to change the issue in the immediate future?
Long-term goal:	**What** permanent changes to do you want?
Tasks:	**What** needs to be done specifically, what steps?
Responsibilities:	**Who** will do **what**? Be very specific, use numbers, title of the person who will do/complete responsibilities.
Time frame:	By **When** will the task be done?
Evaluation:	**How** will we know the issue is solved?
Obstacles:	**What** will get in the way?
Strengths:	**What** will benefit the client in solving the issue?

Example

Area of concern:	**What** is the overall issue?
	Client needs college degree to progress in their chosen profession.
Short-term goals:	**How** do you want to change the issue in the immediate future?
	Client will start college and declare a major.
	Client will meet with advisor and plan academic schedule for time in college.
Long-term goal:	**What** permanent changes to do you want?
	Client will have college degree and progress in field.
Tasks:	**What** needs to be done specifically, what steps?
	Client will apply for financial aid.
	Client will maintain a 3.5 GPA.
	Client will complete university requirements.
	Client will try to gain work experience in the chosen major while in school.
Responsibilities:	**Who** will do **what**? Be very specific, use numbers, title of the person who will complete responsibilities.
	Client will complete FAFSA form by Feb. 15 every year in school.
	Client will study three hours every night. This will include reading, studying, and writing required papers.
	Student will meet with advisor every year in February to review academic plan.
Time frame:	By **when** will the task be done?
	Each task will be done every year by dates indicated in the tasks.
Evaluation:	**How** will we know the issue is solved?
	Student will receive FAFSA report in the mail.
	Student will receive verified schedule in the mail after registration.
	Student will receive grades from registrar's office after each semester.
	Student will graduate when all university requirements are complete.
	Student will be hired for a job in the field.

Obstacles: **What** will get in the way?

Financial aid may not be approved.

Classes may be harder than anticipated.

Class schedules may not coincide with client's personal schedule.

Strengths: **What** will benefit the client in solving the issue?

Desire and motivation

Successful completion of high school

Good SAT scores

Interest in the classroom material

Operationalizing a Intervention Plan with a Theory

Table 10.1 shows you how the treatment differs for Darlene depending on the theory that we use. For this exercise, we use a cognitive-behavioral approach and a family systems approach to see the treatment differences.

Notice the difference in the goals, objectives, and, even more specifically, the people responsible for the objectives. The cognitive-behavioral goals are more about interaction and clearly understanding and then changing the thought process. The family systems approach is more about the collaborative effort of Darlene's system to see that things change. Every problem will follow the same guidelines after you select which theoretical framework you will use. Neither set of treatment objectives is better than the other, at face value. After learning who your client is (better than in the brief summary you have of Darlene), you will be able to choose the best theoretical framework.

Sometimes people intermix theories because each set of objectives listed here has good ideas and could have a synergistic effect if they were all used, thereby increasing the chance of success with Darlene.

Spend a moment thinking about a client at your internship. Use the blank intervention plan at the end of the chapter to write a brief intervention plan for that client. Remember to select a theory first.

Table 10.1 Intervention Plan for Darlene

Cognitive-Behavioral Approach

Area of Concern	Goals	Objectives	Responsibility	Time Frame	Evaluation Procedure
1. Darlene is in trouble with the law.	1. To stop Darlene's illegal activity.	1. Have Darlene research the legal consequences of using alcohol and drugs and shop-lifting. a. Allow Darlene access to online information and the library to find legal repercussions. b. Have Darlene meet with local police juvenile officer to hear stories of other adolescents who have had difficulty with the law.	Darlene	two weeks	Written report to social worker
		2. Have Darlene attend an Outward Bound program that teaches "natural highs" and communication skills. a. Provide structured risk-taking behaviors for one week. b. Increase ability to express thoughts to parents.	Outward Bound program and Darlene	one month	Certificate of completion

Table 10.1 Intervention Plan for Darlene *(continued)*

Area of Concern	Goals	Objectives	Responsibility	Time Frame	Evaluation Procedure
	Anticipated Obstacles: ■ Darlene's willingness to meet with officer ■ Parents' willingness to follow through with Outward Bound program Anticipated Strengths: ■ Darlene's need for challenge and excitement.				
2. *Darlene is having difficulty in school.*	To improve Darlene's progress in school.	1. Have Darlene tested for learning disabilities.	Child Study team	three months	Written report of assessment
		2. Discuss with Darlene her thoughts about education and any importance it may have to her.	Social Worker and Darlene	two weeks	Self-report
		3. Find out what Darlene's goals for the future are and develop plan to achieve.	Social Worker, guidance counselor, and parents	one month	Self-report
	Anticipated Obstacles: ■ Darlene's lack of focus on academics ■ Finding a tutor who will try creative approaches to learning				

Anticipated Strengths:
- Darlene enjoying one-on-one attention from tutor
- Finding ways to access her career choices

Family Systems Theory

Goal	Intervention	Responsible Party	Timeframe	Measurement
1. Darlene is in trouble with the law.				
Stop Darlene's illegal activity	Provide supervision to Darlene on all out-of-house trips.	Parents	Next three months	Self-report from parents
Build relationship with parents to rebuild trust.	1. Darlene to spend quality time with each parent individually one evening a week.	Parents and Darlene	Next two months	Self-report from Darlene
	2. Darlene and parents to increase number of meals together. a. Choose meals to eat together. b. Choose topics of discussion.	Parents and Darlene	Next three months	Self-report from parents
Anticipated Obstacles: - Parents' work schedules - Parents' consistency and willingness				

Table 10.1 Intervention Plan for Darlene *(continued)*

Area of Concern	Goals	Objectives	Responsibility	Time Frame	Evaluation Procedure
	Anticipated Strengths: ▪ Instilling rituals into family lifestyle ▪ Desire of parents to be closer to daughter				
2. Darlene is having difficulty in school.	Improve Darlene's school progress	1. Have Darlene receive an hour of tutoring a week from her parents.	Family	Immediately	Self-report
		2. Establish clear-cut expectations about grades in classes.	Family with teachers	Within three weeks	Self-report
		3. Devise study schedule, routine, and rules for homework time.	Family with social worker	Immediately	Written rules
	Anticipated Obstacles: ▪ Darlene's unwillingness ▪ Parents' time and understanding of homework				
	Anticipated Strengths: ▪ Communication with the school ▪ Support emphasis for importance of school.				

Example of a Macro Community Case

Macro work can take many forms, such as helping unions form, working for a cleaner and greener society, organizing and participating in rallies and demonstrations. For this particular case we again are going to share a project that one of the authors worked on very recently. One of the authors lives in a small community that has a reputation of "dirty politics" and "closed door" decisions. This particular town consists of about 75 percent of people whose families have always lived in this town and somehow by birth or marriage they are all related to one another. The other part of the town are people who have chosen the community for its eclectic nature, its views and proximity to the ocean, and commutability to work.

The town is governed by four town councilpersons and a mayor. The town has financial difficulties and is in need of clear decisive decisions, and someone to help them write grants and enforce policies. A group of concerned citizens met, including the author, to discuss changing the form of government from partisan to nonpartisan government. Partisan government means that each party, Republicans and Democrats, selects a candidate to run in the election. Nonpartisan means there are no party lines. Essentially, not only does that mean people can't declare a party when they run, it also means there can be no financial backing from either party at the county or state level. This evens the playing field and allows for the town's citizens to vote on the person and the issues, not the party.

Our committee started out small with six people. This was good for core decision making, but there was a very detailed list of what needed to be done. First we needed a lawyer who had worked with communities to change government before. We also needed to raise funds to pay that lawyer. A major task would be to acquire enough signatures from the town residents who registered to vote and in fact voted in the last election. As the committee members talked about this we opted to add another six persons to the committee so that we could go in pairs to collect signatures door-to-door. Our group consisted of only one local resident, born in the town. Everyone else had moved to the town within the last ten years. In the group, we had a stock lawyer, a paramedic, a marketing consultant, an organizational consultant, a project manager, an accountant, two construction workers, a computer programmer, a stay-at-home mom, and a sales representative for Legos.

There were several meetings where it appeared that nothing was accomplished as some of the group socialized and got to know each other and others tried to understand the law and develop a task. As we discuss further in the next chapter there are natural stages of group development. This group was no exception as personalities and passions sometimes got in the way, but we worked through them and figured out the plan to move forward. Some of the major decisions included: this group would remain politically neutral and have no actual leader, and we would each use our own money to hire the lawyer. The project manager created a list of tasks, some of which included:

- ✔ acquiring the list of registered voters,
- ✔ developing a petition,
- ✔ dividing the town up into sections for door-to-door petition signing,
- ✔ designing and making lawn signs,
- ✔ creating a Facebook page,
- ✔ making T-shirts,
- ✔ distributing the signs,
- ✔ developing and distributing a brochure,
- ✔ talking with the town clerk,
- ✔ getting access to the larger apartment buildings, and
- ✔ finding a notary.

Our time frame was very short in order to acquire enough good signatures to make it onto the November ballot, about ten weeks. If none of us had other responsibilities ten weeks would have been a lot of time. However this was a voluntary project and we all had life responsibilities as well. The town council said to our face that they supported the idea, even though it threatened their elected positions. However, the political parties spent money to combat our campaign and made robo-calls to all town members encouraging them to vote NO on our issue. The committee was angry at the "business as usual" politics telling us one thing and doing another. We purchased an old-fashioned bullhorn and went through all the neighborhoods in a car with our signs plastered all over it encouraging people to vote. We took advantage of good weather and went out on both weekend days before the election. The project was intense and drained energy and time from the committee. At the same time, having so many people support what we were doing, we knew this was the town's will and we worked harder when we didn't think we had an ounce more energy or time.

We know by now the suspense is killing you. Did we get the form of government changed? The answer is WE WON!!! In the next election two of the council members' terms expired. A person who never ran for office before won. In the next election the position of mayor and another two seats will be up. Two of our committee members have decided to run for those spots. It will be interesting to watch the evolution of the town. If we were right, with new blood and no political party involvement, the town will prosper!

Case Management

One of the traits that makes a social worker different from others who counsel clients is our emphasis on case management. Case management is about providing services to clients that help them access services and coordinate those services. Once there has been a thorough intake and assessment, one of the next tasks is making sure that there is enough support to help the client complete the intervention plan. Case management is a mixture of the micro and macro practices of social work, looking for and securing services for the client. Once those services are secured, the job of the social worker is to ensure that the services are useful and remain in place. If the services don't work or are no longer available, the social worker's role is to develop contingency plans. Case management is a vital cornerstone of social work practice and is one of the jobs most widely available to entry-level graduates.

Thoughts to ponder

✔ Did you have difficulty writing the intervention plan?

✔ What areas were most problematic for you?

✔ Did you make the intervention plan reasonable?

✔ Were you able to see the distinctions between the plans based on the two theories?

✔ What are your concerns about developing an intervention plan?

✔ How close does your agency come to developing intervention plans as explained here?

✔ What are your thoughts about the intervention plan process at your agency?

✔ Whose signatures are needed on an intervention/treatment plan? Why?

Integration of other course material

HBSE	Which part of your assessment will help you with your intervention plan?
Policy	What are the time frames needed for developing an intervention plan in your agency from the time that the client enters your program? Who dictates that policy?
Practice	What are the appropriate ways to develop this intervention plan?
Research	How does this intervention plan expedite your research for this particular case?

Resources

Wodarski, J. S., Rapp-Paglicci, L. A., Dulmus, C. N., & Jongsma, A. E. (2000). *The social work and human services treatment planner.* New York: Wiley.

What does this mean to you?
Does it apply to you?
Write about this aspect of yourself.

Treatment Plan or Intervention Plan

Area of Concern	Goals	Objectives	Responsibility	Time Frame	Evaluation Procedure
	Anticipated Strengths				
	Anticipated Obstacles				
	Anticipated Strengths				
	Anticipated Obstacles				

Chapter 11
Working Together as a Team

No matter where you work—a school, hospital, nursing home, group home, or other agency—you are a part of a team. That team provides a comprehensive program of treatment for all the clients that enter into treatment with your agency. A comprehensive program needs a staff with an array of skill sets and talents. The staff comprises interdisciplinary teams of people who have a variety of degrees. Table 11.1 lists possible teams.

Table 11.1 Personnel in an Interdisciplinary Team

Type of service area	Possible treatment teams
Psychiatric hospital	Psychiatrist, RN, social worker, LPN, adjunctive therapist (recreational therapist, art therapist, etc.)
Nursing home	Medical doctor, nurse practitioner, social worker, dietician, physical therapist
School	Teacher, principal, social worker, learning disability consultant, school psychologist

Team Roles

The role of each person on the team will be based on the setting. For example, in the psychiatric hospital, the psychiatrist generally heads the team, which is the typical medical model. Nurses may facilitate groups and are in charge of medicine and implementation of medical tests and vital signs. Social workers will do the assessment, therapy, and discharge plan. In the nursing home, a registered nurse is generally in charge of the team because the doctor is not always on site. The dietician will recommend proper diets in terms of quantity and the types of food that would be good for the individual based on his or her medical needs. The social worker will work with the families and the residents who may need some tangible resources like clothes. In school settings, teachers lead the child study team. The psychologist and the learning consultant provide testing and observations necessary to complete and implement an individual education plan (IEP or intervention plan) for students who have learning disabilities. Social workers will complete the family assessment and case manage. Social workers' roles vary based on the setting as well. Roles may include intake assessments, therapy sessions, and discharge (psychiatric hospitals); intake, family contact, and discharge planning (nursing home); and assessment and case management (schools).

As with all relationships, the treatment team needs to develop a rapport. The working relationships and the functioning of the team will define themselves based upon historic information (what has always been done), financial considerations (what the agency can afford), legal considerations (what the minimum personnel standards are for the team), and programmatic issues (what is needed for the current makeup of the team). All these factors will enter into the qualifications of the team members as well as how active a role they play. For instance, the nursing home may have a consulting psychiatrist. Not everyone in the nursing home needs a psychiatrist, however; so the psychiatrist will be used only as needed and is therefore not a regular member of the team. Another example may be a school district where the law requires schools to have access to a child study team. If the school district is small and is concerned about budgeting, however, those services may be contracted out to people who work for larger school districts or to new graduates who are less expensive than social workers and psychologists who have years of experience.

Once the team is formed, it must develop a working relationship with an understanding of what each person's responsibilities are. Again, responsibilities could be determined by job descriptions or legal constraints (e.g., social workers can't write prescriptions, so the doctor, physicians assistant, or nurse practioner must). The team must learn to communicate clearly with one another to be sure the client's needs are met in a timely manner that is economically feasible for the client and the agency and accurate in assessment, diagnosis, and treatment.

In order to communicate clearly, it is important that the team meet prior to seeing clients, to get to know one another. This is about knowing one another as *professionals*, not on a personal level. So questions about what type of degree you have, where you received it, how long and where you have been working, and what your experience is with the population you will be working with at this agency are all appropriate and critical to understanding the composition of the team. Other questions to consider are what you are really good at and what you dislike doing; then the team can use everyone's strengths for the benefits of the clients and offer support as needed for jobs that people dislike or cannot do as well.

While getting to know each other on the team, it would be a good time to negotiate tasks if they are not clearly defined or if they are flexible. Things like how often groups are held and who facilitates them can be up for negotiation. One of the benefits of working as a team is that you share the workload to minimize burnout and increase effectiveness.

Stages of Team Development

Anywhere from three to eight people can make up an interdisciplinary team. This is usually the same size as a therapeutic group. Teams will go through the typical stages of group development, and you should expect to be part of that development. Here we will describe the group stages of preaffiliation, power and control, intimacy, differentiation, and separation.

In the interdisciplinary team, preaffiliation involves feelings of ambivalence, fear, and anxiety. People generally don't take risks or disclose their feelings about their strengths and weaknesses or their concerns about the other members. If you were a social worker joining a preexisting team in a hospital, you would probably be professional but quiet and guarded about your contributions to the team or areas where you are unsure about your knowledge and skills.

The phase of power and control is where the negotiation of tasks comes up as well as the roles of each person. At this phase, you discuss who will have what responsibilities within the group. These responsibilities usually include contact with families and external agencies, arranging transportation, tests, ancillary equipment, report writing, chart documentation, discharge planning, therapy sessions, and contact with the client. There certainly is enough to do. Perhaps some responsibilities have to rotate, while others belong specifically to one person and others are shared. All this is addressed in the power-and-control stage.

The third stage is intimacy. The fear and anxiety of the preaffiliation stage is gone, roles and responsibilities were negotiated in the power-and-control stage, and you feel more comfortable about your role and the role of the team. The team comfortableness turns into a caring atmosphere about the general welfare of the other team members, which in turn benefits the clients.

Intimacy then turns into stage four, which is differentiation. Team members have taught each other about their unique contributions to the team and have supported each other enough that team members can anticipate each other's next treatment action and understand fully their own contribution to the team. This is the time when the group begins to act together most efficiently and effectively.

In the final stage, separation, the group usually realizes that each member is an individual and is autonomous. An interdisciplinary treatment team does not separate for individuals to work autonomously. Rather, they come together as one efficient unit, working very well together for their clients.

Joining a Treatment Team

Treatment teams that work with very difficult clients or who stay together for a long time become very close. Usually this closeness transcends the professional relationship and develops into more personal relationships than we recommend for interns. Your relationship with any treatment team that you are placed with is temporary and tangential. In some cases, you may be perceived as an outsider and treated as such. In other cases, the team may welcome you with open arms, but recognize that you are an outsider and need to be incorporated into the team through the stages of the group process. How you are accepted will vary depending on what stage the team is in, the size of the team, and the personalities in it. As an intern be cautious and professional about what you disclose about yourself and how you disclose it (we will discuss boundaries further in chapter 12). As an intern, your job will be the same as the social worker who is your supervisor. If they are filing and developing intervention plans and finalizing discharge plans, you will be as well. If there is any area you want to learn or want to spend time observing, let your supervisor know. Treatment teams, especially those that have been together for a long time, work very fast and efficiently. You will need to show some initiative and let your supervisor know which part of the team responsibilities you want to handle. You may also need to ask what you are legally allowed to handle, because chances are that you cannot legally sign as the social worker on a intervention plan.

Treatment team meetings are usually held at varying times and days. If you can arrange your internship hours to be at the agency when the treatment team is meeting, do so. If you can't because of other commitments, try to arrange to be there at least once or twice during the semester. It is a worthwhile learning experience to observe a high-functioning interdisciplinary team in action.

We should also point out that not only do training and experience contribute to the unique personality of an interdisciplinary team, but culture, gender, and personality do as well. Be aware of the number of people on your team. What are their genders? What are the cultural and ethnic backgrounds of the members? What are their personalities? All of these components make up who the individual members of the teams are. The individual, of course, determine the interactions in the team and how they define who they are, how they will function, and how you as the intern will play a role in the team. They also determine how the team goes through the stages of group process, especially intimacy. If you don't know much about the culture or ethnicity of those represented in your agency (and specifically in your team), you may want to spend time now learning about these cultures or ethnicities, so that you have an appreciation of where people are coming from. You can do that by reading, talking to a fellow classmate who is of the same culture or ethnicity, or talking to your coworkers about their culture. This exercise may give you a greater awareness of that culture that helps make your interactions more meaningful and you a better social worker.

Education, specifically within colleges and universities, is creating more and more opportunities for shared learning and research. Social work has always relied on the other social services (criminal justice, sociology, psychology) to inform our profession. Joint learning, by more than one teacher teaching the same course so learning integrates both majors and both sets of research, is now becoming a common occurrence. Research is also being done collaboratively. This is a natural precursor to our work in teams in the field. Yet, at this time, it is being put in place *after* the teamwork in the field was put in place.

Working on a Team in a Community

When working in the community, you will build a team that should be able to help you accomplish your goals. The team you develop will be specific to what you are trying to accomplish and so will change with each project you take on. These teams will often include people in your organization along with people outside of your organization. In community work, we are usually more successful when we take on large projects with the help of others. Often, community work means building a coalition of groups or organizations that can all lend some of their expertise and their membership to the goal or final outcome.

The NASW Code of Ethics in section 2.03 outlines the role of social workers on interdisciplinary teams.

(a) Social workers who are members of an interdisciplinary team should participate in and contribute to decisions that affect the well-being of clients by drawing on the perspectives, values, and experiences of the social work profession. Professional and ethical obligations of the interdisciplinary team as a whole and of its individual members should be clearly established.

(b) Social workers for whom a team decision raises ethical concerns should attempt to resolve the disagreement through appropriate channels. If the disagreement cannot be resolved, social workers should pursue other avenues to address their concerns consistent with client well-being.

In section 3.0, "Ethical Responsibilities to Colleagues," the CASW Guidelines for Ethical Practice also delineates the social worker's role when he or she is working with other professionals in other disciplines.

3.1 *Respect* Social workers relate to both social work colleagues and colleagues from other disciplines with respect, integrity, and courtesy and seek to understand differences in viewpoints and practice.

3.2 *Collaboration and Consultation* When collaborating with other professionals, social workers utilize the expertise of other disciplines for the benefit of their clients. Social workers participate in and contribute to decisions that affect the well-being of clients by drawing on the knowledge, values, and experiences of the social work profession.

Social workers have a status in the team in the agency. Depending on the setting of your field placement, social workers as a whole will have a status and reputation. Before we go on, take time as a class to discuss your opinions about how social workers are treated at your agency. Answer the following questions:

How the agency treats social workers

✔ What type of agency are you placed in?

✔ What is the reputation/status of social workers in the agency?

✔ How are you treated as a social work intern?

✔ Are there any BSWs there?

✔ Is there a difference between how BSWs and MSWs are treated?

✔ Is there anyone there who is from another school? How does your educational experience compare to theirs? Are you feeling well prepared?

If your internship experience is anything like what our students have felt, your reactions to the above questions will vary. Most of you will be observed and treated as who you are. But sometimes, especially where social workers are the minority (hospitals and schools), you may feel that you are the "low man on the totem pole," so to speak. We have had a social worker from a school district say she felt like the lone ranger hung out to dry because she tried to advocate for the students, had no support from anyone, and was the only social worker in the school. Another social worker who worked in a hospital said that she felt she was next to the janitor in order of importance on the staff and that sometimes even the janitor was more important. Often the social workers that came before you in the job help establish (or hinder) the reputation and perceptions of social workers.

Remember that many places need and require social workers, but because social workers are in the minority, they do not have a lot of support. For that reason your job becomes even more important. You alone possess the social work skills, resources, and knowledge base that are necessary to help the clients. In your mind, that should rank you as equal to the rest of the people in the agency. Unfortunately, the hospital, a traditional medical model, has always had a pecking order where doctors come first, followed by nurses, and so on. It would take a very special setting or a very mindful doctor to make the rest of the people feel equal.

It also becomes your responsibility as the newest member of the social work profession to represent the profession and your school appropriately. The more professional and proficient you are, the more respect the profession receives, and the better social workers' reputations will become. Nationally, social workers have a reputation of being "do gooders" and "bleeding hearts." We may have those traits among us, but we also have a unique set of skills, an individual knowledge base, and a profession that we all can be proud of and represent in a strong manner every chance we get. This will help eliminate stereotypes of social workers and show people what we are capable of and what we are worth to an agency and its client base.

Section 5 of the NASW Code of Ethics, "Social Workers' Ethical Responsibilities to the Social Work Profession," delineates standards for integrity of the profession (section 5.01) and of evaluation and research (section 5.02). The section on integrity of the profession is very relevant to our discussion here.

(a) Social workers should work toward the maintenance and promotion of high standards of practice.

(b) Social workers should uphold and advance the values, ethics, knowledge, and mission of the profession. Social workers should protect, enhance, and improve the integrity of the profession through appropriate study and research, active discussion, and responsible criticism of the profession.

(c) Social workers should contribute time and professional expertise to activities that promote respect for the value, integrity, and competence of the social work profession. These activities may include teaching, research, consultation, service, legislative testimony, presentations in the community, and participation in their professional organizations.

(d) Social workers should contribute to the knowledge base of social work and share with colleagues their knowledge related to practice, research, and ethics. Social workers should seek to contribute to the profession's literature and to share their knowledge at professional meetings and conferences.

(e) Social workers should act to prevent the unauthorized and unqualified practice of social work.

One last thought. You received a very specialized degree, that is, you are a social worker. Be proud of that title. "Clinician" or just "worker" could be used instead of "social worker" in some settings. But avoid calling yourself a life coach or therapist.

Thoughts to ponder

✔ How can you alter people's perception about stereotypes of social workers?

✔ What skills and knowledge do you have to offer an interdisciplinary team?

✔ When you meet a new group of people professionally, how do you want them to perceive you?

✔ Are you representing yourself accurately?

Integration of other course material	
HBSE	How might your assessment of a client differ from that of another person on your team, such as a nurse, doctor, or teacher?
Policy	What are the legal mandates for social workers in your agency setting?
Practice	How many social work teams have you come across in your internship experiences? How are they the same? How are they different?
Research	What practice literature can you find either supporting or not supporting interdisciplinary teams?

Resources

University of Washington School of Medicine
http://depts.washington.edu/bioethx/topics/

National Association of Social Workers
http://www.naswdc.org/practice/adolescent_health/ah0303.pdf

 When have you needed to take a detour in the field? How did this occur, how did you feel, and was it beneficial?

Chapter 12
Boundaries:
The Invisible Lines of Trust

The concept of boundaries has been part of your life as long as you can remember, but not always the word *boundaries*. Phrases like "come to my house," "that's my sweater," or "you're invading my space" indicate you are setting or acknowledging a boundary. Boundaries are the limits we place on another human being around physical, emotional, and mental space.

Boundaries are easier to understand when we think about the concept of physical space, which we discussed in chapter 6. Most of us have a comfort zone about how close we allow strangers to get to us, 4 to 12 feet. We have another zone for acquaintances, 18 inches to 4 feet, which might be a little closer to your person, and we have an even closer zone for family, friends, and loved ones, no more than 18 inches. The space we allow people into is the boundary we establish. Usually it is not a physical boundary, yet a strange uncomfortable feeling comes over us if someone gets too close to us physically. That amount of space is different in every culture.

We have those same boundaries in terms of emotional space and cognitive space. We don't let everyone we meet know what we are thinking and feeling; remember the Johari window in chapter 7? We choose whom to share information with and when. These are personal boundaries, and we begin to establish those boundaries early on in our development. Throughout our development, we refine these boundaries by clarifying what feels right and setting limits with people. Sometimes we have help developing these boundaries because of laws and social rules. If you live in a house, you know where your property line is. Maybe your family has a rule about when the phone can be used or not used (such as, no calls during dinner or after 10 p.m.).

You also have probably met someone who gave you too much information within the first few minutes of meeting them, at a party, on a bus, or on the first day of class. They don't have appropriate boundaries. Everyone needs to learn what to say, how to say it, when to say it, and to whom. For some this does not come naturally, and it is usually a hard lesson to learn. For all of us when we enter a new environment we need to tweak the rules about boundaries again. This occurs when we move to a new area and don't know anyone, when we start at a new school, or when we start a new job or internship. So think before sharing information with new people at a new job in a new career.

Why Is It Important to Have Boundaries?

Boundaries protect us, both physically and emotionally. They establish structure, create order in our lives, and give us clear indications of hierarchy. For example, parents have a particular role to fulfill, both with each other and with their children. If a parent crosses the parent–child boundary, we have physical abuse, sexual abuse, emotional issues, or at minimum children very confused about what their role is within the family. These issues often continue through generations, where boundaries are violated and the cycle of abuse continues. One of our tasks as a social worker is to help clients develop appropriate boundaries and teach them how to maintain those boundaries. Clients, like ourselves, learn boundaries through cultural and societal norms but usually have to maintain them without the support of that same society. It is expected that you will learn to recognize when you have violated boundaries.

Why Do Boundary Violations Occur?

Some people don't have clearly defined boundaries because of crisis, poor role modeling, and many other reasons. Most of you can probably recall experiences where you found out information that you should not know. The person who shared that information with you likely has poor boundaries or does not maintain boundaries. Or maybe that person had a hidden agenda to create some drama or trouble. You also have probably broken a few boundaries yourself. Perhaps you went snooping in your house for Christmas presents, read your sister's diary, eavesdropped on your roommate's phone calls, or looked at your significant other's cell phone—whom they talked to and all their texts. Even just curiosity, a very innocuous feeling, causes trouble when you violate not only the boundary but the trust between you and that other person.

People who have a hard time creating and maintaining appropriate boundaries are considered vulnerable, impulsive, confused, alone, or isolated. Usually these people have low self-esteem and need to be validated. They may be very dependent or manipulative and may have had some kind of childhood trauma that causes relationship difficulties. Clients are not responsible for maintaining the boundaries between themselves and their social workers, and they will test the boundaries and see how far they can go. It is a natural human instinct. Do you remember having a substitute teacher in grade school or high school and telling the substitute lies, like "we already did that," or "we don't get homework"? Those students are testing the limits. Clients may also do this, it is what happens in all new relationships, and it is how we know where we stand and that we can trust the person.

So if it is normal for a client to test the limits and test boundaries, then it is the social worker's responsibility to maintain the boundary. Sometimes it is hard for the social worker for several reasons. Sometimes the social worker is so stressed or burned-out that it is hard to maintain the boundaries. Maintaining boundaries takes work, and you must be actively thinking about your interactions with your clients. As students, more likely than not, the reason you may have difficulty maintaining a boundary is inexperience. You are new to the field and are accustomed to spending time with people developing and maintaining other types of relationships. You will now be clarifying, developing, maintaining, and reinforcing professional boundaries. Be patient, as it will take practice.

Often, as social workers, we are helping our clients do the same things with their boundaries. In order to teach them to effectively manage their boundaries, you need to model appropriate boundaries—both personal and professional. It is important to define these boundaries and understand why they are needed. Professional boundaries exist to protect the social worker and the client. They put limits on the relationship, which helps the client feel safe. Professional boundaries also frame the role(s) the social worker will take on.

The first set of boundaries consists of explaining the rules of treatment: how often it will occur, when it will occur, how long it will take, how much it will cost, and what the expected outcome is. These preliminary boundaries set the tone for how the relationship will develop between you and the client. They create a safe space and allow the client to develop trust. There may be other boundaries that your agency or program overlays on this relationship as well, like whom to contact in an emergency, and what constitutes an emergency. Boundaries are established to make sure that the client's best interests are being considered. Boundaries also support the relationship that forms between the client and the social worker, protecting and guarding them both. The final set of boundaries are the NASW Code of Ethics and the CASW Code of Ethics and their guidelines.

When you enter into a relationship as a social worker with a client, you need to understand that the relationship is uneven in terms of power. As a professional, you have a knowledge base and experience that your client does not have. You become the expert in the room because of your knowledge, because it is your office space, and because you are in charge of what happens. This power differential makes you responsible for what happens in the agency between you and the client. That power differential makes you responsible for the boundaries of the relationship.

Thoughts to ponder

✔ What do you think of the power differential between you and your client? Are there ways to decrease the inequality?

✔ Would you want to change the power differential? Why or why not? In what settings would it be good to balance the power and where would it not be good?

Boundary violations can be divided into categories. Here we will discuss sexual boundaries, other physical contact, overfamiliarity, personal gain, gift giving, treating family and friends, and social contact. These categories were delineated by The College of Psychologists of Ontario in 1998; see end of chapter for Web address.

Sexual Boundaries

When researching professional boundaries in the social work literature, almost everything you find is focused on sexual boundaries and preventing sexual encounters with clients, including sexual harassment. The rule on sexual contact with clients is really simple to state, but apparently difficult for some to adhere to: there is *no sexual contact of any kind* for any reason with clients. Sexual contact includes intercourse, kissing, flirting, inappropriate conversation, or requiring sexual favors in exchange for treatment. The NASW Code of Ethics is very clear about sexual relationships (section 1.09).

(a) Social workers should under no circumstances engage in sexual activities or sexual contact with current clients, whether such contact is consensual or forced.

(b) Social workers should not engage in sexual activities or sexual contact with clients' relatives or other individuals with whom clients maintain a close personal relationship when there is a risk of exploitation or potential harm to the client. . . . Social workers—not their clients, their clients' relatives, or other individuals with whom the client maintains a personal relationship— assume the full burden for setting clear, appropriate, and culturally sensitive boundaries.

(c) Social workers should not engage in sexual activities or sexual contact with former clients.

(d) Social workers should not provide clinical services to individuals with whom they have had a prior sexual relationship.

In section 2.6, CASW Guidelines for Ethical Practice specifically address romantic and sexual relationships with clients:

2.6.1 Social workers do not engage in a romantic relationship, sexual activities, or sexual contact with clients, even if such contact is sought by clients.

2.6.2 Social workers who have provided psychotherapy or in-depth counseling do not engage in romantic relationships, sexual activities, or sexual contact with former clients. It is the responsibility of the social worker to evaluate that nature of the professional relationship they had with a client and to determine whether the social worker is in a position of power and/or authority that many unduly and/or negatively affect the decisions and actions of their former client.

2.6.3 Social workers do not engage in a romantic relationship, sexual activities, or sexual contact with social work students whom they are supervising or teaching.

Other Physical Contact

Touching clients needs further elaboration besides a blanket rule of DO NOT TOUCH. This touching includes comforting someone who is crying in your office. A natural instinct for some social workers might include a hug, hand-holding, or a pat on the shoulder. All of these would be appropriate if they met the following criteria: (1) you have asked the client's permission first, (2) your intentions are only momentary comfort, and (3) the client is clear about your intentions. These criteria are important, because then there is no misunderstanding about what occurred. Something important to note here is that many times our clients have a history of boundary violations that could involve sexual abuse, rape, sexual harassment, and domestic violence. An unexpected or unwanted touch, no matter how well-intentioned, may violate their boundaries and ruin the relationship that could help others heal: the relationship with you, the social worker.

Another population, little children, may want you to touch them all the time, for example, getting a hug every morning when they come to see you. Make sure that the children and the caretakers are OK with it, that your intentions are clear, and that the child knows what you are doing. Again, the child might have been abused, and your touching him or her, although well meaning, could cause anxiety and fear. For example, for a child with a cold who is crying, you might naturally take a tissue to help them blow their nose and wipe their eyes. Yet if someone once tried to suffocate this child, your innocent and helpful act could trigger some very sensitive memories, making things worse for the client. Remember, physical boundaries are very delicate and are the first layer of defense mechanisms that some clients may have established for good reasons.

Once again, the NASW Code of Ethics speaks to this type of situation.

> Social workers should not engage in physical contact with clients when there is a possibility of psychological harm to the client as a result of the contact (such as cradling or caressing clients). Social workers who engage in appropriate physical contact with clients are responsible for setting clear, appropriate, and culturally sensitive boundaries that govern such physical contact. (section 1.10)

Likewise, CASW Guidelines for Ethical Practice discuss physical contact with clients in sections 2.5, "Avoid Physical Contact with Clients," and 2.6, "No Romantic or Sexual Relationships with Clients."

> 2.5.1 Social workers avoid engaging in physical contact with clients when there is a possibility of harm to the client as a result of the contact. Social workers who engage in appropriate physical contact with clients are

responsible for setting clear, appropriate and culturally sensitive boundaries to govern such physical contact.

2.6.1 Social workers do not engage in romantic relationships, sexual activities, or sexual contact with clients, even if such contact is sought by clients.

The remaining boundary issues—overfamiliarity, personal gain, gift giving, treating family and friends, and social contact—are not as clear as the rules on sexual contact. Sometimes these areas do not have definitive answers, but we will explain each one to help you understand these different boundary areas.

Overfamiliarity

When discussing overfamiliarity, we include things such as discussing topics that have no relation to the issue the client is seeing you about. For instance, your client is a teenager who sees you to discuss problems in school, and you spend time talking about how much his or her parents make and the type of car they drive. Or your client is an elderly woman on a fixed income who can't afford her medicine, and you discuss instead how your parents grew up in the same neighborhood that she did. Another form of overfamiliarity is, having known the client for a long time, you start assuming you know why he or she acted in a certain way, which may stop communication or cause a power struggle over who is right. Never make assumptions about what your clients are thinking or feeling, and always verify your thoughts and hunches.

Personal Gain

Another boundary violation is personal gain. For instance, your client works at a clothing store and offers you their discount if you buy clothes at the store. Or your client works at a movie theater and offers to let you see movies for free. Clients have those perks from jobs for themselves and maybe family members (depending on how the benefits are explained to them). You cannot exploit that benefit because you will put the client in an uncomfortable position.

Personal gain can also crop up when you take a client's case only because it will benefit you, make you look good, get you a promotion at work, or be a case to publish in a presentation or a journal article. One real example that we know of involved a client who owned an automotive detailing shop. He offered his social worker a huge discount on the detailing of his car. The social worker accepted the discount, and while the car was being detailed, the client requested longer sessions and wanted to pay less for those sessions. It is awkward to barter with your social worker. How difficult would it have been if the social worker's car had been stolen while it was being detailed? It could make it impossible to be objective in helping the client, no matter how hard the social worker tried.

Conflicts of interest like those mentioned above are covered by the Code of Ethics in section 1.06.

(a) Social workers should be alert to and avoid conflicts of interest that interfere with the exercise of professional discretion and impartial judgment.

(b) Social workers should not take unfair advantage of any professional relationship or exploit others to further their personal, religious, political, or business interests.

(c) Social workers should not engage in dual or multiple relationships with clients or former clients in which there is a risk of exploitation or potential harm to the client.

(d) When social workers provide services to two or more people who have a relationship with each other (for example, couples, family members), social workers should clarify with all parties which individuals will be considered clients and the nature of social workers' professional obligations to the various individuals who are receiving services.

Conflicts of interest are addressed twice in the CASW Guidelines for Ethical Practice in sections 2.3, "Declare Conflicts of Interest," and 5.2, "Avoid and Declare Conflicts of Interest." Clearly, social workers must be very careful of any conflicts of interest they have that may interfere with their work in the best interest of the client.

Gift Giving

According to the NASW Code of Ethics and CASW Guidelines for Ethical Practice, social workers cannot accept gifts from clients. Section 1.13 of the NASW code, "Payment for Services" states: "Social workers should avoid accepting goods or services from clients as payment for professional service." Accepting gifts for what we do in our capacity as social workers is awkward and creates many unanswered questions. What if you didn't like the gift? What if you feel obligated to give the client a gift? Does it mean that you should offer more services, better services, or discounted services because of the gift? Does the client think that he or she is better than other clients now or feel we owe him or her special considerations? Gift giving can create a conflict of interest. The idea of gift-giving from a client to a social worker has been deemed inappropriate by the Code of Ethics because of all the potential problems, but it also presents a few ambiguities. What if you are working with a child who brings you a stuffed animal for your office or some Halloween candy after he or she went trick-or-treating? Learning to share and trust you enough to want to give you a gift may be significant in the child's treatment process, and refusing the gift may impede progress. When this occurs, it is one of those gray areas in ethics, and you should discuss it with your supervisor.

Thoughts to ponder

✔ How would you tell a client you cannot accept a gift without hurting his or her feelings or jeopardizing the relationship?

✔ Is there a cultural imperative for gift giving?

There will come a time when you are offered a gift by a client for the assistance you gave them. Clients who are from other cultures may want to give you a token of their appreciation—perhaps something they baked, an item from their country, or some other acknowledgment of your work. You must use your best cultural sensitivity in these cases, as refusing the gift could be quite offensive to your client. Accepting it, however, could be the beginning of a dual relationship. Here are some suggestions of what to say to people when they try to give you a gift:

- I am sorry; my profession doesn't allow me to accept gifts.
- Thank you for thinking of me; our agency doesn't allow me to accept gifts.
- Please keep the money and buy yourself something nice or donate to the agency.

If you feel like you must accept the gift, donate it to a place that the client won't know about.

Treating Family and Friends

A clear boundary violation is offering to treat family and friends. One of the first things taught in social work classes is not to try social work with any of your family members. Family roles and systems are constantly trying to maintain homeostasis without adding any unnecessary new roles to the system. Besides, as a social worker and a family member, the issues are too close to your heart and you can't offer the objectivity that is so needed and expected of a social worker. An example might arise if a doctor suggests that your sick parent sign a living will. As an adult child, if you are not ready for your parent to sign a living will (an order of "do not resuscitate"), you might not hear what your parent wants and might not be able to take the role of social worker in conversation with your family members, because of your emotional involvement.

Similar things could be said about friends. There are things you may need to say as a social worker that you can't say as a friend. For instance, a friend may have a serious drug problem, and you are concerned. If you confront as a social worker and offer treatment options, the friend may see you as a betrayer, because you knew about the drug use only because of your friendship. Your friend may feel that you violated his or her trust, and may never again talk to you as a friend, and may not want to see a social worker, either.

Social Contact

The last area where boundary violations tend to occur is in social contact. This is probably the grayest area of all, especially if you live in the community where you work. Social contact involves any contact with clients outside the social work relationship, such as patronizing their business, serving on committees together, or seeing each other socially. Perhaps your children and your client's children go to the same school, and you and your client both want to be active members of the Parent–Teacher Association (PTA), or maybe you and your client attend the same twelve-step meeting for Alcoholics Anonymous.

On the surface this sounds harmless. However, further examination turns up some issues. What happens if the PTA makes a strong stand to change the school rule requiring that children all wear uniforms? You disagree with the idea, but your client is spearheading the initiative. How would you keep your social work/client relationship separate from the adversarial role on the PTA issue? Likewise, what if your favorite clothing store somehow confuses a major special order for you or loses your layaway but refuses to reimburse you for your loss, and your client is the one refusing to give you back your money? You may need to sue to get your money back. How does that work in your relationship with your client in your capacity as a social worker? These are awkward situations, and best avoided. In an AA meeting you may not be able to share on a personal level because a client is thbere, again a very gray area.

Social Media

In the past few years opportunities to connect electronically have grown exponentially. When we wrote the first edition of the book social media was just on the horizon of being the new best thing. MySpace was the thing, Facebook didn't exist and only birds twittered. As we write this, everyone is tweeting, posting to Instagram, writing their own specialty blog, and "face timing" their friends when they want to talk "in person." Facebook, Tumblr, Instagram, FaceTime, Skype, Google Circles, LinkedIn, texting, Twittering and Second Life have connected the world. By the time this book is published some of these programs will be "old school" and something else will be the rage. These sites add a whole new dimension to social contact with clients outside work. Do you want your clients to know what you are doing on the weekends? What if they see the pictures you have posted of your family in front of your house? What if your avatar is more provocative or wild than you appear in the workplace? Be sure to recognize that even with all the safeguards and computer savvy you may have, the World Wide Web is pretty easily accessed by someone with computer knowledge.

In the past, our concerns about boundaries were physical and not electronic. The age of technology brings multiple issues up that need to be explored. Before graduating with your degree, we urge you to think before you post anything on the Internet. By now your professors and family members have warned you about whatever you put out on the Web; it is there forever. Be careful of those candid shots from your last spring break and your selfie from the good time at that bar the night before graduation. Employers now regularly Google you to see what they can discover about you. An agency's reputation is partially based on employees and they want to be careful to hire the right people, and your content on the Internet helps them decide about you. Obviously, if an employer can Google you, so too can a client. Be sure they don't find the proverbial skeleton in the closet when they search! Googling people is a common occurrence now and you want employers to find only positive things about you. If you are going to continue to post, watch your privacy settings on all social media sites.

Once you are employed, your personal relationships and your professional life ought to be as separate as possible. Your coworkers may eventually become friends. But clients, according to the NASW Code of Ethics, always remain as clients. They should not be your friends or connected to you in personal social media sites. Don't accept friend requests or let clients follow you on Twitter or whatever social media platform is the newest rage. If you have a good reason and your supervisor supports social media, keep a separate work Twitter account or a separate work Facebook page. If your agency has a social media site, you, of course, can post there about professional events like an open house or a fundraising event. When clients or their families ask to be part of your network let them know politely but firmly that you're unable to connect with them. If a request does come through, ignore or deny the request and let the client or their family member know that you appreciate the request but you just couldn't accept. If it helps and you feel you cannot say that to the client, you can blame it on your professional code of ethics or agency policy.

In our experience students have tried a few options to stay anonymous on the Web. Examples include using your middle name or your mother's maiden name to set up your private accounts and keeping all your data and privacy profiles as closed as possible. Be sure to know your agency's policy about social media.

Other social media faux pas to avoid are examples that we have seen that we were sure were not intentional on the student's part but could have been problematic if not caught quickly. Two examples that we can share are the following. A student was working with children and wanted to show the parents the pictures. She took the picture, posted it on Facebook and friended the parent. The second was an alumnus who was working with a twenty-something-year-old who died in a car accident. Somehow, the alumnus had posted several pictures of the client at her death and on the anniversary of her death. Both of these situations are not only illegal but also unethical. At **NO** time can you post any identifying information about a client on the Web (including after they pass away). This includes pictures, birthdays, addresses, and/or names. Client's information is always kept confidential. In the social media world, it is so easy to connect people. Personally one of the authors has been asked several times to be connected to someone on their LinkedIn accounts. Several of those people were clients. When approaching the client about the inability to connect via social media the client told the author they didn't request the connection. Somehow in the world of cyberspace the Internet had found a way to connect the two, a very awkward piece of knowledge to be wary about in the future. It is unusual and disconcerting when you try your best to keep appropriate boundaries with clients and a machine connects you!

We also want to include texting here. Almost everyone texts now, proposing marriage, breaking up relationships, and having very serious and real conversations. Those texting conversations belong between you and your family and friends. (Although we still don't encourage breaking up with your significant other over text!) ☺. Do not carry on long-term conversations over text with clients or your supervisor, whether it is your personal phone or a work phone. We all know how quickly texting, and e-mail, conversations go awry. It could be very hard to restore the relationship you have with your client if texting and e-mailing goes wrong. It is certainly appropriate to confirm a time, date, and place of a meeting with a client via a *work* cell phone, but not appropriate for a client to have your personal phone number. Be sure to follow the latest textiquette rules. Unless given permission by your supervisor do not use texting to call in sick or say that you will be late coming in to work. These are not the appropriate mediums for such an important communication. And finally, a student of ours once quit her internship via a text. Remember the earlier information that the social work world is a small community. Doing something as inappropriate as quitting by a text also may follow you in your future career. We cannot stress enough the importance of scheduling a time, and conducting all important conversations, like quitting a job or internship, in person.

Geographical Boundaries

Whenever possible, especially in very large metropolitan areas, try not to live in the area that you work. When this is not possible, make your connections in the community clear and businesslike. You will probably run into clients all the time outside of your agency setting, so be polite and friendly, but distant. When faced with more than a social-work relationship with a client, try to keep it at a minimum, don't initiate anything more than what is expected in that setting, and acknowledge the awkwardness with the client from the beginning, so that you can talk about avoiding difficulty in the future. It is always best to let your clients know how you will greet them in public before it happens the first time (or if you will let them decide to greet you or not). They will then know what to expect. Many rural agencies have policies/practices in place to address boundaries. If they don't, talk to·your supervisor about the agency's expectations when these circumstances occur.

Signs That a Boundary Violation Is Occurring

As a social worker you are responsible for maintaining the professional boundaries. The best way to do this is to constantly assess your practice both independently and with your supervisor. You can ask yourself questions about your relationship with the client to assure yourself that the boundaries are intact. Boundaries generally erode slowly; sometimes it is not very obvious, so look at the relationship from the beginning to the present when assessing the change.

Are you still objective? Can you see both sides of the issue and understand where the client is incorrect or losing his or her own objectivity? Are you treating that client as special or different? Is it OK that they are late or don't have to be responsible for their actions? Do you allow that client to do things that you wouldn't let other clients do? If so, these are all signs that the boundaries are becoming diffuse or cloudy. Have you disclosed information to this client about other clients? Maybe it's not even a name but information about their case, like "I had another client go through the same thing as you" and similar situations. This is, of course, inappropriate and borders on breaking confidentiality.

It is really not hard for clients to learn about who is being treated by whom and for what. You think an agency is an anonymous place, but most agencies are just a microcosm of where we live. Clients know each other and talk to one another, when we as social workers can't. Most social workers and agencies rely on word of mouth for referral, and clients will share conversations frequently. Wouldn't it be awful if a client said to a friend, "My social worker is treating someone who did blah, blah, blah," and the second person recognized his or her own story?

Finally, you know you are getting too close to a client when you start self-disclosing. Clients should know little about you, if anything. Self-disclosure can be one of the hardest areas to define. It can be hard to be a social worker without having some ability to self-disclose in professional use of self. When you use humor correctly in a session, it's good use of self—but it also shows you have a sense of humor. When you say to a child, "My favorite ice cream is vanilla, too," that boundary is self-disclosure but is not inherently harmful. When discussing self-disclosure as a bonding issue, you are using the session to share that you have had similar problems or that you are concerned about this situation because of what you went through. When this type of self-disclosure occurs it changes you from a social worker providing services to a person sharing their issue with another person. Once boundaries are gone, they are difficult to restore, and you may have lost the therapeutic relationship you had.

If in your self-analysis any of these issues come up, make sure you discuss them in supervision. These signs are clues that boundaries are being violated and that you need assistance in reestablishing them.

Consequences of Boundary Violation

The consequences of boundary violations vary. Sometimes you can apologize for them, boundaries can be clarified and reinforced, and it is OK. For the client, becoming dependent on the worker can immobilize the client, or even cause regression. The client may mistrust and feel unsafe with that social worker (and maybe with the entire helping profession), preventing the client from seeking help and causing more difficulties in his or her life. For the social worker, boundary violations can ruin his or her career. If a client feels violated and shares that feeling with other people in the agency or community, how likely is it that anyone else will go to that worker? If the boundary violation is serious enough, a social worker's license can be revoked or suspended, leaving the social worker without the ability to work.

Other Boundaries

This chapter started out discussing boundaries as a general concept and a part of all relationships. But most of this chapter has been a delineation of boundaries between social workers and clients. There are other boundaries that as a student you must be aware of, between you and your teacher, you and your supervisor, and you and your coworkers. Your teacher and your supervisor are mostly responsible for maintaining those boundaries, and you and your coworkers are equally responsible for your relationship. But if a teacher or supervisor breaks a boundary, especially in the context of sex, take all necessary action to address the issue, bringing in other people if you have to.

The best way to maintain boundaries is to be clear about what they are from the beginning. Know what the expectations are about dress code; for instance, when violations are frequent or severe, there are consequences to both the social worker and the client.

In residential settings for kids, you may be expected to dress to be ready to play or restrain, but that doesn't mean your torn jeans or your shirt with one arm or no back is appropriate. Clothing in most settings will tell you who are staff and who are the clients. Other things to consider are the boundaries for e-mails and phone calls. What is appropriate to discuss in the office and what is not? When and where do you answer phone calls from clients?

The same type of questions can be asked about your professor. They include boundaries regarding assignments and class attendance. Is your teacher firm about assignment deadlines? Do you know who will be flexible and when?

Expect that maintaining boundaries takes as much work as establishing relationships. Sometimes you don't know if you are crossing a boundary until it's too late. Keeping watch on your boundaries is a way of maintaining relationships and keeping them healthy within the appropriate context (e.g., a friend/friend relationship or a social work/client relationship). When establishing boundaries, it is always a good idea to have firm, clear boundaries with people first. Once the relationship is established, it is easy to make them a little closer and more flexible. It is always harder to start with really flexible, close boundaries and have to establish firmer boundaries. Most people, including clients, will have a hard time understanding why the boundaries changed from flexible and close to rigid and distant.

Integration of other course material	
HBSE	How can you determine what the formal and informal boundaries are in a community?
Policy	What are the options available to a client if a boundary violation occurs?
Practice	What strategies can you think of to help you develop and maintain appropriate professional boundaries with your clients?
Research	What does the research show regarding how often boundary violations occur and in what areas?

Resources

The College of Psychologists of Ontario
http://www.cap.ab.ca/pdfs/capmonitor08.pdf

Life Quality Institute
http://www.capnm.ca/Prof_Boundaries_Packet_2010.pdf

New York State Office of the Professions
http://www.op.nysed.gov/prof/sw/swboundaries.htm

Ever feel taken advantage of in your internship? When did this happen? Describe the circumstances, how you felt, and what you did about it.

Did you speak with your supervisor? Why or why not?

Chapter 13
Difficult Issues and Difficult Situations

What can we write that would help you through difficult issues that you will face or difficult cases that you will need to work out for your clients? Each of us will find different aspects of social work more appealing and more exciting than others. For instance, one of the authors of this book likes clinical work with people who are drug-addicted and alcoholic. The other author would prefer to organize a union around workplace-safety issues or to increase the awareness of social work issues internationally. Although we respect each other's differences and are both trained to do either job, we choose to specialize in particular areas because of our interests.

The point is that throughout your career each of you will define for yourself what a difficult issue or population is for you to work with. Our intention in this chapter is to explore issues that come up frequently for students in their fieldwork, so that you may know what to expect. The common issues that always seem to come up are

conflicts between personal and agency values;

use of alternative methods, techniques, or skills to work with clients;

transference and countertransference;

recognizing when you, the social worker, are being difficult;

working within your own community;

negotiating collaborative agreements between a variety of agencies and communities;

chronic psychiatric impairments of individual clients or their family members;

the reluctant or resistant client; and

disapproval of how other colleagues treat clients.

Ethical Conflicts

In each chapter of this book we have pointed out the section from the NASW Code of Ethics and the Canadian Code of Social Work that has some bearing on the content of the chapter. The Code of Ethics is a very useful tool that you should keep readily available. You can purchase the code in booklet form from NASW, and it is probably also in a number of your textbooks (including this one;

see appendix A), or it can be easily downloaded or bookmarked on the Internet. The NASW Code of Ethics started out as a very short document (less than two pages) and over the years has increased in depth and breadth, especially in areas that were vague or in areas where new issues arose. Although the code tries to be inclusive, there is no way that it can cover every issue that arises in social work practice. Our suggestion is to start with the Code of Ethics when struggling with an issue, and hopefully it will give you guidance.

Sometimes the code cannot give an answer because your problem is too vague or too specific. Several social work ethicists have spent a large part of their careers looking at ethical dilemmas and trying to provide guidance to social work practitioners and educators on how to best approach difficult issues. There are many textbooks and articles written on the subject. You will have to find a social work ethicist that you enjoy reading and understand to be a personal guide for you. Because, unfortunately for you, as a new social worker, the dilemmas faced by social workers do not always have clear-cut answers. Ethical dilemmas are rarely black and white—there is so much gray area associated with ethical issues. In fact, when attending training or classes on ethics, you will often walk out with more questions than you walked in with! You may even get different answers to the same question from experienced, respected social workers.

Here are some questions and guidelines for you to follow:

1. Have you looked at your personal values on the subject?

2. Have you looked at societal values on the subject?

3. What insight can the NASW Code of Ethics or the CASW Guidelines give for Ethical Practice give in this situation?

4. Are there legal statutes that can give light to the subject?

5. What is the agency's view on the issue?

6. Think about all of the consequences of your decision for you, your client, and the agency. Are you willing to accept the actions of your decision?

7. Don't make any decisions based upon one answer from the above list; take everything into consideration.

8. Before enacting any decision that went through the above process, be sure that your supervisor is in agreement with what you will do.

After consulting the Code of Ethics, if the answer to your question is unclear or unsatisfactory, you can always consult colleagues and your supervisor. We must warn you, however, that each social worker is an individual, and you may end up with as many answers as people that you asked. The dialogue that takes place will usually help you clarify your response. Together, you and your colleagues can usually come up with a solution that all can live with, by selecting components of many ideas and forming one direction to pursue. When in doubt many agencies and NASW have attorneys that you can consult. Always check with your supervisor before calling a lawyer, as that may be costly to the agency. If you opt for liability insurance the companies usually also have attorneys readily available to answer questions. After all, they have a vested interest in keeping you out of trouble. They also prefer to answer questions before the incident occurs rather than after the fact. Your ethical dilemma is just that; it is not a moral, religious, or personal decision. The several answers you receive from colleagues and supervisors are their interpretation of the agency policy and the code of ethics, not their opinions about how the client will live their life.

Conflicts between Personal and Agency Values

Ethics become an issue when your personal values come into direct conflict with professional boundaries. This usually occurs when a client makes a choice, under the guise of self-determination, to do something that is in direct violation of your own values. This personal and professional dilemma can also occur at the macro level when you disagree with a decision your agency has made. An obvious micro level example of this is when a client decides to get an abortion and your personal belief is that abortions are wrong. A macro level example is if an organizational decision is made by your agency, a drug treatment program, to start a needle-exchange program to minimize the risk of HIV. You don't believe that those programs are a good idea because you think that needle-exchange programs encourage the same drug use that you are trying to treat. These scenarios highlight a difference in values between you and your client or you and your agency. You have several options to pursue while you try to sort out where you stand on these dilemmas.

The first is to say nothing, regardless of your feelings, and let the agency and your client choose to do what they want. This sounds easy, but it entails that you put your personal values aside, and this decision may come back again and again. It could make working in your agency uncomfortable.

Your second choice is to ask questions and provide information on the pros and cons of the decision, so that your client and your agency are sure they made the right decision and that you have raised your awareness of other viewpoints on the issue. It is very inappropriate to force a client to change his or her mind. But it is your responsibility to be sure the client has all the objective facts (NOT your opinion slanted and presented as facts) and has sorted out all feelings regarding his or her decision before acting on it. It is appropriate to discuss with your agency administrators their stance on an issue. Be aware that challenging agency policy may make you unpopular, and it could become difficult to work there—the agency attitude toward change and resistance to change will affect how you are perceived if you do this. It could, however, make you well respected and regarded as an up-and-coming leader in the agency if your points are well taken and change people's minds.

Your third option is to seek supervision and reflect on why you feel the way you do. Sometimes talking out loud with another person can clarify your stance and the origin of that opinion or value. Individual reflection can also help. Ask yourself, where does my value come from? Do I believe that for myself, or is it a value I carry from my parents that I have not questioned? Or is it a value I acquired somewhere else (e.g., religion or former community) that I have not fully discerned and need to rethink? These types of questions are not easy but are essential in the realm of ethical decision making. While you are still a student, you can use a teacher or your peers for this discernment process.

Your final option is to refuse to work with that client or for that agency any longer. If you cannot set aside your personal values and you feel uncomfortable with your or the agency's actions, it may be time to move on. Recognize the reason that you can't change your values and be sure to clearly and thoroughly research the next agency you go to. You will have to explain to a new employer what type of issues you cannot work with or what conditions you cannot work under. Remember, this could limit the places you can work and the supervisors who are willing to give you a chance within their agencies. In the end, you have to be comfortable and confident wherever you work. If your beliefs can't be reconciled with the Code of Ethics and social work agency's policy it may be that you were not meant to be a social worker, despite how many people you want to help.

Thoughts to ponder

✔ How do you make your decisions?

✔ Do you have values that you adopted because they were your parents' and that you no longer feel as strongly about as when you were taught them?

✔ Have you had any ethical dilemmas in the field?

✔ If so, what did you do to resolve them?

✔ If you haven't had any yet, do you anticipate any such issues?

Use of Alternative Methods

Another set of difficult issues that we believe to be problematic for students is the use of alternative techniques to deal with clients. In your classes, both in psychology and social work, you will be exposed to many theories and techniques. The ones you will use with clients are the theories and skills that you practice in class and that your supervisor has competence in, so he or she can guide you.

The longer you are in the field, the more opportunities you will have to receive specialized training in other areas. The longer you are in the field, the more you will see clients who will not respond to the skills and theories you have learned thus far. There are many other techniques and skills being taught to advance your level of practice. Treatment approaches such as hypnotism, eye movement desensitization and reprocessing (EMDR), rapid eye movement (REM), and psychodrama are techniques that many people receive specialized training in. Just as now you explain to your clients that you are an intern, you must also explain to your clients when you are practicing a new technique or method. For ethical reasons you need to tell clients that you are doing something new and that you are unsure how it will be as an experience for you or them. It is expected that if you are trying something new with a client, you have been properly trained and you feel confident that you can successfully complete the tasks that are part of the new technique.

If your teacher discusses a new technique in class that you want to try now, check with your supervisor. Make sure he or she is aware of what you want to do, why you think it will work, and if it fits the therapeutic milieu of the agency. Make sure your supervisor or someone else knows the technique, in case you need help. There is something known as best practice with clients: Best practices are well researched and are known to work for that specific client group or issue. Many people in your agency will know about best practices and be able to help you with the technique and/or theory.

Transference and Countertransference

Transference and countertransference can be difficult for new social workers. Transference is when clients associate the social worker with someone in their life and start treating the social worker like that person, sometimes negatively, sometimes positively. Countertransference is the same thing for the social worker, who associates the client with someone else. It is the reverse of transference.

When the issue occurs in your practice as a social worker, it may not be obvious right away. You may feel like the relationship is not building as fast as most of your client-worker relationships, or it just feels like it's not working and you are not sure what is happening. You need to reflect on your practice by yourself and with your supervisor to determine why this relationship is not working. Chances are good that countertransference or transference is getting in the way. Once made aware that this is the issue, you can address it fairly easily with supervision. If it is your issue, talk about it in supervision and adjust your behavior accordingly with your client.

If it is your client's issue, try to explore with them who you might be reminding them of from their life. Identifying the transference will allow the client the opportunity to resolve any issues that remain about that relationship. Transference becomes an issue only when it's not identified. Used appropriately, it can assist clients and help them make great strides in their treatment.

Recognizing When You Are Being Difficult

As well as being a social worker, you are also a human being who has personality quirks that will occasionally get in the way of your work. This is not the same as transference because it has nothing to do with your interaction with the client. Instead, it is an area of life that impedes your work as a social worker. An example of this may be that you are a morning person, very energetic and cheerful as soon as you wake up. You know that your down time is late afternoon, but you are working in a school-based youth service program where you see most clients after school. As you may know, most adolescents are not morning people and may just be waking up after school! A client who is half asleep may find your energy level very unpleasant in the morning, and because you are tired in the afternoon, you may find it difficult to engage a client in meaningful conversation later in the day. It is easy to report, "Client was quiet and did not engage in meaningful conversation," making it appear that it is the client's issue. Your responsibility as the social worker is to assess your part in the relationship and see what you can do to alter it. Acknowledging the issue and putting the onus on the client is irresponsible.

Another example would be if you made culturally insensitive comments to a client and they stopped talking to you. Labeling that client as unresponsive or reluctant puts the responsibility on the client, when you should understand the difficulty is on your end.

Working within Your Own Community

An additional area that causes some difficulty for many students is working within their own community. We already mentioned problems with this when we discussed boundaries in chapter 12. The main issue is how much self-disclosure is comfortable for you. When you live in the community where you work, people know a lot about you. They will see you shopping, going out to dinner, attending church, and visiting your child's school. Some social workers also feel awkward about the dual relationships that can occur as we discussed previously (e.g., your child playing with the child of your client). It is better to avoid these situations whenever possible. If you are in a position where you must live and work in the same community, set up boundaries that will help clients understand when to approach you about work issues and when you are not on duty. Monitor those boundaries carefully on a fairly regular basis. This protects you from burnout and stress and protects clients from awkward moments as well.

Negotiation with Other Agencies

Another area of difficulty for many social workers is negotiating collaborative agreements among agencies. As funding gets cut and as our world seems to get smaller and smaller, it becomes ever more necessary for all of us to work together to assist everyone in need. Many agencies within a community are working on similar issues and maybe even with similar clients. To be the most effective and efficient, many agencies are now working together and hiring consultants to do pieces of their program (e.g., evaluation).

When agencies decide to collaborate, a social worker usually brokers the deal. This includes negotiating the various components of the program. For example, who will be the lead agency? The lead agency usually receives the funding and is ultimately responsible for the program. Which agency will provide the evaluation? Which agency will design and implement the different segments of the program? There are a lot of pieces to negotiate and whether the agencies will work together well depends on how firmly established the relationships are between the agencies. The social worker that leads this effort will be responsible for keeping communication lines open, keeping track of the tasks and responsibilities of each agency, and overseeing everyone's accountability to the project. If you ever have this task, be clear, open, and honest with everyone. The job is much less stressful when everyone is doing his or her share and everyone is reliable and competent. It becomes difficult when some are not always honest—the agencies involved want their funds but do not always want to produce the work to the agreed quality, or are unable to produce the work for other reasons. When this occurs you need to scramble to get all the tasks done, and it causes strained relations.

A similar situation can arise in a group project for class. We are sure that at some point you have been in a group where another student did not fulfill his or her piece of the project in the specified amount of time. Or maybe it was in on time but was not the quality the group expected. Someone has to step forward to tell the person the problem and to correct the situation. Afterward, because the class is still going on, you need to continue to get along. So not only is the negotiation important, but so is the relationship building and the leadership used to get the agencies to work together. Remember, open, clear, and honest communication will see you through.

Partnering with Multiple Agencies

Many times when working in the community, social workers find it far more beneficial to partner with other agencies and groups to accomplish some of their work that is related to their goals. Sometimes this is done to share resources—both logistically and in kind. For example, you might find several nonprofit groups sharing a building together and sharing the expenses for the operation and maintenance of that building. Some groups might share staff—like an accountant or auditor—to help manage their budgets.

You also will see community groups partnering together to accomplish goals, and this is also called coalition building. This happens frequently when new legislation is introduced at the city, state, or national level that would benefit a number of groups or constituencies. In order to pool resources, build a larger power base, increase their impact, and develop new leaders, community groups will build coalitions around this issue to try and win a campaign. These are just some of the benefits of this work and this process. There are a number of books that are devoted to coalition building, and you might be reading some of these in your studies. Of course, there are drawbacks, as coalition building takes time and effort and distracts you from the regular routine of your agency work. And, as with all groups, there will be members who do not put in as much work and effort as other group members do, but overall, working in coalitions is a great way to promote and accomplish large-scale work in communities.

Chronic Psychiatric Impairments

Another difficulty faced by social workers is when the client or the client's family members have mental health issues. Not all social workers choose to work in mental health. At the bachelor's level you probably receive little classroom education on the topic of mental health unless you choose to take an abnormal psychology class. Just because your career path is not in mental health does not mean that you will not come across the issue. Many clients who are in social work settings have multiple issues, and some may very well have mental health issues. It is important for you to have a general understanding of diagnosis and medications. When you take a complete biopsychosocial, ask about the client's mental health history and the family's relevant history. You, as the social worker, should be familiar enough with the DSM-5 to learn about the criteria for a diagnosis and what types of medicine clients are taking.

As you continue to work with your clients, you will be able to observe if they are following treatment. You will also be able to tell when they may be having difficulty and need assistance. When the general population thinks about mental health issues, there is a general fear for their own safety. As social workers you need to be aware that most people who have a mental illness are not a danger to you or society. If they are having a difficult day, they are probably more a danger to themselves than to others. As a responsible student, and soon-to-be social worker, you are encouraged to become familiar with diagnoses like depression, bipolar disorder, and schizophrenia. Recognize the obstacles your clients may be facing, and assist them within your scope of practice the best you know how, with encouragement, support, and education as needed from your supervisor. We just mentioned the term scope of practice. One of the important items to keep in mind is to work only with issues that you are competent to treat. When you are not competent within an area you are not permitted to assist that client or group or to gain training and supervision until you have competence. When you don't get training and supervision and choose to work with the particular issue, you are working "out of the scope of your practice" and that is certainly unethical and could be illegal as well.

Substances of Abuse and Those That Use Them

Most of what was just said about the chronic psychiatric impairments could be said about substance use. You may choose not to work with people who have an addiction problem, but between alcohol, illegal drugs like cocaine and heroin, prescription drugs, over-the-counter drugs, and nicotine being abused at record highs, it is even more likely that you will encounter people who have substance abuse issues. It is important that you have a working knowledge (not first-hand knowledge) of what happens when people use specific substances, 12-step meetings, and treatment facilities in your area. It would also be useful if you follow drug policies in your state (or province) and the country, as marijuana for medical use is a quickly growing phenomena.

The Reluctant or Resistant Client

Depending on where you work, you may meet clients that do not necessarily want the services your agency provides. You may be at a nursing home where clients don't want to be but cannot care for themselves at home and have no one else to care for them. You may work in a drug and alcohol rehabilitation program where a judge has assigned a client to complete a drug program or go to jail instead, and the client does not believe they have a drug problem. Some of the clients you will see as a social worker may fall into this category. These clients are known as involuntary, reluctant, or resistant and appear in many agencies in various ways fairly frequently. These clients can be harder to engage, get to know, and help. There is a good chance they may refuse to talk to you.

Our first suggestion to you is not to get discouraged when talking to the reluctant client. Instead, embrace the challenge. Try each of your social work skills to try to get the person engaged in conversation with you. Once you start conversing, it may be easier to engage the client in treatment.

Your challenge is to break through that barrier and provide the care that your client needs and you want to give. There are semester-long courses spent on how to assist this type of client; here we can only suggest to keep trying. Your perseverance will not go unnoticed and often will be all it takes to persuade the person to speak. Another idea is to give clients time and space to get used to the idea that they have no choice about being here and that it is not as bad an experience as they thought or that you are going to make the best of the situation. You will need to try a variety of techniques and be patient.

Difficulty in the Community

Just as working with clients can be challenging at times, working in communities can also be challenging, and for some of the same reasons. Personalities are interesting and you work with many of them in the community. Part of the challenge of being a community social worker is figuring out all the various personalities of the people you work with in the community and how to work with them and how to get them to work with each other. It is group work notched up about five degrees! The same principles that you apply in group work also apply to community groups in many ways, as to how to work with people in a large setting interpersonally.

What also confounds community work and adds to the difficulty sometimes are the resource issues—lack of staff, space, money, etc., can make this work very challenging.

Community work also takes place over a longer time span sometimes than individual work with clients and their families, so it can take longer to see results, or you have to go back to the drawing board more often and start over. This can be frustrating and can hinder progress on issues, which then can be personally unfulfilling.

Concern of Colleagues' Treatment of Clients

The final area social work students have told us can be difficult is when they disapprove of how another colleague treats clients. It is our teaching and belief that all people, not just clients, should be treated with respect and dignity as human beings. So it doesn't matter what setting we are in; it matters that care and compassion are present in our dealings with others. Not everyone holds that belief, however, even some people in the helping profession. When students experience this in the field, we try to do a variety of things. The first is to educate students that not everyone has the same underlying principles about basic human rights, or sometimes people may be so burned out that they treat clients with disdain or disrespect. Your coworker may also be so burned out or fed up with a client population or a particular client that they have difficulty being patient and respectful. Thjs issue needs to be addressed.

When students see inappropriate treatment of clients, we encourage them to talk to their coworker about it. We recognize it is not easy to confront colleagues about how they are working or treating clients. But before you go over their head and talk to your supervisor, your colleague needs a chance to give their point of view. We never really know what is happening with another person—there could be medical problems, personal issues, difficulties at home, and so on. Your colleagues are under no obligation to tell you all their private affairs, but by speaking with them first, you allow them to speak up and to see how others perceive their actions. They can also reflect on their behavior.

If things do not improve, you may be forced to report the incidents to your supervisor. It is important that the situation change, and if you have knowledge of an issue, especially regarding the treatment of clients, you have a responsibility to address it. If the person is burned out, you might suggest to them to take vacation time or a different job. Help your coworker, and don't make issues worse by not acknowledging them.

We could have spent weeks of the semester on each type of difficult issue and probably added some new topics as well. This is not a comprehensive explanation or an exhaustive list of the issues you may face in this profession. We can say with confidence that the longer you are in the field, the more knowledge and experience you will have to address these issues. Hopefully you won't see difficult issues constantly in your daily routine as a social worker. You may even get to the point where you see difficult issues as challenges that can be faced in a positive way.

The environment in which we practice has changed a great deal since the beginnings of social work. There are more people in the world, and there have been many inventions that make life easier, cures have been developed for many illnesses, and advances in technology have been made that no one in centuries past could have dreamed possible. Along with those wonderful things have come additional issues: more illnesses, including mental health issues; more substance abuse; more and different crimes than could ever be imagined years ago; and an enormous amount of poverty. As a social worker, you will be encountering multiple issues and, unfortunately, a dwindling set of resources. These two issues combined make it more important to assist our clients in getting what they need. When we can, we need to create new resources and help decrease social issues through programs like drug prevention and education programs. Our training in micro, mezzo, and macro social work will be very useful for tackling multiple issues even with a lack of resources.

Integration of other course material

HBSE   During the assessment process with a client, is there anything you could do to anticipate and alleviate any difficulties that you might encounter?

Policy   What is your agency policy regarding how to handle difficult situations with clients?

Practice   What is the benefit to your practice as a social worker of having difficult practice issues?

Research   Is there a research project you could set up to determine, when there is difficulty between social worker and client, how often this difficulty lies with the social worker?

Resources

National Mental Health Association
http://www.nmha.org/

Value Conflicts
http://www.jswvearchives.com/

Transference and Countertransference
http://www.crisiscounseling.com/Articles/Transference.htm

 **Ethical dilemmas are prevalent throughout the field internship experience. Take a moment to process an ethical question or dilemma you were faced with.**

Describe the ethical dilemma or question.

Who did you turn to for help?

What happened?

Did you follow any particular ethical decision-making model? Which one? How did it work?

Chapter 14
Self-Evaluation

Guess what? You are coming into the home stretch! Only a few weeks left and you'll have finished the semester! For some of you, it may mean you are done with fieldwork completely; others might have another semester or two. Whatever the case, we are sure that you have been exposed to many new situations where you have been able to do things that you would not have believed possible when you declared yourself to be a social work major. Now it is time to reflect on your experience over the semester and see what you have accomplished, and how far you have come in your professional development. In other words, it is time for self-evaluation.

For many of you, your internship was your first professional work experience. That means you are about to have your first evaluation. Work evaluations are done on multiple levels—there is usually a ninety-day probationary period for all employees, and if you pass that, you will have an annual review. The annual review is much like your field evaluation. It can include personal work ethics, your competency, how you fit into the agency's work culture, and your effectiveness with clients and staff. We will take a look at what all this means in a moment.

Many of you have had jobs before. Whether they were in the field of social work or not, you probably had a performance appraisal. Maybe this appraisal was informal (Hey, you are doing a great job!), or formal, where you sat down and signed an evaluation. Your field evaluation will be similar in many respects, because it is time to receive feedback.

We would like you to evaluate *yourself* before your supervisor evaluates you. In order to do this, you will need some materials. Gather your journal, your contract, your chapter 1 exercise about preparing your agency contract, and the blank evaluation used by your social work program or the agency you are at. Spend time reviewing these materials. You'll use them as we discuss work expectations and evaluation. First, we'll discuss your personal inventory.

Work Ethic Revisited

Let's return now to the concept of work ethic discussed at the end of chapter 1. You are probably familiar with what has been called the "Protestant work ethic," which encompasses commitment, hard work, loyalty, dedication, passion, and self-sacrifice. Most employers still expect hard work and commitment, but the workforce has changed. People are not willing to sacrifice themselves for their employers. Workers' loyalty has changed because their sense is that organizations are not loyal now, due to downsizing, layoffs, closures, and mergers. Permanent employment is not guaranteed, and employees never know how long the job will be there.

We'd like to contend that all the pieces of the Protestant work ethic still need to exist for you as an employee, as a human being. While at your job, for your own career development, you need to be hard-working, committed, loyal, and dedicated. For those who have never worked or who have worked only in temporary jobs, we'd like to take a few moments to operationalize those words. Take some time to answer these questions.

Work Ethic

✔ What does it mean to be a good employee?

✔ What personal qualities do employers look for when hiring someone?

✔ What personal qualities do employers look for when promoting someone?

✔ What are things you should not do because they will get you in trouble at work?

✔ Share your answers in small groups and see what similarities exist.

Does your list include any of the following things?

Punctuality

Following the dress code

Making sure your cell phone is off

Not checking your personal e-mail while at the office

Not taking off every possible minute of time as soon as you accrue it

These are just a few examples of things to be aware of when thinking about working hard and doing a good job. One of us worked for a social work agency that was a real stickler for promptness. At that place a 9 a.m. start time meant 9:00 at your desk, already having your coffee and having been to the restroom. One employee was fired because she couldn't get to work by 9:00, even though she stayed almost every well night past 6:00 and had all her work done, despite that 5:00 was the end of the day.

One way to understand what employers look for in an employee is to work every day as though you are the owner or director of the agency. Short-term hard work, dedication, commitment, and positive attitude will get you far. Building your abilities, your knowledge, and your reputation, you will be ready to handle most other jobs later in your career. If you are willing to work in a team, a strong communicator, intrinsically motivated (motivated inside yourself, not outside by money or fear or punishment), productive, prepared, organized, and dependable, you have the essential qualities that will help you go far in your career.

Here are some work habits that are frowned upon:

1. Packing up and organizing your work area to leave before quitting time while you watch the clock;
2. Not following the dress code;
3. Being late;
4. Forgetting to share information (communication is key in any organization);
5. Acting as an individual, not as a team member;
6. Using company resources for personal use—computers, copiers, fax machines, postage machines, etc.;
7. Inappropriate language (cursing, swearing, gossiping). Making personal calls from your office;
8. Lack of initiative;
9. Consistently putting personal life in front of the job; and
10. Keeping personal cell phone on and texting or making/taking personal calls on work time.

Here are some work habits that will benefit your career and make you invaluable to any agency:

1. Being prepared to work until the job is done;
2. Taking on additional responsibilities;
3. Being creative;
4. Pointing out issues only when you can also give solutions;
5. Showing respect;
6. Being dependable and reliable;
7. Being responsible for the work of the organization, not just your work within the team;
8. Having a positive attitude; and
9. Good critical thinking skills.

Perhaps you already have good work habits, developed at your first job at the local mall or when you babysat. If this is the first time you are reading about developing a work ethic, be sure you understand it thoroughly and incorporate it as your own. Not everyone has this work ethic, and they will lose out through their work experience and you will benefit. As you enter the profession, ignore what others do, because it may be against your career goals and the work ethic you are building. It may frustrate you when you believe you are working very hard and others are not doing their part. You will benefit later on, as you are looking at long-term gain and the benefit for your clients. You also need to keep in mind that you do have a personal life and need to balance it appropriately with your work ethic. You also must be careful that you are not doing more than you should for clients; they need to become independent, not look to you to do everything for them.

The traits discussed above are the first level of evaluation that your supervisor will make prior to looking at your social work skills or the individual points on your individual agreement or job description. So this is where we will start in your own evaluation. Your personal inventory is critical to successful employment in any field.

Thoughts to ponder

✔ What can you say about your own work ethic?

✔ Where can you improve your work ethic?

✔ Are you satisfied with your personal inventory?

Fulfilling the Contract

Now that your personal inventory is complete, it is appropriate to look at your professional inventory. Look at the materials you collected at the beginning of the chapter. Consider your work performance now as if you are your supervisor. What were your expectations when you completed the exercise in chapter 1 about developing your agreement? Did all your expectations get written into this semester's field agreement? If not, do you still need to learn those specific tasks? How are the essential roles that you need to learn as a generalist social work practitioner playing out in this agency? Your evaluation should take all of these items into account and try to accurately reflect what you have done, how you did it, and what you should do next.

Your learning agreement with the agency is a contract between two parties. You agreed to certain activities that you have knowledge about but no practical experience in. The agency has social work tasks to give you practical experience and supervision. Select the tasks and objectively examine your completion and mastery of them. For instance, maybe one of the tasks in your learning agreement was to facilitate a group. Ask yourself these questions about that activity.

1. Have I facilitated a group yet? How often? How did I do?

2. Am I comfortable facilitating a group?

3. Have I dealt with the behavioral challenges that have occurred in group? Did I start the group on time?

4. Did I use the time well, being prepared with enough material that was appropriate for the populations that I was working with?

5. Most important, did I put my best effort into this specific component of the agreement?

6. How was my documentation of the group process?

These are the types of questions you need to ask for every item of your agreement. Once you have completed each item of the agreement, give your overall impressions of your work at the internship this semester. Rate yourself on the questions in table 14.1.

Table 14.1 Self-Evaluation

	Needs immediate attention	Poor	Adequate	Good	Excellent
	1	2	3	4	5
How was your overall performance?					
Do you have the potential to be an effective social worker?					
Are your personal values consistent with social work values?					
Is this the population you would consider working with after you graduate?					
Is social work the profession for you?					

Developing a New Learning Agreement

When you have completed this evaluation, think about next semester and developing a new agreement. Questions to ask yourself include:

1. What areas of this semester's agreement still need improvement or refinement?

2. What areas of this semester's contract were not started, because of the needs of the agency?

3. What do I want to learn that I have not been exposed to?

4. What things on the agreement do I think I can do independently and would like to continue to do?

5. Is there an area of coursework that I have not yet integrated into my internship and that I need help learning how to apply (a particular theory or skill)?

6. Is there anything else I want to include for my personal development or knowledge?

7. Is there a task that I have been avoiding because I am fearful or uncertain and I am unwilling and unhappy to perform?

You have just established your new learning goals for your professional development next semester. It is time to set up a meeting with your supervisor to discuss these items, your evaluation, and your new learning agreement for next semester. You should let your supervisor know that you want to discuss all this when you set up the meeting. Sharing the subject you wish to talk about gives them time to prepare for the meeting as well.

The NASW Code of Ethics covers evaluation from the perspectives of both students and employees. Section 3.02b states, "Social workers who function as educators or field instructors for students should evaluate students' performance in a manner that is fair and respectful." Further on, section 3.03 speaks to evaluation of employees: "Social workers who have responsibility for evaluating the performance of others should fulfill such responsibility in a fair and considerate manner and on the basis of clearly stated criteria."

CASW Guidelines for Ethical Practice also discusses evaluation in section 3.4.3: "Social workers evaluate supervisees in a manner that is fair and respectful and consistent with the expectations of the place of employment." The guidelines go on to state in section 3.5.8: "Social workers evaluate a student's performance in a manner that is fair and respectful and consistent with the expectations of the student's educational institution."

In the meeting with your supervisor, a variety of outcomes are possible. The easiest is that you and your supervisor agree on the goals that you have achieved and the areas where you need to grow. The agreement is the best possible scenario. You should be prepared for the more common situation, however, where you don't see eye to eye on every item of the learning agreement. Your supervisor could evaluate you higher than you evaluate yourself, or you might evaluate yourself higher than your supervisor does.

If your supervisor sees you as a much stronger student than you have given yourself credit for, one agenda item for supervision is your self-perception. Why do you expect so much from yourself, why are you so critical of yourself, and why is your self-confidence not yet fully developed, are all questions that need to be explored. When you get insight into this issue and work on it, usually it is beneficial in your professional and personal life. These questions, of course, assume that you were not just downplaying your answers to please your supervisor.

The other scenario, your rating yourself higher than your supervisor does, happens much less often than the other two possibilities. The reasons for your difference of opinion may be limited insight about how others perceive you, an unclear expectation, miscommunication, lack of supervision, and a personality conflict. Regardless of the reason, this evaluation will be unpleasant for you to sit through. It is important that you receive this feedback in a nondefensive manner, hoping that it will improve your performance as a social work intern. Our hope is that this information is not new to you, and that you and your supervisor have spoken about these areas prior to the formal evaluation. If that's the case, you shouldn't be shocked, but it always looks worse on paper.

It is important to assess the reason for a discrepancy between your thoughts about the evaluation and your supervisor's thoughts. The reason will help you proceed with the feedback. If you had no idea that you were being perceived in a certain way, we suggest you get a reality check by talking to your field coordinator, your field instructor, and your adviser, and perhaps family, friends, and former employers. They might be able to present the information so that you can learn from it and determine why your perception is an issue.

For instance, because of your personality you may not like to sit through meetings where things are discussed for a long time, you may be avoiding frustration by not focusing fully on the discussion. Your supervisor may consider that an uncaring attitude and lack of concentration. You may not understand that, but with a teacher's help you may be able to see how that particular mannerism may come across differently than intended. You may understand the need to change your behavior, even if you can't change your personality and the meetings are still difficult to sit through. If the problem ends up being about unclear expectations or miscommunications, you need to work really hard next semester toward being open to feedback (without being defensive). Work on communicating clearly how you feel and ask a lot of questions to be sure you and your supervisor understand the same thing. Often field supervisors expect interns to be self-starters and people who initiate their own tasks, when you thought you should be waiting for direction. Be clear about what the agency expects.

If the issue is about personality or lack of supervision, you will need to discuss your thoughts and feelings with your supervisor and your field instructor. Please be sure that you are tactful and diplomatic but also assertive. This may include writing on your evaluation that you don't agree with all parts of the evaluation, and asking that the evaluation that you prepared be attached to the document your supervisor created.

This piece of development (doing separate evaluations) is extremely important for you as a professional social worker. It is great if both of you agree on your performance and it was a good evaluation. But if anything else happens, you have a unique learning opportunity. You can learn how to make a more complete appraisal, comparing yourself to where you started when you joined the field, or you can learn how to negotiate, accept constructive criticism, advocate for yourself, and work with someone in an awkward and difficult situation.

Let us detour for a second on this important point. As you enter the professional world, recognize that you won't like everyone that you work with. Sometimes you won't get along with everyone you work with, including your supervisor. This in itself is not a good reason to leave a job. You have to take into consideration your responsibility to your clients or the program you are working on. Clients have the right to services and some consistency in a social worker. You have to consider your own marketability. Soon you will no longer be a student who can work one place for a semester and change jobs without consequences. You are now a professional, and your next employer will be wondering why you change jobs so frequently. For your own benefit, you need to stay at a job for at least a year. Learning how to deal with a difficult relationship with your supervisor will be your challenge while you also complete your job functions. Trust us when we say that in the long run you will benefit from this tremendously. It will be important to hear your supervisor's feedback and let him or her know, in a very professional way, with respect toward the position in the agency, why you disagree. Remain composed and level but express your opinion as clearly as possible.

Back to the evaluation and negotiation of the second-semester learning agreement: If the evaluation does not go well, you can ask that the renegotiation of your next semester agreement be postponed. You can say that you want to use the time to take into account your supervisor's comments and revise the agreement. This gives you time to get some feedback from others and figure out what you want to say to your supervisor. Based upon that information, you may want to change your learning agreement for next semester.

In rare instances your field placement may be changed if your school official (field coordinator and/or field instructor) decides that the relationship between you and your supervisor won't work. If that is the case, you will need to leave professionally and terminate responsibly (discussed further in the next chapter). This situation could arise when your supervisor refuses to let you do some basic social work tasks on your own and you cannot get experience. Once we had a supervisor who went on maternity leave and the person covering for her believed social workers could only case manage. The supervisor would not let the intern cofacilitate groups, complete biopsychosocials, or develop treatment plans. This person's bias prevented a good learning environment for our student, and we found another field placement.

Although self-evaluation may be difficult for you at first, it is an excellent habit to get into both for your annual performance appraisal and for your own daily activities. During your daily activities, you may not have the opportunity to process a session after it has occurred. But try to answer the questions below.

Self-Supervision Questions

✔ Do I have all the information I need for this case?

✔ Is there information missing, or am I assuming information that is not there?

✔ Did I use the right approach with the client?

✔ What is my next step?

✔ Do I need to review or read about any new material before I see the client again?

✔ Do I know how to access resources that my client may need?

✔ What skills or tools do I need to hone before I work with this client again?

✔ Was I culturally sensitive in my dealings with my client?

✔ Was I ethical in my dealings with my client?

✔ Do I know and understand my individual style yet?

✔ What do I need to discuss in supervision about this case?

By the time you reach this chapter, your supervisor may have already completed your evaluation. Even if the evaluation is complete it does not mean that you cannot evaluate yourself. We encourage you to give yourself an opportunity to complete the evaluation. If there is disparity, ask yourself why. If you need to have another conversation with your supervisor, ask for one and discuss the discrepancies. If you still disagree, ask for an addendum that you have written, explaining your opinion of the evaluation.

We wish you luck with this process. It takes training, discipline, and objectivity to accurately evaluate your own social work practice. Yet it is an important component of developing a professional and personal inventory that will build character and responsibility.

Integration of other course material	
HBSE	What do you think about the assessment process that you have employed with your clients thus far? What can be added or deleted from the process?
Policy	What does the law say about your need for continuing evaluation and education?
Practice	What can you do to evaluate your practice with clients?
Research	What are ways that you can evaluate your practice with clients?

Resources

Self-Evaluation
http://www.joe.org/joe/1999april/tt1.html

Field Evaluation Forms
http://monmouth.edu/school-of-social-work/office-of-field-and-professional-education.aspx

Revise your learning contract. Answer these questions. Take your notes with you when you sit down with your supervisor to discuss your second-semester learning contract.

What haven't I experienced at my internship that I still hope to experience?

What specific knowledge do I still need to be exposed to?

What specific skills or techniques do I need to sharpen?

How should supervision change for the next semester?

Do I have the ability to work independently, or do I need more experience working with close supervision?

Where do I stand in terms of my commitment to the agency? How are my hours? Have I experienced or seen all aspects of the agency and its services?

Are there other agency activities I want to be exposed to (e.g., budgeting, administration, board meetings, grant writing)?

Have I been exposed to collaborating agencies and learned about all the resources that the clients need to have access to?

Add other thoughts you have about your internship.

Chapter 15
Termination and Evaluation of Client Progress

It seems appropriate that the last chapter of the book should be about endings! Termination is probably one of the most important components of the social work relationship and may be one of the least well addressed areas of social work. Not thoroughly addressing termination could be because it's an ending and many people are in a hurry to finish things or they do not like endings themselves. Those endings can be at the appropriate time (i.e., the client has successfully completed treatment) or premature because you or the client is leaving prior to successful completion. This chapter explains why termination is important and how to terminate successfully.

Termination

The easiest way to explain why termination is so important is to look at the case of a young child. Tyrone, an African American thirteen-year-old male, was left in a bus station by his mother when he was five. His mother took his two older sisters to the bathroom, and told him to stay right there and she would be right back. Two days later, a passenger waiting for a bus found him crying and huddled under a bench. (True story, the name was changed.) Tyrone became a ward of the state and by the age of thirteen had been removed from ten foster homes. He was removed from some homes because he tried to run away to find his mother, other homes because he got too big and the foster parents wanted little children, and the most recent move was because he was too angry and acted out often. By the time Tyrone came to the group home where he stayed until he was eighteen, he had had eleven sets of parents and six case workers from the county where he resided, all of whom worked for children's protective services. His mother still had legal custody because none of the workers took action to terminate parental rights. They had found Mom but had failed to develop a reunification plan that she abided by. Mom expressed interest in wanting Tyrone back.

Empathize for a moment. Wouldn't you be angry if you were Tyrone? He was all over the system with biological and foster parents and no consistency in case workers. Eventually, Tyrone was able to verbalize that he had no trust in anyone. Every time he trusted people, they left him, most of the time without notice.

Tyrone said that twice he was picked up at school and told he would not be returning to his foster home. One time it was a new case worker who picked him up and told him his old case worker had quit last month. Everyone left Tyrone, without notice or explanation. Even after sessions with the social worker, he could never trust that anyone would be there for him or that people wouldn't leave without saying good-bye.

The moral of this story is that termination should be done ethically and professionally for your benefit and for the benefit of your clients. Tyrone moved on and never kept in touch with the group home. To some of us, his story will be less traumatic because he will be older, and so much time will have elapsed between his traumatic childhood and his adulthood. Some people will figure he needs to get over it and see no connection to any issues he faces now and the lack of endings in his life. Think of Tyrone and every other client you have met thus far in your internship while we discuss termination.

When do you think the termination process begins? A week before a client leaves? A month? Two months? Actually, the termination process begins when the client arrives for intake. It is your goal from the beginning to have your client successfully complete your program. Even if your client is chronically mentally ill or developmentally disabled, your hope is that they will do well enough in your program to live independently (if you are a group home) or attend fewer days (if you are a partial program or sheltered workshop). That being said, you take a biopsychosocial assessment, develop a treatment plan, and work on the goals that the client needs to achieve so that he or she no longer needs your services. When that day comes, it does not mean that you send your client off and say you are "done," nor does it mean that your client has nothing else to work on.

Review of the Client's Progress

In the ideal world, you are constantly reviewing your client's treatment plan and revising it along the way. As you become aware that your client is completing the goals, you need to discuss progress and begin thinking about an appropriate time for discharge. Talking about it, planning for it, and discussing options make the ending of treatment real for both you and the client. It is an opportunity to discuss what the client's plans are after treatment and the feelings associated with ending a relationship. Remember when you started working with the client? You developed a rapport, you came to know your client as an individual, and now you will put an end to the relationship in the same manner you spent time developing the relationship.

As you discuss termination, share with your clients your assessment of their progress, any memorable stories you have about them, and areas that you see they will need to work on for the future. When you start this process will depend on the types of clients you have (age, level of functioning) and how long they will stay in your program. Ask your supervisor for guidance within your agency.

Review of Community Progress

Progress in a community is not reviewed by one outcome or method. There are multiple factors to take into consideration when looking at what is happening in a community. Even when you do not win a campaign, it does not mean that a community has lost, because good things have happened along the way in the process of developing the campaign and trying to succeed. Some of these may include educating the community about the issue, raising new funds for one or more community organizations, developing new community leaders, changing elected leadership, establishing new rules or laws that occurred because of your campaign, etc.

Client Termination

Some agencies are very short term (inpatient psychiatric, whose average length of stay is under a week). You may not need to work much on termination with these clients, except to go over what you worked on and their appointments for follow-up care. Some agencies offer treatment care where clients may live in the program for two years or longer (independent living, correctional facilities, and drug/alcohol rehabilitation programs). These clients will obviously have a stronger relationship with you, and the termination process will be longer and more detailed. Often the longer programs have formal graduations or terminations where everyone, residents and staff (clients and social workers), celebrates the accomplishment and come together to say good-bye.

The process described above works well if you are staying with the agency and the client is terminating successfully. Usually that means talking about growth while in treatment, what the client has accomplished, and what he or she needs to work on after leaving. If the client is going to another program, you will usually send paperwork summarizing treatment, but It is probably more important to have this conversation with clients.

At that point some clients may want to thank you for your help or give some feedback to you about the program. All of that is unsurprising and usual. Sometimes at this point, especially if you and a client got along very well, the client may ask permission to still call you, or ask you for your personal phone number. Clients, not totally inaccurately, think that now that they are not clients, you can have a personal relationship with them. You will need to explain that the boundary must remain in place in case they ever need your services again. The Code of Ethics is clear—once a client, always a client. If the client still wants to contact you at work, you will need to determine when he or she would want to do that and what your agency policy is. Many programs encourage clients to call when they are in trouble. One phone call could prevent a relapse or a readmission and be very beneficial. Other programs discourage former clients from calling because they do not have time to do the work required for the new clients, and no resources to offer the old clients. Find out what your agency policy is.

The other two ways termination occurs is when you the social worker (or intern) are leaving or when the client leaves prematurely. Many of you will leave your place of employment or your internship while in the middle of working with a client. Once you have decided to leave, or your internship hours are up, read your agency policy manual to determine if you need to give two weeks' notice or longer. Many of you may need to give one month's notice. The first person you will tell is your supervisor. Do *not* be tempted to tell your coworkers first. Nothing is more damaging than your supervisor finding out from someone else.

Once you tell your supervisor you are leaving, a few things need to be decided. First, you will establish your last day, how your responsibilities will be divided (including your clients), and in what order to tell people. Once you start telling people, everyone knows and will be talking. Don't wait long (more than a day) before starting to tell your clients. Depending on your agency and your relationships with your clients, you may tell them individually or you may tell them in a group. Remember the clients have to be served by the agency after you are gone, so if you are leaving because you dislike your supervisor or your agency, your clients do not need to know that. All you need to say is that you are moving on, when you are going, and that you wish them well. Some clients will be closer to you than others. Those who are closer to you are going to have a harder time; those who are not as close may not even care. When an appropriate amount of time is available a few things make the termination process very useful when you are leaving but the client is continuing treatment. You can update a client's ecomap and genogram with documentation in a one-page summary for the person who is taking over. This allows you and the client to recognize changes and gives the new social worker a brief synopsis of treatment issues to address. Ideally, discuss the history and intervention plan in a joint session with the client, yourself, and the new worker. The client hears what you are saying, adds any relevant material, and is part of the transition. They can see you passing the information on, and if the client's relationship with you is good, they will trust the person you are giving the case to. This makes the transition easier than if the client meets the person individually after you are gone.

Some clients may need time to process your leaving and will want to speak to you later on or individually. Making time for those conversations is one reason why you need to give them time to process and think. The two-week minimum is important. Clients who say you are critical to their treatment may begin to regress or act out, mostly because they are not sure how they will manage without you. If this part of the process is done properly, the client will not only survive the loss of you, but heal from other losses that were not resolved in the past. For some clients, this will take more than just one session. Reassure them that *they* made changes and that you were just guiding them, which is what the next worker will do.

Termination When You Are Struggling

If you are leaving because you don't like an agency, don't say anything negative, for your own sake. You don't want to burn your bridges. You never know when you may need assistance or when you may be working with some of the same people in a different agency somewhere.

Termination When the Client Leaves Prematurely

If the client is leaving before treatment is completed, it usually is because he or she is noncompliant, lacks funding, or is moving to another area. If the client is noncompliant or the program is out of funding, you need to be clear that the client still needs more treatment and refer them elsewhere, as the Code of Ethics indicates. If it is because the client is moving and you don't know the area to make a referral, at minimum you need to get phone numbers for the local mental health clinics and department of social services so the client has a lead on where to go. Ideally, you can find out more specific numbers than the client can. Just because the client's departure prompts the termination does not mean the termination process can't occur. Tell the client what they have completed and what areas still need work, and wish the client well. If a client is leaving prematurely they may just stop coming to the program and the termination process with the client may not occur. You can reach out to the client to encourage their participation or to give them a list of other services but you cannot force their attendance. Whenever a client leaves prematurely there may still be discharge paperwork and discussion with other clients in the program about how they feel about the departure. There also may be formal discussions with the staff to reflect on what went wrong with this particular incident and see if there are programmatic changes or policies that need to be altered.

Termination When the Client Is the Community

In community work, we often do not talk about termination. When our campaigns come to a close, or we win our legislative battles, we move on to our next project, and we don't formally terminate with the community like we would with individual clients. What we do, however, is celebrate if we win and regroup if we lose and think about next steps. The community itself will often decide the natural course of what should happen next.

The NASW Code of Ethics has a very detailed section on termination of services, section 1.16:

> (a) Social workers should terminate services to clients and professional relationships with them when such services and relationships are no longer required or no longer serve the clients' needs or interests.

(b) Social workers should take reasonable steps to avoid abandoning clients who are still in need of services. Social workers should withdraw services precipitously only under unusual circumstances, giving careful consideration to all factors in the situation, and taking care to minimize possible adverse effects. Social workers should assist in making appropriate arrangements for continuation of services when necessary.

(c) Social workers in fee-for-service settings may terminate services to clients who are not paying an overdue balance if the financial contractual arrangements have been made clear to the client, if the client does not pose an imminent danger to self or others, and if the clinical and other consequences of the current nonpayment have been addressed and discussed with the client.

(d) Social workers should not terminate services to pursue a social, financial, or sexual relationship with a client.

(e) Social workers who anticipate the termination or interruption of services to clients should notify clients promptly and seek the transfer, referral, or continuation of services in relation to the clients' needs and preferences.

(f) Social workers who are leaving an employment setting should inform clients of appropriate options for the continuation of services and of the benefits and risks of the options.

Canadian social workers have many guidelines to follow for appropriate termination of services in CASW Guidelines for Ethical Practice. These are outlined in section 1.8, "Practices for Termination or Interruption of Services."

1.8.1 Social workers renegotiate or terminate professional services when these services are no longer required or no longer meet the needs of the client.

1.8.2 Social workers respect the right of voluntary clients to discontinue service, engage another practitioner, or seek a second opinion.

1.8.3 Whether the decision to renegotiate or terminate is that of the client or the social worker, social workers (where appropriate) initiate a discussion with the client to appreciate, and, if possible, address any difficulties or misunderstandings that may have occurred. If the client desires other professional services, the social worker may assist in referral.

1.8.4 Social workers discuss clients' needs, options, and preferences before continuing or discontinuing services, or offering to seek transfer or referral.

1.8.5 Social workers at the earliest opportunity inform clients of any factor, condition, or pressure that affects their ability to practice adequately and competently.

1.8.6 When obliged to interrupt or terminate a professional relationship, social workers advise clients regarding the discontinuation of service and, if possible, ensure their referral to another professional.

Coworkers and Supervisors

Up until now, we've just dealt with saying good-bye to clients. But you also have to terminate with your coworkers and supervisor. It is not uncommon to have a good-bye party, sometimes without clients, sometimes with them. Be prepared to say a few words and thank people who assisted you. Leaving coworkers is not the same as leaving clients. You can contact former coworkers. In fact, they become part of your network in your professional development and can be asked for information or resources whenever you think they may be helpful. Some of those relationships may continue as friendships after you no longer work at the agency. The good-bye process can be very draining and stressful. Just because you are leaving does not mean that you don't have feelings for your clients, your coworkers, or your supervisor. Sometimes you need to move on for other reasons (like your internship is over), and it will be hard to leave. It is OK that people know that and for you to show your sadness (in an appropriate way).

As interns you hopefully have enjoyed your experience and learned a lot. Sometimes you like it so much that when you complete your hours you want to stay and volunteer. We want to caution you not to do that for a few reasons. First, it is valuable for you to learn how to terminate appropriately, especially if you have had losses in your life that you have not dealt with. Second, it's important early in your career to learn how to set up boundaries so you don't burn out. It is very easy to give a few hours here and a few hours there and suddenly be aware that you don't have time to breathe because you have overcommitted yourself. The third reason is that eventually, when you have your degree, agencies will need to compensate you for your time. Once you're established in your career, you may volunteer once again for other things, like your church, your local school system, or another nonrelated location. The last reason you should not stay on to work is that you need to finish the process you started, completing your degree and moving on to your next step in pursuing your ultimate career goal (if you even know what that is yet!). Keep your focus: who knows, maybe your agency will even hire you when you graduate. In Canada, you are not permitted to work for pay until after graduation for liability reasons.

Self-Care

Several times throughout the book we have mentioned burnout. You have probably already felt it yourself regarding school, toward mid-term time or at the end of the semester. This is a field where you will see and hear many harsh stories and situations. Not only do you have to learn how to leave the stories at work but you also need to take care of yourself. Everyone will have their own way to self-care. Some of you will get a massage, some will eat your favorite ice cream, others journal or sleep, and still others will exercise. Whatever means you have of self-care both long term and short term, please do so regularly. Preventing burnout is the best way to self-care. If you ever feel burnout, use supervision, a mental health day (planned time off without leaving the agency short-handed; this could be sick time or vacation days) or use the weekend to lay low.

Miscellaneous Yet Important Information

One last unrelated comment. If you are finishing this part of your internship in the fall, it is the beginning of the holiday season. This time is particularly difficult for our clients because of the termination issue. Many clients can't be with family during the holidays. All the messages on television, radio, and billboards are focused on giving gifts and being with family. If you were in a situation where you had no family (or could not be with them) and had no one giving you gifts, no one to give gifts to, and no one to spend the holidays with, how would you feel? Suicides increase during this time of year. Hospitalizations increase as does acting out behavior. Be aware that this is a difficult time for most clients and you should have a little more patience and a whole lot more empathy. It will help the holidays go much more smoothly.

As a new social worker, if you choose to work in a twenty-four-hour facility, be aware that you will probably be working at least one (and maybe more than one) holiday for a few years, at least until you get seniority. Plan activities that will be fun and healing for the clients. Also plan accordingly in your personal life, and if work disrupts your personal time, don't let clients know that you are upset about being there. At least you can celebrate later on or the next day with your family, whereas your clients cannot.

We expect as you finish this book that you are near the completion of your program. Please make it a point to take time to know and understand your state laws around licensing and continuing education coursework (usually workshops are not an actual college class). You worked hard to get the degree; make sure you work to get and keep the license by following your state laws, federal laws, and code of ethics and maintaining your continuing education requirements.

Conclusions

We would like to terminate appropriately by thanking you for being receptive to the activities and ideas in this book. We wish you well in your journey to enter this profession we care so deeply about. We are happy to have shared this part of the journey with you, and we invite you to use any of the activities you tried this semester with your clients and see how they respond!

Thoughts to ponder

✔ How do you deal with saying good-bye to other people?

✔ What are your thoughts as you think about leaving school and going into the workforce?

✔ Can you think of situations where you experienced termination that left you feeling very upset? What could have been done differently?

Integration of other course material

HBSE   What HBSE content deals with endings? What do you know about client life stages and how clients handle endings?

Policy   What are the policies at your agency regarding termination with clients? Do these differ if you leave your job? Go on vacation? The client terminates first?

Practice   How have you experienced successful endings? What do you already do now to help your clients experience successful endings?

Research   What does the literature have to say about the termination process?

Resources

Women's Business Association on Effective Termination Techniques
http://www.piperlemoine.com/2004/01/

More about "Endings," from a Social Work Perspective
http://www.communitycare.co.uk/2010/10/21/how-to-end-a-working-relationship-with-a-service-user/#.UzttpFdgDGc

Green means go . . .

Now that you have finished this semester of field, where do you want to go from here?

Appendix A
National Association of Social Workers Code of Ethics 2008

Approved by the 1996 NASW Delegate Assembly and revised by the 2008 NASW Delegate Assembly

The 2008 NASW Delegate Assembly approved the following revisions to the NASW Code of Ethics:

1.05 Cultural Competence and Social Diversity

(c) Social workers should obtain education about and seek to understand the nature of social diversity and oppression with respect to race, ethnicity, national origin, color, sex, sexual orientation, gender identity or expression, age, marital status, political belief, religion, immigration status, and mental or physical disability.

2.01 Respect

(a) Social workers should treat colleagues with respect and should represent accurately and fairly the qualifications, views, and obligations of colleagues.

(b) Social workers should avoid unwarranted negative criticism of colleagues in communications with clients or with other professionals. Unwarranted negative criticism may include demeaning comments that refer to colleagues' level of competence or to individuals' attributes such as race, ethnicity, national origin, color, sex, sexual orientation, gender identity or expression, age, marital status, political belief, religion, immigration status, and mental or physical disability.

4.02 Discrimination

Social workers should not practice, condone, facilitate, or collaborate with any form of discrimination on the basis of race, ethnicity, national origin, color, sex, sexual orientation, gender identity or expression, age, marital status, political belief, religion, immigration status, or mental or physical disability.

6.04 Social and Political Action

(d) Social workers should act to prevent and eliminate domination of, exploitation of, and discrimination against any person, group, or class on the basis of race, ethnicity, national origin, color, sex, sexual orientation, gender identity or expression, age, marital status, political belief, religion, immigration status, or mental or physical disability.

Preamble

The primary mission of the social work profession is to enhance human well-being and help meet the basic human needs of all people, with particular attention to the needs and empowerment of people who are vulnerable, oppressed, and living in poverty. A historic and defining feature of social work is the profession's focus on individual well-being in a social context and the well-being of society. Fundamental to social work is attention to the environmental forces that create, contribute to, and address problems in living.

Social workers promote social justice and social change with and on behalf of clients. "Clients" is used inclusively to refer to individuals, families, groups, organizations, and communities. Social workers are sensitive to cultural and ethnic diversity and strive to end discrimination, oppression, poverty, and other forms of social injustice. These activities may be in the form of direct practice, community organizing, supervision, consultation, administration, advocacy, social and political action, policy development and implementation, education, and research and evaluation. Social workers seek to enhance the capacity of people to address their own needs. Social workers also seek to promote the responsiveness of organizations, communities, and other social institutions to individuals' needs and social problems.

The mission of the social work profession is rooted in a set of core values. These core values, embraced by social workers throughout the profession's history, are the foundation of social work's unique purpose and perspective:

- service
- social justice
- dignity and worth of the person
- importance of human relationships
- integrity
- competence.

This constellation of core values reflects what is unique to the social work profession. Core values, and the principles that flow from them, must be balanced within the context and complexity of the human experience.

Purpose of the NASW Code of Ethics

Professional ethics are at the core of social work. The profession has an obligation to articulate its basic values, ethical principles, and ethical standards. The *NASW Code of Ethics* sets forth these values, principles, and standards to guide social workers' conduct. The *Code* is relevant to all social workers and social work students, regardless of their professional functions, the settings in which they work, or the populations they serve.

The *NASW Code of Ethics* serves six purposes:

1. The Code identifies core values on which social work's mission is based.

2. The *Code* summarizes broad ethical principles that reflect the profession's core values and establishes a set of specific ethical standards that should be used to guide social work practice.

3. The *Code* is designed to help social workers identify relevant considerations when professional obligations conflict or ethical uncertainties arise.

4. The *Code* provides ethical standards to which the general public can hold the social work profession accountable.

5. The *Code* socializes practitioners new to the field to social work's mission, values, ethical principles, and ethical standards.

6. The *Code* articulates standards that the social work profession itself can use to assess whether social workers have engaged in unethical conduct. NASW has formal procedures to adjudicate ethics complaints filed against its members. In subscribing to this *Code*, social workers are required to cooperate in its implementation, participate in NASW adjudication proceedings, and abide by any NASW disciplinary rulings or sanctions based on it.

The *Code* offers a set of values, principles, and standards to guide decision making and conduct when ethical issues arise. It does not provide a set of rules that prescribe how social workers should act in all situations. Specific applications of the *Code* must take into account the context in which it is being considered and the possibility of conflicts among the *Code's* values, principles, and standards. Ethical responsibilities flow from all human relationships, from the personal and familial to the social and professional.

Further, the *NASW Code of Ethics* does not specify which values, principles, and standards are most important and ought to outweigh others in instances when they conflict. Reasonable differences of opinion can and do exist among social workers with respect to the ways in which values, ethical principles, and ethical standards should be rank ordered when they conflict. Ethical decision making in a given situation must apply the informed judgment of the individual social worker and should also consider how the issues would be judged in a peer-review process where the ethical standards of the profession would be applied.

Ethical decision making is a process. There are many instances in social work where simple answers are not available to resolve complex ethical issues. Social workers should take into consideration all the values, principles, and standards in this *Code* that are relevant to any situation in which ethical judgment is warranted. Social workers' decisions and actions should be consistent with the spirit as well as the letter of this *Code*.

In addition to this *Code*, there are many other sources of information about ethical thinking that may be useful. Social workers should consider ethical theory and principles generally, social work theory and research, laws, regulations, agency policies, and other relevant codes of ethics, recognizing that among codes of ethics social workers should consider the *NASW Code of Ethics* as their primary source. Social workers also should be aware of the impact on ethical decision making of their clients' and their own personal values and cultural and religious beliefs and practices. They should be aware of any conflicts between personal and professional values and deal with them responsibly. For additional guidance, social workers should consult the relevant literature on professional ethics and ethical decision making and seek appropriate consultation when faced with ethical dilemmas. This may involve consultation with an agency-based or social work organization's ethics committee, a regulatory body, knowledgeable colleagues, supervisors, or legal counsel.

Instances may arise when social workers' ethical obligations conflict with agency policies or relevant laws or regulations. When such conflicts occur, social workers must make a responsible effort to resolve the conflict in a manner that is consistent with the values, principles, and standards expressed in this *Code*. If a reasonable resolution of the conflict does not appear possible, social workers should seek proper consultation before making a decision.

The *NASW Code of Ethics* is to be used by NASW and by individuals, agencies, organizations, and bodies (such as licensing and regulatory boards, professional liability insurance providers, courts of law, agency boards of directors, government agencies, and other professional groups) that choose to adopt it or use it as a frame of reference. Violation of standards in this *Code* does not automatically imply legal liability or violation of the law. Such determination can only be made in the context of legal and judicial proceedings. Alleged violations of the *Code* would be subject to a peer-review process. Such processes are generally separate from legal or administrative procedures and insulated from legal review or proceedings to allow the profession to counsel and discipline its own members.

A code of ethics cannot guarantee ethical behavior. Moreover, a code of ethics cannot resolve all ethical issues or disputes or capture the richness and complexity involved in striving to make responsible choices within a moral community. Rather, a code of ethics sets forth values, ethical principles, and ethical standards to which professionals aspire and by which their actions can be judged. Social workers' ethical behavior should result from their personal commitment to engage in ethical practice. The *NASW Code of Ethics* reflects the commitment of all social workers to uphold the profession's values and to act ethically. Principles and standards must be applied by individuals of good character who discern moral questions and, in good faith, seek to make reliable ethical judgments.

Ethical Principles

The following broad ethical principles are based on social work's core values of service, social justice, dignity and worth of the person, importance of human relationships, integrity, and competence. These principles set forth ideals to which all social workers should aspire.

Value: Service

Ethical Principle: Social workers' primary goal is to help people in need and to address social problems.

Social workers elevate service to others above self-interest. Social workers draw on their knowledge, values, and skills to help people in need and to address social problems. Social workers are encouraged to volunteer some portion of their professional skills with no expectation of significant financial return (pro bono service).

Value: Social Justice

Ethical Principle: Social workers challenge social injustice.

Social workers pursue social change, particularly with and on behalf of vulnerable and oppressed individuals and groups of people. Social workers' social change efforts are focused primarily on issues of poverty, unemployment, discrimination, and other forms of social injustice. These activities seek to promote sensitivity to and knowledge about oppression and cultural and ethnic diversity. Social workers strive to ensure access to needed information, services, and resources; equality of opportunity; and meaningful participation in decision making for all people.

Value: Dignity and Worth of the Person

Ethical Principle: Social workers respect the inherent dignity and worth of the person.

Social workers treat each person in a caring and respectful fashion, mindful of individual differences and cultural and ethnic diversity. Social workers promote clients' socially responsible self-determination. Social workers seek to enhance clients' capacity and opportunity to change and to address their own needs. Social workers are cognizant of their dual responsibility to clients and to the broader society. They seek to resolve conflicts between clients' interests and the broader society's interests in a socially responsible manner consistent with the values, ethical principles, and ethical standards of the profession.

Value: Importance of Human Relationships

Ethical Principle: Social workers recognize the central importance of human relationships.

Social workers understand that relationships between and among people are an important vehicle for change. Social workers engage people as partners in the helping process. Social workers seek to strengthen relationships among people in a purposeful effort to promote, restore, maintain, and enhance the well-being of individuals, families, social groups, organizations, and communities.

Value: Integrity

Ethical Principle: Social workers behave in a trustworthy manner.

Social workers are continually aware of the profession's mission, values, ethical principles, and ethical standards and practice in a manner consistent with them. Social workers act honestly and responsibly and promote ethical practices on the part of the organizations with which they are affiliated.

Value: Competence

Ethical Principle: Social workers practice within their areas of competence and develop and enhance their professional expertise.

Social workers continually strive to increase their professional knowledge and skills and to apply them in practice. Social workers should aspire to contribute to the knowledge base of the profession.

Ethical Standards

The following ethical standards are relevant to the professional activities of all social workers. These standards concern (1) social workers' ethical responsibilities to clients, (2) social workers' ethical responsibilities to colleagues, (3) social workers' ethical responsibilities in practice settings, (4) social workers' ethical responsibilities as professionals, (5) social workers' ethical responsibilities to the social work profession, and (6) social workers' ethical responsibilities to the broader society.

Some of the standards that follow are enforceable guidelines for professional conduct, and some are aspirational. The extent to which each standard is enforceable is a matter of professional judgment to be exercised by those responsible for reviewing alleged violations of ethical standards.

1. Social Workers' Ethical Responsibilities to Clients

1.01 Commitment to Clients

Social workers' primary responsibility is to promote the well-being of clients. In general, clients' interests are primary. However, social workers' responsibility to the larger society or specific legal obligations may on limited occasions supersede the loyalty owed clients, and clients should be so advised. (Examples include when a social worker is required by law to report that a client has abused a child or has threatened to harm self or others.)

1.02 Self-Determination

Social workers respect and promote the right of clients to self-determination and assist clients in their efforts to identify and clarify their goals. Social workers may limit clients' right to self-determination when, in the social workers' professional judgment, clients' actions or potential actions pose a serious, foreseeable, and imminent risk to themselves or others.

1.03 Informed Consent

(a) Social workers should provide services to clients only in the context of a professional relationship based, when appropriate, on valid informed consent. Social workers should use clear and understandable language to inform clients of the purpose of the services, risks related to the services, limits to services because of the requirements of a third-party payer, relevant costs, reasonable alternatives, clients' right to refuse or withdraw consent, and the time frame covered by the consent. Social workers should provide clients with an opportunity to ask questions.

(b) In instances when clients are not literate or have difficulty understanding the primary language used in the practice setting, social workers should take steps to ensure clients' comprehension. This may include providing clients with a detailed verbal explanation or arranging for a qualified interpreter or translator whenever possible.

(c) In instances when clients lack the capacity to provide informed consent, social workers should protect clients' interests by seeking permission from an appropriate third party, informing clients consistent with the clients' level of understanding. In such instances social workers should seek to ensure that the third party acts in a manner consistent with clients' wishes and interests. Social workers should take reasonable steps to enhance such clients' ability to give informed consent.

(d) In instances when clients are receiving services involuntarily, social workers should provide information about the nature and extent of services and about the extent of clients' right to refuse service.

(e) Social workers who provide services via electronic media (such as computer, telephone, radio, and television) should inform recipients of the limitations and risks associated with such services.

(f) Social workers should obtain clients' informed consent before audiotaping or videotaping clients or permitting observation of services to clients by a third party.

1.04 Competence

(a) Social workers should provide services and represent themselves as competent only within the boundaries of their education, training, license, certification, consultation received, supervised experience, or other relevant professional experience.

(b) Social workers should provide services in substantive areas or use intervention techniques or approaches that are new to them only after engaging in appropriate study, training, consultation, and supervision from people who are competent in those interventions or techniques.

(c) When generally recognized standards do not exist with respect to an emerging area of practice, social workers should exercise careful judgment and take responsible steps (including appropriate education, research, training, consultation, and supervision) to ensure the competence of their work and to protect clients from harm.

1.05 Cultural Competence and Social Diversity

(a) Social workers should understand culture and its function in human behavior and society, recognizing the strengths that exist in all cultures.

(b) Social workers should have a knowledge base of their clients' cultures and be able to demonstrate competence in the provision of services that are sensitive to clients' cultures and to differences among people and cultural groups.

(c) Social workers should obtain education about and seek to understand the nature of social diversity and oppression with respect to race, ethnicity, national origin, color, sex, sexual orientation, age, marital status, political belief, religion, and mental or physical disability.

1.06 Conflicts of Interest

(a) Social workers should be alert to and avoid conflicts of interest that interfere with the exercise of professional discretion and impartial judgment. Social workers should inform clients when a real or potential conflict of interest arises and take reasonable steps to resolve the issue in a manner that makes the clients' interests primary and protects clients' interests to the greatest extent possible. In some cases, protecting clients' interests may require termination of the professional relationship with proper referral of the client.

(b) Social workers should not take unfair advantage of any professional relationship or exploit others to further their personal, religious, political, or business interests.

(c) Social workers should not engage in dual or multiple relationships with clients or former clients in which there is a risk of exploitation or potential harm to the client. In instances when dual or multiple relationships are unavoidable, social workers should take steps to protect clients and are responsible for setting clear, appropriate, and culturally sensitive boundaries. (Dual or multiple relationships occur when social workers relate to clients in more than one relationship, whether professional, social, or business. Dual or multiple relationships can occur simultaneously or consecutively.)

(d) When social workers provide services to two or more people who have a relationship with each other (for example, couples, family members), social workers should clarify with all parties which individuals will be considered clients and the nature of social workers' professional obligations to the various individuals who are receiving services. Social workers who anticipate a conflict of interest among the individuals receiving services or who anticipate having to perform in potentially conflicting roles (for example, when a social worker is asked to testify in a child custody dispute or divorce proceedings involving clients) should clarify their role with the parties involved and take appropriate action to minimize any conflict of interest.

1.07 Privacy and Confidentiality

(a) Social workers should respect clients' right to privacy. Social workers should not solicit private information from clients unless it is essential to providing services or conducting social work evaluation or research. Once private information is shared, standards of confidentiality apply.

(b) Social workers may disclose confidential information when appropriate with valid consent from a client or a person legally authorized to consent on behalf of a client.

(c) Social workers should protect the confidentiality of all information obtained in the course of professional service, except for compelling professional reasons. The general expectation that social workers will keep information confidential does not apply when disclosure is necessary to prevent serious, foreseeable, and imminent harm to a client or other identifiable person. In all instances, social workers should disclose the least amount of confidential information necessary to achieve the desired purpose; only information that is directly relevant to the purpose for which the disclosure is made should be revealed.

(d) Social workers should inform clients, to the extent possible, about the disclosure of confidential information and the potential consequences, when feasible before the disclosure is made. This applies whether social workers disclose confidential information on the basis of a legal requirement or client consent.

(e) Social workers should discuss with clients and other interested parties the nature of confidentiality and limitations of clients' right to confidentiality. Social workers should review with clients circumstances where confidential information may be requested and where disclosure of confidential information may be legally required. This discussion should occur as soon as possible in the social worker/client relationship and as needed throughout the course of the relationship.

(f) When social workers provide counseling services to families, couples, or groups, social workers should seek agreement among the parties involved concerning each individual's right to confidentiality and obligation to preserve the confidentiality of information shared by others. Social workers should inform participants in family, couples, or group counseling that social workers cannot guarantee that all participants will honor such agreements.

(g) Social workers should inform clients involved in family, couples, marital, or group counseling of the social worker's, employer's, and agency's policy concerning the social worker's disclosure of confidential information among the parties involved in the counseling.

(h) Social workers should not disclose confidential information to third-party payers unless clients have authorized such disclosure.

(i) Social workers should not discuss confidential information in any setting unless privacy can be ensured. Social workers should not discuss confidential information in public or semipublic areas such as hallways, waiting rooms, elevators, and restaurants.

(j) Social workers should protect the confidentiality of clients during legal proceedings to the extent permitted by law. When a court of law or other legally authorized body orders social workers to disclose confidential or privileged information without a client's consent and such disclosure could cause harm to the client, social workers should request that the court withdraw the order or limit the order as narrowly as possible or maintain the records under seal, unavailable for public inspection.

(k) Social workers should protect the confidentiality of clients when responding to requests from members of the media.

(l) Social workers should protect the confidentiality of clients' written and electronic records and other sensitive information. Social workers should take reasonable steps to ensure that clients' records are stored in a secure location and that clients' records are not available to others who are not authorized to have access.

(m) Social workers should take precautions to ensure and maintain the confidentiality of information transmitted to other parties through the use of computers, electronic mail, facsimile machines, telephones and telephone answering machines, and other electronic or computer technology. Disclosure of identifying information should be avoided whenever possible.

(n) Social workers should transfer or dispose of clients' records in a manner that protects clients' confidentiality and is consistent with state statutes governing records and social work licensure.

(o) Social workers should take reasonable precautions to protect client confidentiality in the event of the social worker's termination of practice, incapacitation, or death.

(p) Social workers should not disclose identifying information when discussing clients for teaching or training purposes unless the client has consented to disclosure of confidential information.

(q) Social workers should not disclose identifying information when discussing clients with consultants unless the client has consented to disclosure of confidential information or there is a compelling need for such disclosure.

(r) Social workers should protect the confidentiality of deceased clients consistent with the preceding standards.

1.08 Access to Records

(a) Social workers should provide clients with reasonable access to records concerning the clients. Social workers who are concerned that clients' access to their records could cause serious misunderstanding or harm to the client should provide assistance in interpreting the records and consultation with the client regarding the records. Social workers should limit clients' access to their records, or portions of their records, only in exceptional circumstances when there is compelling evidence that such access would cause serious harm to the client. Both clients' requests and the rationale for withholding some or all of the record should be documented in clients' files.

(b) When providing clients with access to their records, social workers should take steps to protect the confidentiality of other individuals identified or discussed in such records.

1.09 Sexual Relationships

(a) Social workers should under no circumstances engage in sexual activities or sexual contact with current clients, whether such contact is consensual or forced.

(b) Social workers should not engage in sexual activities or sexual contact with clients' relatives or other individuals with whom clients maintain a close personal relationship when there is a risk of exploitation or potential harm to the client. Sexual activity or sexual contact with clients' relatives or other individuals with whom clients maintain a personal relationship has the potential to be harmful to the client and may make it difficult for the social worker and client to maintain appropriate professional boundaries. Social workers—not their clients, their clients' relatives, or other individuals with whom the client maintains a personal relationship—assume the full burden for setting clear, appropriate, and culturally sensitive boundaries.

(c) Social workers should not engage in sexual activities or sexual contact with former clients because of the potential for harm to the client. If social workers engage in conduct contrary to this prohibition or claim that an exception to this prohibition is warranted because of extraordinary circumstances, it is social workers—not their clients—who assume the full burden of demonstrating that the former client has not been exploited, coerced, or manipulated, intentionally or unintentionally.

(d) Social workers should not provide clinical services to individuals with whom they have had a prior sexual relationship. Providing clinical services to a former sexual partner has the potential to be harmful to the individual and is likely to make it difficult for the social worker and individual to maintain appropriate professional boundaries.

1.10 Physical Contact

Social workers should not engage in physical contact with clients when there is a possibility of psychological harm to the client as a result of the contact (such as cradling or caressing clients). Social workers who engage in appropriate physical contact with clients are responsible for setting clear, appropriate, and culturally sensitive boundaries that govern such physical contact.

1.11 Sexual Harassment

Social workers should not sexually harass clients. Sexual harassment includes sexual advances, sexual solicitation, requests for sexual favors, and other verbal or physical conduct of a sexual nature.

1.12 Derogatory Language

Social workers should not use derogatory language in their written or verbal communications to or about clients. Social workers should use accurate and respectful language in all communications to and about clients.

1.13 Payment for Services

(a) When setting fees, social workers should ensure that the fees are fair, reasonable, and commensurate with the services performed. Consideration should be given to clients' ability to pay.

(b) Social workers should avoid accepting goods or services from clients as payment for professional services. Bartering arrangements, particularly involving services, create the potential for conflicts of interest, exploitation, and inappropriate boundaries in social workers' relationships with clients. Social workers should explore and may participate in bartering only in very limited circumstances when it can be demonstrated that such arrangements are an accepted practice among professionals in the local community, considered to be essential for the provision of services, negotiated without coercion, and entered into at the client's initiative and with the client's informed consent. Social workers who accept goods or services from clients as payment for professional services assume the full burden of demonstrating that this arrangement will not be detrimental to the client or the professional relationship.

(c) Social workers should not solicit a private fee or other remuneration for providing services to clients who are entitled to such available services through the social workers' employer or agency.

1.14 Clients Who Lack Decision-Making Capacity

When social workers act on behalf of clients who lack the capacity to make informed decisions, social workers should take reasonable steps to safeguard the interests and rights of those clients.

1.15 Interruption of Services

Social workers should make reasonable efforts to ensure continuity of services in the event that services are interrupted by factors such as unavailability, relocation, illness, disability, or death.

1.16 Termination of Services

(a) Social workers should terminate services to clients and professional relationships with them when such services and relationships are no longer required or no longer serve the clients' needs or interests.

(b) Social workers should take reasonable steps to avoid abandoning clients who are still in need of services. Social workers should withdraw services precipitously only under unusual circumstances, giving careful consideration to all factors in the situation and taking care to minimize possible adverse effects. Social workers should assist in making appropriate arrangements for continuation of services when necessary.

(c) Social workers in fee-for-service settings may terminate services to clients who are not paying an overdue balance if the financial contractual arrangements have been made clear to the client, if the client does not pose an imminent danger to self or others, and if the clinical and other consequences of the current nonpayment have been addressed and discussed with the client.

(d) Social workers should not terminate services to pursue a social, financial, or sexual relationship with a client.

(e) Social workers who anticipate the termination or interruption of services to clients should notify clients promptly and seek the transfer, referral, or continuation of services in relation to the clients' needs and preferences.

(f) Social workers who are leaving an employment setting should inform clients of appropriate options for the continuation of services and of the benefits and risks of the options.

2. Social Workers' Ethical Responsibilities to Colleagues

2.01 Respect

(a) Social workers should treat colleagues with respect and should represent accurately and fairly the qualifications, views, and obligations of colleagues.

(b) Social workers should avoid unwarranted negative criticism of colleagues in communications with clients or with other professionals. Unwarranted negative criticism may include demeaning comments that refer to colleagues' level of competence or to individuals' attributes such as race, ethnicity, national origin, color, sex, sexual orientation, age, marital status, political belief, religion, and mental or physical disability.

(c) Social workers should cooperate with social work colleagues and with colleagues of other professions when such cooperation serves the well-being of clients.

2.02 Confidentiality

Social workers should respect confidential information shared by colleagues in the course of their professional relationships and transactions. Social workers should ensure that such colleagues understand social workers' obligation to respect confidentiality and any exceptions related to it.

2.03 Interdisciplinary Collaboration

(a) Social workers who are members of an interdisciplinary team should participate in and contribute to decisions that affect the well-being of clients by drawing on the perspectives, values, and experiences of the social work profession. Professional and ethical obligations of the interdisciplinary team as a whole and of its individual members should be clearly established.

(b) Social workers for whom a team decision raises ethical concerns should attempt to resolve the disagreement through appropriate channels. If the disagreement cannot be resolved, social workers should pursue other avenues to address their concerns consistent with client well-being.

2.04 Disputes Involving Colleagues

(a) Social workers should not take advantage of a dispute between a colleague and an employer to obtain a position or otherwise advance the social workers' own interests.

(b) Social workers should not exploit clients in disputes with colleagues or engage clients in any inappropriate discussion of conflicts between social workers and their colleagues.

2.05 Consultation

(a) Social workers should seek the advice and counsel of colleagues whenever such consultation is in the best interests of clients.

(b) Social workers should keep themselves informed about colleagues' areas of expertise and competencies. Social workers should seek consultation only from colleagues who have demonstrated knowledge, expertise, and competence related to the subject of the consultation.

(c) When consulting with colleagues about clients, social workers should disclose the least amount of information necessary to achieve the purposes of the consultation.

2.06 Referral for Services

(a) Social workers should refer clients to other professionals when the other professionals' specialized knowledge or expertise is needed to serve clients fully or when social workers believe that they are not being effective or making reasonable progress with clients and that additional service is required.

(b) Social workers who refer clients to other professionals should take appropriate steps to facilitate an orderly transfer of responsibility. Social workers who refer clients to other professionals should disclose, with clients' consent, all pertinent information to the new service providers.

(c) Social workers are prohibited from giving or receiving payment for a referral when no professional service is provided by the referring social worker.

2.07 Sexual Relationships

(a) Social workers who function as supervisors or educators should not engage in sexual activities or contact with supervisees, students, trainees, or other colleagues over whom they exercise professional authority.

(b) Social workers should avoid engaging in sexual relationships with colleagues when there is potential for a conflict of interest. Social workers who become involved in, or anticipate becoming involved in, a sexual relationship with a colleague have a duty to transfer professional responsibilities, when necessary, to avoid a conflict of interest.

2.08 Sexual Harassment

Social workers should not sexually harass supervisees, students, trainees, or colleagues. Sexual harassment includes sexual advances, sexual solicitation, requests for sexual favors, and other verbal or physical conduct of a sexual nature.

2.09 Impairment of Colleagues

(a) Social workers who have direct knowledge of a social work colleague's impairment that is due to personal problems, psychosocial distress, substance abuse, or mental health difficulties and that interferes with practice effectiveness should consult with that colleague when feasible and assist the colleague in taking remedial action.

(b) Social workers who believe that a social work colleague's impairment interferes with practice effectiveness and that the colleague has not taken adequate steps to address the impairment should take action through appropriate channels established by employers, agencies, NASW, licensing and regulatory bodies, and other professional organizations.

2.10 Incompetence of Colleagues

(a) Social workers who have direct knowledge of a social work colleague's incompetence should consult with that colleague when feasible and assist the colleague in taking remedial action.

(b) Social workers who believe that a social work colleague is incompetent and has not taken adequate steps to address the incompetence should take action through appropriate channels established by employers, agencies, NASW, licensing and regulatory bodies, and other professional organizations.

2.11 Unethical Conduct of Colleagues

(a) Social workers should take adequate measures to discourage, prevent, expose, and correct the unethical conduct of colleagues.

(b) Social workers should be knowledgeable about established policies and procedures for handling concerns about colleagues' unethical behavior. Social workers should be familiar with national, state, and local procedures for handling ethics complaints. These include policies and procedures created by NASW, licensing and regulatory bodies, employers, agencies, and other professional organizations.

(c) Social workers who believe that a colleague has acted unethically should seek resolution by discussing their concerns with the colleague when feasible and when such discussion is likely to be productive.

(d) When necessary, social workers who believe that a colleague has acted unethically should take action through appropriate formal channels (such as contacting a state licensing board or regulatory body, an NASW committee on inquiry, or other professional ethics committees).

(e) Social workers should defend and assist colleagues who are unjustly charged with unethical conduct.

3. Social Workers' Ethical Responsibilities in Practice Settings

3.01 Supervision and Consultation

(a) Social workers who provide supervision or consultation should have the necessary knowledge and skill to supervise or consult appropriately and should do so only within their areas of knowledge and competence.

(b) Social workers who provide supervision or consultation are responsible for setting clear, appropriate, and culturally sensitive boundaries.

(c) Social workers should not engage in any dual or multiple relationships with supervisees in which there is a risk of exploitation of or potential harm to the supervisee.

(d) Social workers who provide supervision should evaluate supervisees' performance in a manner that is fair and respectful.

3.02 Education and Training

(a) Social workers who function as educators, field instructors for students, or trainers should provide instruction only within their areas of knowledge and competence and should provide instruction based on the most current information and knowledge available in the profession.

(b) Social workers who function as educators or field instructors for students should evaluate students' performance in a manner that is fair and respectful.

(c) Social workers who function as educators or field instructors for students should take reasonable steps to ensure that clients are routinely informed when services are being provided by students.

(d) Social workers who function as educators or field instructors for students should not engage in any dual or multiple relationships with students in which there is a risk of exploitation or potential harm to the student. Social work educators and field instructors are responsible for setting clear, appropriate, and culturally sensitive boundaries.

3.03 Performance Evaluation

Social workers who have responsibility for evaluating the performance of others should fulfill such responsibility in a fair and considerate manner and on the basis of clearly stated criteria.

3.04 Client Records

(a) Social workers should take reasonable steps to ensure that documentation in records is accurate and reflects the services provided.

(b) Social workers should include sufficient and timely documentation in records to facilitate the delivery of services and to ensure continuity of services provided to clients in the future.

(c) Social workers' documentation should protect clients' privacy to the extent that is possible and appropriate and should include only information that is directly relevant to the delivery of services.

(d) Social workers should store records following the termination of services to ensure reasonable future access. Records should be maintained for the number of years required by state statutes or relevant contracts.

3.05 Billing

Social workers should establish and maintain billing practices that accurately reflect the nature and extent of services provided and that identify who provided the service in the practice setting.

3.06 Client Transfer

(a) When an individual who is receiving services from another agency or colleague contacts a social worker for services, the social worker should carefully consider the client's needs before agreeing to provide services. To minimize possible confusion and conflict, social workers should discuss with potential clients the nature of the clients' current relationship with other service providers and the implications, including possible benefits or risks, of entering into a relationship with a new service provider.

(b) If a new client has been served by another agency or colleague, social workers should discuss with the client whether consultation with the previous service provider is in the client's best interest.

3.07 Administration

(a) Social work administrators should advocate within and outside their agencies for adequate resources to meet clients' needs.

(b) Social workers should advocate for resource allocation procedures that are open and fair. When not all clients' needs can be met, an allocation procedure should be developed that is nondiscriminatory and based on appropriate and consistently applied principles.

(c) Social workers who are administrators should take reasonable steps to ensure that adequate agency or organizational resources are available to provide appropriate staff supervision.

(d) Social work administrators should take reasonable steps to ensure that the working environment for which they are responsible is consistent with and encourages compliance with the *NASW Code of Ethics*. Social work administrators should take reasonable steps to eliminate any conditions in their organizations that violate, interfere with, or discourage compliance with the *Code*.

3.08 Continuing Education and Staff Development

Social work administrators and supervisors should take reasonable steps to provide or arrange for continuing education and staff development for all staff for whom they are responsible. Continuing education and staff development should address current knowledge and emerging developments related to social work practice and ethics.

3.09 Commitments to Employers

(a) Social workers generally should adhere to commitments made to employers and employing organizations.

(b) Social workers should work to improve employing agencies' policies and procedures and the efficiency and effectiveness of their services.

(c) Social workers should take reasonable steps to ensure that employers are aware of social workers' ethical obligations as set forth in the *NASW Code of Ethics* and of the implications of those obligations for social work practice.

(d) Social workers should not allow an employing organization's policies, procedures, regulations, or administrative orders to interfere with their ethical practice of social work. Social workers should take reasonable steps to ensure that their employing organizations' practices are consistent with the *NASW Code of Ethics*.

(e) Social workers should act to prevent and eliminate discrimination in the employing organization's work assignments and in its employment policies and practices.

(f) Social workers should accept employment or arrange student field placements only in organizations that exercise fair personnel practices.

(g) Social workers should be diligent stewards of the resources of their employing organizations, wisely conserving funds where appropriate and never misappropriating funds or using them for unintended purposes.

3.10 Labor Management Disputes

(a) Social workers may engage in organized action, including the formation of and participation in labor unions, to improve services to clients and working conditions.

(b) The actions of social workers who are involved in labor management disputes, job actions, or labor strikes should be guided by the profession's values, ethical principles, and ethical standards. Reasonable differences of opinion exist among social workers concerning their primary obligation as professionals during an actual or threatened labor strike or job action. Social workers should carefully examine relevant issues and their possible impact on clients before deciding on a course of action.

4. Social Workers' Ethical Responsibilities as Professionals

4.01 Competence

(a) Social workers should accept responsibility or employment only on the basis of existing competence or the intention to acquire the necessary competence.

(b) Social workers should strive to become and remain proficient in professional practice and the performance of professional functions. Social workers should critically examine and keep current with emerging knowledge relevant to social work. Social workers should routinely review the professional literature and participate in continuing education relevant to social work practice and social work ethics.

(c) Social workers should base practice on recognized knowledge, including empirically based knowledge, relevant to social work and social work ethics.

4.02 Discrimination

Social workers should not practice, condone, facilitate, or collaborate with any form of discrimination on the basis of race, ethnicity, national origin, color, sex, sexual orientation, gender identity or expression, age, marital status, political belief, religion, immigration status, or mental or physical disability.

4.03 Private Conduct

Social workers should not permit their private conduct to interfere with their ability to fulfill their professional responsibilities.

4.04 Dishonesty, Fraud, and Deception

Social workers should not participate in, condone, or be associated with dishonesty, fraud, or deception.

4.05 Impairment

(a) Social workers should not allow their own personal problems, psychosocial distress, legal problems, substance abuse, or mental health difficulties to interfere with their professional judgment and performance or to jeopardize the best interests of people for whom they have a professional responsibility.

(b) Social workers whose personal problems, psychosocial distress, legal problems, substance abuse, or mental health difficulties interfere with their professional judgment and performance should immediately seek consultation and take appropriate remedial action by seeking professional help, making adjustments in workload, terminating practice, or taking any other steps necessary to protect clients and others.

4.06 Misrepresentation

(a) Social workers should make clear distinctions between statements made and actions engaged in as a private individual and as a representative of the social work profession, a professional social work organization, or the social worker's employing agency.

(b) Social workers who speak on behalf of professional social work organizations should accurately represent the official and authorized positions of the organizations.

(c) Social workers should ensure that their representations to clients, agencies, and the public of professional qualifications, credentials, education, competence, affiliations, services provided, or results to be achieved are accurate. Social workers should claim only those relevant professional credentials they actually possess and take steps to correct any inaccuracies or misrepresentations of their credentials by others.

4.07 Solicitations

(a) Social workers should not engage in uninvited solicitation of potential clients who, because of their circumstances, are vulnerable to undue influence, manipulation, or coercion.

(b) Social workers should not engage in solicitation of testimonial endorsements (including solicitation of consent to use a client's prior statement as a testimonial endorsement) from current clients or from other people who, because of their particular circumstances, are vulnerable to undue influence.

4.08 Acknowledging Credit

(a) Social workers should take responsibility and credit, including authorship credit, only for work they have actually performed and to which they have contributed.

(b) Social workers should honestly acknowledge the work of and the contributions made by others.

5. Social Workers' Ethical Responsibilities to the Social Work Profession

5.01 Integrity of the Profession

(a) Social workers should work toward the maintenance and promotion of high standards of practice.

(b) Social workers should uphold and advance the values, ethics, knowledge, and mission of the profession. Social workers should protect, enhance, and improve the integrity of the profession through appropriate study and research, active discussion, and responsible criticism of the profession.

(c) Social workers should contribute time and professional expertise to activities that promote respect for the value, integrity, and competence of the social work profession. These activities may include teaching, research, consultation, service, legislative testimony, presentations in the community, and participation in their professional organizations.

(d) Social workers should contribute to the knowledge base of social work and share with colleagues their knowledge related to practice, research, and ethics. Social workers should seek to contribute to the profession's literature and to share their knowledge at professional meetings and conferences.

(e) Social workers should act to prevent the unauthorized and unqualified practice of social work.

5.02 Evaluation and Research

(a) Social workers should monitor and evaluate policies, the implementation of programs, and practice interventions.

(b) Social workers should promote and facilitate evaluation and research to contribute to the development of knowledge.

(c) Social workers should critically examine and keep current with emerging knowledge relevant to social work and fully use evaluation and research evidence in their professional practice.

(d) Social workers engaged in evaluation or research should carefully consider possible consequences and should follow guidelines developed for the protection of evaluation and research participants. Appropriate institutional review boards should be consulted.

(e) Social workers engaged in evaluation or research should obtain voluntary and written informed consent from participants, when appropriate, without any implied or actual deprivation or penalty for refusal to participate; without undue inducement to participate; and with due regard for participants' well-being, privacy, and dignity. Informed consent should include information about the nature, extent, and duration of the participation requested and disclosure of the risks and benefits of participation in the research.

(f) When evaluation or research participants are incapable of giving informed consent, social workers should provide an appropriate explanation to the participants, obtain the participants' assent to the extent they are able, and obtain written consent from an appropriate proxy.

(g) Social workers should never design or conduct evaluation or research that does not use consent procedures, such as certain forms of naturalistic observation and archival research, unless rigorous and responsible review of the research has found it to be justified because of its prospective scientific, educational, or applied value and unless equally effective alternative procedures that do not involve waiver of consent are not feasible.

(h) Social workers should inform participants of their right to withdraw from evaluation and research at any time without penalty.

(i) Social workers should take appropriate steps to ensure that participants in evaluation and research have access to appropriate supportive services.

(j) Social workers engaged in evaluation or research should protect participants from unwarranted physical or mental distress, harm, danger, or deprivation.

(k) Social workers engaged in the evaluation of services should discuss collected information only for professional purposes and only with people professionally concerned with this information.

(l) Social workers engaged in evaluation or research should ensure the anonymity or confidentiality of participants and of the data obtained from them. Social workers should inform participants of any limits of confidentiality, the measures that will be taken to ensure confidentiality, and when any records containing research data will be destroyed.

(m) Social workers who report evaluation and research results should protect participants' confidentiality by omitting identifying information unless proper consent has been obtained authorizing disclosure.

(n) Social workers should report evaluation and research findings accurately. They should not fabricate or falsify results and should take steps to correct any errors later found in published data using standard publication methods.

(o) Social workers engaged in evaluation or research should be alert to and avoid conflicts of interest and dual relationships with participants, should inform participants when a real or potential conflict of interest arises, and should take steps to resolve the issue in a manner that makes participants' interests primary.

(p) Social workers should educate themselves, their students, and their colleagues about responsible research practices.

6. Social Workers' Ethical Responsibilities to the Broader Society

6.01 Social Welfare

Social workers should promote the general welfare of society, from local to global levels, and the development of people, their communities, and their environments. Social workers should advocate for living conditions conducive to the fulfillment of basic human needs and should promote social, economic, political, and cultural values and institutions that are compatible with the realization of social justice.

6.02 Public Participation

Social workers should facilitate informed participation by the public in shaping social policies and institutions.

6.03 Public Emergencies

Social workers should provide appropriate professional services in public emergencies to the greatest extent possible.

6.04 Social and Political Action

(a) Social workers should engage in social and political action that seeks to ensure that all people have equal access to the resources, employment, services, and opportunities they require to meet their basic human needs and to develop fully. Social workers should be aware of the impact of the political arena on practice and should advocate for changes in policy and legislation to improve social conditions in order to meet basic human needs and promote social justice.

(b) Social workers should act to expand choice and opportunity for all people, with special regard for vulnerable, disadvantaged, oppressed, and exploited people and groups.

(c) Social workers should promote conditions that encourage respect for cultural and social diversity within the United States and globally. Social workers should promote policies and practices that demonstrate respect for difference, support the expansion of cultural knowledge and resources, advocate for programs and institutions that demonstrate cultural competence, and promote policies that safeguard the rights of and confirm equity and social justice for all people.

(d) Social workers should act to prevent and eliminate domination of, exploitation of, and discrimination against any person, group, or class on the basis of race, ethnicity, national origin, color, sex, sexual orientation, gender identity or expression, age, marital status, political belief, religion, immigration status, or mental or physical disability.

Appendix B

Canadian
Code of Ethics
2005

Table of Contents

Acknowledgements

The Canadian Association of Social Workers (CASW) acknowledges with thanks the National Association of Social Workers (NASW) for permission to use sections of the copyrighted NASW 1999 *Code of Ethics* in the development of the CASW 2005 *Code of Ethics* and CASW 2005 *Guidelines for Ethical Practice*.

The CASW also acknowledges that other codes of ethics and resources were used in the development of this *Code* and the *Guidelines for Ethical Practice*, in particular the *Code of Ethics* of the Australian Association of Social Workers (AASW). These resources can be found in the Reference section of each document.

Purpose of the CASW Code of Ethics

Ethical behaviour lies at the core of every profession. The Canadian Association of Social Workers (CASW) *Code of Ethics* sets forth values and principles to guide social workers' professional conduct. A code of ethics cannot guarantee ethical behaviour. Ethical behaviour comes from a social worker's individual commitment to engage in ethical practice. Both the spirit and the letter of this *Code of Ethics* will guide social workers as they act in good faith and with a genuine desire to make sound judgements.

This *Code of Ethics* is consistent with the International Federation of Social Workers (IFSW) *International Declaration of Ethical Principles of Social Work* (1994, 2004), which requires members of the CASW to uphold the values and principles established by both the CASW and the IFSW. Other individuals, organizations and bodies (such as regulatory boards, professional liability insurance providers, courts of law, boards of directors of organizations employing social workers and government agencies) may also choose to adopt this *Code of Ethics* or use it as a basis for evaluating professional conduct. In Canada, each province and territory is responsible for regulating the professional conduct of social workers to ensure the protection of the public. Social workers are advised to contact the regulatory body in their province or territory to determine whether it has adopted this *Code of Ethics*. To find the IFSW declarations or information about your relevant regulatory body, visit the CASW Web site: http://www.casw-acts.ca.

Recognition of Individual and Professional Diversity

The CASW *Code of Ethics* does not provide a set of rules that prescribe how social workers should act in all situations. Further, the *Code of Ethics* does not specify which values and principles are most important and which outweigh others in instances of conflict. Reasonable differences of opinion exist among social workers with respect to which values and principles should be given priority in a particular situation. Further, a social worker's personal values, culture, religious beliefs, practices and/or other important distinctions, such as age, ability, gender or sexual orientation can affect his/her ethical choices. Thus, social workers need to be aware of any conflicts between personal and professional values and deal with them responsibly.

Ethical Behaviour Requires Due Consideration of Issues and Judgement

Social work is a multifaceted profession. As professionals, social workers are educated to exercise judgement in the face of complex and competing interests and claims. Ethical decision-making in a given situation will involve the informed judgement of the individual social worker. Instances may arise when social workers' ethical obligations conflict with agency policies, or relevant laws or regulations. When such conflicts occur, social workers shall make a responsible effort to resolve the conflicts in a manner that is consistent with the values and principles expressed in this *Code of Ethics*. If a reasonable resolution of the conflict does not appear possible, social workers shall seek appropriate consultation before making a decision. This may involve consultation with an ethics committee, a regulatory body, a knowledgeable colleague, supervisor or legal counsel.

Preamble

The social work profession is dedicated to the welfare and self-realization of all people; the development and disciplined use of scientific and professional knowledge; the development of resources and skills to meet individual, group, national and international changing needs and aspirations; and the achievement of social justice for all. The profession has a particular interest in the needs and empowerment of people who are vulnerable, oppressed, and/or living in poverty. Social workers are committed to human rights as enshrined in Canadian law, as well as in international conventions on human rights created or supported by the United Nations.

As professionals in a country that upholds respect for diversity, and in keeping with democratic rights and freedoms, social workers respect the distinct systems of beliefs and lifestyles of individuals, families, groups, communities and nations without prejudice (United Nations Centre for Human Rights, 1992). Specifically, social workers do not tolerate discrimination[1] based on age, abilities, ethnic background, gender, language, marital status, national ancestry, political affiliation, race, religion, sexual orientation or socio-economic status.

Core Social Work Values and Principles

Social workers uphold the following core social work values:

Value 1: Respect for Inherent Dignity and Worth of Persons

Value 2: Pursuit of Social Justice

Value 3: Service to Humanity

Value 4: Integrity in Professional Practice

Value 5: Confidentiality in Professional Practice

Value 6: Competence in Professional Practice

---

1. Throughout this document the term "discrimination" refers to treating people unfavourably or holding negative or prejudicial attitudes based on discernable differences or stereotypes. It does **not refer** to the positive intent behind programs, such as affirmative action, where one group may be given preferential treatment to address inequities created by discrimination.

The following section describes each of these values and discusses their underlying principles.

Value 1: Respect for the Inherent Dignity and Worth of Persons

Social work is founded on a long-standing commitment to respect the inherent dignity and individual worth of all persons. When required by law to override a client's wishes, social workers take care to use the minimum coercion required. Social workers recognize and respect the diversity of Canadian society, taking into account the breadth of differences that exist among individuals, families, groups and communities. Social workers uphold the human rights of individuals and groups as expressed in *The Canadian Charter of Rights and Freedoms* (1982) and the United Nations *Universal Declaration of Human Rights* (1948).

Principles:

- Social workers respect the unique worth and inherent dignity of all people and uphold human rights.

- Social workers uphold each person's right to self-determination, consistent with that person's capacity and with the rights of others.

- Social workers respect the diversity among individuals in Canadian society and the right of individuals to their unique beliefs consistent with the rights of others.

- Social workers respect the client's right to make choices based on voluntary, informed consent.

- Social workers who have children as clients determine the child's ability to consent and where appropriate, explain to the child and to the child's parents/guardians, the nature of the social worker's relationship to the child.

- Social workers uphold the right of society to impose limitations on the self-determination of individuals, when such limitations protect individuals from self-harm and from harming others.

- Social workers uphold the right of every person to be free from violence and threat of violence.

Value 2: Pursuit of Social Justice

Social workers believe in the obligation of people, individually and collectively, to provide resources, services and opportunities for the overall benefit of humanity and to afford them protection from harm. Social workers promote social fairness and the equitable distribution of resources, and act to reduce barriers and expand choice for all persons, with special regard for those who are marginalized, disadvantaged, vulnerable, and/or have exceptional needs.

Social workers oppose prejudice and discrimination against any person or group of persons, on any grounds, and specifically challenge views and actions that stereotype particular persons or groups.

Principles:

- Social workers uphold the right of people to have access to resources to meet basic human needs.
- Social workers advocate for fair and equitable access to public services and benefits.
- Social workers advocate for equal treatment and protection under the law and challenge injustices, especially injustices that affect the vulnerable and disadvantaged.
- Social workers promote social development and environmental management in the interests of all people.

Value 3: Service to Humanity

The social work profession upholds service in the interests of others, consistent with social justice, as a core professional objective. In professional practice, social workers balance individual needs, and rights and freedoms with collective interests in the service of humanity. When acting in a professional capacity, social workers place professional service before personal goals or advantage, and use their power and authority in disciplined and responsible ways that serve society. The social work profession contributes to knowledge and skills that assist in the management of conflicts and the wide-ranging consequences of conflict.

Principles:

- Social workers place the needs of others above self-interest when acting in a professional capacity.
- Social workers strive to use the power and authority vested in them as professionals in responsible ways that serve the needs of clients and the promotion of social justice.
- Social workers promote individual development and pursuit of individual goals, as well as the development of a just society.
- Social workers use their knowledge and skills in bringing about fair resolutions to conflict and in assisting those affected by conflict.

Value 4: Integrity in Professional Practice

Social workers demonstrate respect for the profession's purpose, values and ethical principles relevant to their field of practice. Social workers maintain a high level of professional conduct by acting honestly and responsibly, and promoting the values of the profession. Social workers strive for impartiality in their professional practice, and refrain from imposing their personal values, views and preferences on clients. It is the responsibility of social workers to establish the tenor of their professional relationship with clients, and others to whom they have a professional duty, and to maintain professional boundaries. As individuals, social workers take care in their actions to not bring the reputation of the profession into disrepute. An essential element of integrity in professional practice is ethical accountability based on this *Code of Ethics*, the IFSW *International Declaration of Ethical Principles of Social Work*, and other relevant provincial/territorial standards and guidelines. Where conflicts exist with respect to these sources of ethical guidance, social workers are encouraged to seek advice, including consultation with their regulatory body.

Principles:

- Social workers demonstrate and promote the qualities of honesty, reliability, impartiality and diligence in their professional practice.

- Social workers demonstrate adherence to the values and ethical principles of the profession and promote respect for the profession's values and principles in organizations where they work or with which they have a professional affiliation.

- Social workers establish appropriate boundaries in relationships with clients and ensure that the relationship serves the needs of clients.

- Social workers value openness and transparency in professional practice and avoid relationships where their integrity or impartiality may be compromised, ensuring that should a conflict of interest be unavoidable, the nature of the conflict is fully disclosed.

Value 5: Confidentiality in Professional Practice

A cornerstone of professional social work relationships is confidentiality with respect to all matters associated with professional services to clients. Social workers demonstrate respect for the trust and confidence placed in them by clients, communities and other professionals by protecting the privacy of client information and respecting the client's right to control when or whether this information will be shared with third parties. Social workers only disclose confidential information to other parties (including family members) with the informed consent of clients, client's legally authorized representatives or when required by law or court order. The general expectation that social workers will keep information confidential does not apply when disclosure is necessary to prevent serious, foreseeable and imminent harm to a client or others. In all instances, social workers disclose the least amount of confidential information necessary to achieve the desired purpose.

Principles:

- Social workers respect the importance of the trust and confidence placed in the professional relationship by clients and members of the public.
- Social workers respect the client's right to confidentiality of information shared in a professional context.
- Social workers only disclose confidential information with the informed consent of the client or permission of client's legal representative.
- Social workers may break confidentiality and communicate client information without permission when required or permitted by relevant laws, court order or this *Code*.
- Social workers demonstrate transparency with respect to limits to confidentiality that apply to their professional practice by clearly communicating these limitations to clients early in their relationship.

Value 6: Competence in Professional Practice

Social workers respect a client's right to competent social worker services. Social workers analyze the nature of social needs and problems, and encourage innovative, effective strategies and techniques to meet both new and existing needs and, where possible, contribute to the knowledge base of the profession. Social workers have a responsibility to maintain professional proficiency, to continually strive to increase their professional knowledge and skills, and to apply new knowledge in practice commensurate with their level of professional education, skill and competency, seeking consultation and supervision as appropriate.

Principles:

- Social workers uphold the right of clients to be offered the highest quality service possible.
- Social workers strive to maintain and increase their professional knowledge and skill.
- Social workers demonstrate due care for client's interests and safety by limiting professional practice to areas of demonstrated competence.
- Social workers contribute to the ongoing development of the profession and its ability to serve humanity, where possible, by participating in the development of current and future social workers and the development of new professional knowledge.
- Social workers who engage in research minimize risks to participants, ensure informed consent, maintain confidentiality and accurately report the results of their studies.

Glossary

Capacity

The ability to understand information relevant to a decision and to appreciate the reasonably foreseeable consequences of choosing to act or not to act. Capacity is specific to each decision and thus a person may be capable of deciding about a place of residence, for example, but not capable with respect to deciding about a treatment. Capacity can change over time (Etchells, Sharpe, Elliot and Singer, 1996).

Recent references in law point to the concept of "a mature minor," which Rozovsky and Rozovsky (1990) define as ". . . one with capacity to understand the nature and consequences of medical treatment. Such a person has the power to consent to medical treatment and parental consent is not necessary" (p. 55). They quote the comments by The Honorable Justice Lambert in *Van Mol v. Ashmore,* which help clarify common law with respect to a minor's capacity to consent. He states:

> At common law, without reference to statute law, a young person, still a minor, may give, on his or her own behalf, a fully informed consent to medical treatment if he or she has sufficient maturity, intelligence and capacity of understanding what is involved in making informed choices about the proposed medical treatment. Once the capacity to consent has been achieved by the young person reaching sufficient maturity, intelligence and capability of understanding, the discussions about the nature of the treatment, its gravity, the material risks and any special and unusual risks, and the decisions about undergoing treatment, and about the form of the treatment, must all take place with and be made by the young person whose bodily integrity is to be invaded and whose life and health will be affected by the outcome.

Child

The *Convention on the Rights of the Child,* passed by the United Nations in 1959 and ratified by Canada in 1990, defines a child as a person under the age of 18 years unless national law recognizes an earlier age of majority (Alberta Law Reform Institute, 1991). The age of majority differs in provinces and territories in Canada. Under the *Criminal Code of Canada,* the age of consent is held to be over the age of 14 years; age in the context of the criminal code frequently refers to capacity to consent to sexual relations. All jurisdictions in Canada have legislation regarding child protection, which defines the age of a child for the purposes of protection. In Canada, in the absence of provincial or territorial legislation, courts are governed by common law. Social workers are encouraged to maintain current knowledge with respect to legislation on the age of a child, as well as capacity and consent in their jurisdiction.

Client

A person, family, group of persons, incorporated body, association or community on whose behalf a social worker provides or agrees to provide a service or to whom the social worker is legally obligated to provide a service. Examples of legal obligation to provide service include a legislated responsibility (such as in child welfare) or a valid court order. In the case of a valid court order, the judge/court is the client and the person(s) who is ordered by the court to participate in assessment is recognized as an involuntary client.

Conduct Unbecoming

Behaviour or conduct that does not meet social work standard of care requirements and is, therefore, subject to discipline. In reaching a decision in Matthews and Board of Directors of Physiotherapy (1986) 54 O.R. (2d) 375, Saunders J. makes three important statements regarding standards of practice, and by implication, professional codes of ethics:

1. Standards of practice are inherent characteristics of any profession.

2. Standards of practice may be written or unwritten.

3. Some conduct is clearly regarded as misconduct and need not be written down, whereas other conduct may be the subject of dispute within a profession.

(See "Standard of Practice.")

Confidentiality

A professional value that demands that professionally acquired information be kept private and not shared with third parties unless the client provides informed consent or a professional or legal obligation exists to share such information without client informed consent.

Discrimination

Treating people unfavourably or holding negative or prejudicial attitudes based on discemable differences or stereotypes (AASW, 1999).

Informed Consent

Voluntary agreement reached by a capable client based on information about foreseeable risks and benefits associated with the agreement (e.g., participation in counselling or agreement to disclose social work report to a third party).

Human Rights

The rights of an individual that are considered the basis for freedom and justice, and serve to protect people from discrimination and harassment. Social workers may refer to the *Canadian Charter of Rights and Freedoms* enacted as Schedule B to the *Canada Act* 1982 (U.K.) 1982, c. 11, which came into force on April 17, 1982, as well as the *Universal Declaration of Human Rights* (1948) proclaimed by the United Nations General Assembly December 10, 1948.

Malpractice and Negligence

Behaviour that is included in "conduct unbecoming" and relates to social work practice behaviour within the parameters of the professional relationship that falls below the standard of practice and results in, or aggravation of, injury to a client. It includes behaviour that results in assault, deceit, fraudulent misrepresentations, defamation of character, breach of contract, violation of human rights, malicious prosecution, false imprisonment or criminal conviction.

Self-Determination

A core social work value that refers to the right to self-direction and freedom of choice without interference from others. Self-determination is codified in practice through mechanisms of informed consent. Social workers may be obligated to limit self-determination when a client lacks capacity or in order to prevent harm (Regehr and Antle, 1997).

Social Worker

A person who is duly registered to practice social work in a province or territory; or where mandatory registration does not exist, a person with social work education from an institution recognized by the Canadian Association of Schools of Social Work (CASSW) or an institution from outside of Canada that has been approved by the CASW, who is practising social work and who voluntarily agrees to be subject to this *Code of Ethics*. **Note:** Social workers living in Quebec and British Columbia, whose social work education was obtained outside of Canada, follow a separate approval process within their respective provinces.

Standard of Practice

The standard of care ordinarily expected of a competent social worker. It means that the public is assured that a social worker has the training, the skill and the diligence to provide them with social work services. Social workers are urged to refer to standards of practice that have been set by their provincial or territorial regulatory body or relevant professional association (see "Conduct Unbecoming").

Voluntary

"In the context of consent, 'voluntariness' refers to a patient's right to make treatment decisions free of any undue influence, such as ability of others to exert control over a patient by force, coercion or manipulation. . . . The requirement for voluntariness does not imply that clinicians should refrain from persuading patients to accept advice. Persuasion involves appealing to the patient's reason in an attempt to convince him or her of the merits of a recommendation. In attempting to persuade the patient to follow a particular course of action, the clinician still leaves the patient free to accept or reject this advice." (Etchells, Sharpe, Dykeman, Meslin and Singer, 1996, p. 1083).

Appendix C

Canadian Guidelines for Ethical Practice 2005

CASW ACTS

Canadian Association
Association canadienne

Social Workers des travailleuses et travailleurs sociaux

Table of Contents

Acknowledgements

The Canadian Association of Social Workers (CASW) acknowledges with thanks the National Association of Social Workers (NASW) for permission to use sections of the copyrighted NASW 1999 *Code of Ethics* in the development of the CASW 2005 *Code of Ethics* and *Guidelines for Ethical Practice*.

The CASW also acknowledges that other codes of ethics and resources were used in the development of this *Code* and *Guidelines for Ethical Practice,* in particular, the *Code of Ethics* of the Australian Association of Social Workers (AASW). These resources can be found in the "Reference" section of each document.

Guidelines for Ethical Practice

These guidelines serve as a companion document to the CASW *Code of Ethics* and provide guidance on ethical practice by applying values and principles in the *Code* to common areas of social work practice. While detailed, these guidelines for ethical practice are not intended to be exhaustive, or entirely prescriptive, but rather are intended to provide social workers with greater clarity on how to interpret and apply the ethical values and principles in the *Code*.

The extent to which each guideline is enforceable is a matter of professional judgement. Social workers are encouraged to consult their relevant provincial/territorial regulatory body or professional association for more specific guidance with respect to the application of these ethical guidelines in their own jurisdiction.

Core Social Work Values and Principles

Social workers uphold the following core values of the profession as outlined below. For a more detailed description of these values and principles please see the CASW *Code of Ethics* (2005). While all of these values and principles inform social work practice, to facilitate practical application a cross-reference is provided below between values from the *Code* and values from sections in the *Guidelines to Ethical Practice*. The reader is cautioned that this is not an exhaustive cross-reference and is meant only to enhance reader familiarity. The reader may also use the "Index" at the back of this document to help locate relevant sections of the *Guidelines to Ethical Practice*.

Value 1: Respect for Inherent Dignity and Worth of Persons

See Section 1, "Ethical Responsibilities to Clients."
See also Sections 5.3 and 6.

Value 2: Pursuit of Social Justice

See Section 8, "Ethical Responsibilities to Society."
See also Sections 1.4, 1.6, 4.1.3 and 4.2.

Value 3: Service to Humanity

See Section 2, "Ethical Responsibilities in Professional Relationships."
See also Sections 3.3, 5.2, 6.4 and 8.

Value 4: Integrity of Professional Practice

See Section 2, "Ethical Responsibilities in Professional Relationships";
Section 3, "Ethical Responsibilities to Colleagues"; Section 4, "Ethical Responsibilities to the Workplace"; and Section 5, "Ethical Responsibilities in Private Practice." See also Sections 1.1 and 7.4.

Value 5: Confidentiality in Professional Practice

See Sections 1.5, 1.4, 6.3 and 7.3.2.

Value 6: Competence in Professional Practice

See Section 6, "Ethical Responsibilities in Research," and Section 7, "Ethical Responsibilities to the Profession." See also Sections 3.2.1, 3.2.3, 3.4.1, 3.5.1, 3.5.2 and 8.2.5.

1.0 Ethical Responsibilities to Clients

1.1 Priority of Clients' Interests

1.1.1 Social workers maintain the best interests of clients as a priority, with due regard to the respective interests of others.

1.1.2 Social workers do not discriminate against any person on the basis of age, abilities, ethnic background, gender, language, marital status, national ancestry, political affiliation, race, religion, sexual orientation or socio-economic status.

1.1.3 Social workers collaborate with other professionals and service providers in the interests of clients with the client's knowledge and consent. Social workers recognize the right of client determination in this regard and include clients (or legally mandated client representatives when clients are not capable of giving consent) in such consultations.

1.1.4 Social workers limit their involvement in the personal affairs of clients to matters related to service being provided.

1.1.5 In exceptional circumstances, the priority of clients' interests may be outweighed by the interests of others, or by legal requirements and conditions. In such situations clients are made aware of the obligations the social worker faces with respect to the interests of others (see section 1.5), unless such disclosure could result in harm to others.

1.1.6 Social workers seek to safeguard the rights and interests of clients who have limited or impaired decision-making capacity when acting on their behalf, and/or when collaborating with others who are acting for the client (see section 1.3).

1.2 Demonstrate Cultural Awareness and Sensitivity

1.2.1 Social workers strive to understand culture and its function in human behaviour and society, recognizing the strengths that exist in all cultures.

1.2.2 Social workers acknowledge the diversity within and among individuals, communities and cultures.

1.2.3 Social workers acknowledge and respect the impact that their own heritage, values, beliefs and preferences can have on their practice and on clients whose background and values may be different from their own.

1.2.4 Social workers seek a working knowledge and understanding of clients' racial and cultural affiliations, identities, values, beliefs and customs.

1.2.5 Where possible, social workers provide or secure social work services in the language chosen by the client. If using an interpreter, when possible, social workers preferentially secure an independent and qualified professional interpreter.

1.3 Promote Client Self-Determination and Informed Consent

1.3.1 Social workers promote the self-determination and autonomy of clients, actively encouraging them to make informed decisions on their own behalf.

1.3.2 Social workers evaluate a client's capacity to give informed consent as early in the relationship as possible.

1.3.3 Social workers who have children as clients determine the child's capacity to consent and explain to the child (where appropriate), and to the child's parents/guardians (where appropriate) the nature of the social worker's relationship to the child and others involved in the child's care (see section 1.5.5 regarding confidentiality).

1.3.4 Social workers, at the earliest opportunity, discuss with clients their rights and responsibilities and provide them with honest and accurate information regarding the following:

- the nature of the social work service being offered;
- the recording of information and who will have access to such information;
- the purpose, nature, extent and known implications of the options open to them;
- the potential risks and benefits of proposed social work interventions;
- their right to obtain a second opinion or to refuse or cease service (recognizing the limitations that apply when working with involuntary clients);
- the client's right to view professional records and to seek avenues of complaint; and
- the limitations on professional confidentiality (see section 1.5 regarding confidentiality).

1.3.5 Social workers provide services to clients only on valid informed consent or when required to by legislation or court-ordered (see section 1.4 regarding involuntary clients).

1.3.6 Social workers obtain clients' informed consent before audio taping or video taping clients or permitting observation of services to clients by a third party.

1.4 Responsibilities to Involuntary Clients and Clients Not Capable of Consent

1.4.1 Social workers recognize that in some cases their ability to promote self-determination is limited because clients may not be capable of making their own decisions, are involuntary or because clients' actions pose a serious threat to themselves or others.

1.4.2 Social workers endeavour to minimize the use of compulsion. Any action that violates or diminishes the civil or legal rights of clients is taken only after careful evaluation of the situation (see section 1.6 regarding protection of vulnerable members of society).

1.4.3 When a social worker is court-ordered or agrees to conduct a legally-mandated assessment, the social worker's primary obligation is to the judge or designate. The social worker, however, continues to have professional obligations toward the person being assessed with respect to dignity, openness regarding limits to confidentiality and professional competence.

1.4.4 In all cases where clients' right to self-determination is limited by duty of care (e.g., client intent to self-harm), the law (e.g., child abuse), or court order, social workers assist clients to negotiate and attain as much self-determination as possible. In particular, involuntary clients are made aware of any limitations that apply to their right to refuse services and are advised how information will be shared with other parties.

1.4.5 Social workers, wherever possible or warranted, notify clients regarding decisions made about them, except where there is evidence that this information may bring about, or exacerbate, serious harm to individuals or the public.

1.4.6 In instances when clients lack the capacity to provide informed consent, social workers protect clients' interests by advocating that their interests are represented by an appropriate third party, such as a substitute decision-maker.

1.5 Protect Privacy and Confidentiality

Social workers respect clients' right to privacy. Social workers do not solicit private information from clients unless it is required to provide services or to conduct social work research. Once information is shared or observed in a professional context, standards of confidentiality apply. Social workers protect clients' identity and only disclose confidential information to other parties (including family members) with the informed consent of clients or the clients' legally authorized representatives, or when required by law or court order. This obligation continues indefinitely after the social worker has ceased contact with the client. The general expectation that social workers will keep information confidential does not apply when disclosure is necessary to prevent serious, foreseeable, and imminent harm to a client or others (see section 1.6 regarding protection of vulnerable members of society). In all instances, social workers disclose the least amount of confidential information necessary to achieve the desired purpose.

1.5.1 Social workers discuss with clients the nature of confidentiality and limitations of clients' right to confidentiality at the earliest opportunity in their relationship. Social workers review with clients when disclosure of confidential information may be legally or ethically required. Further discussion of confidentiality may be needed throughout the course of the relationship.

1.5.2 Social workers ascertain and take into account the manner in which individual clients wish confidentiality to apply within their cultural context.

1.5.3 Social workers inform clients, to the extent possible, about the disclosure of confidential information and its potential consequences before the disclosure is made. This applies in all circumstances of disclosure, except when, in the professional judgement of the social worker, sharing this information with the client may bring about, or exacerbate, serious harm to individuals or the public.

1.5.4 When social workers provide services to families, couples, or groups, social workers seek agreement among the parties involved concerning each individual's right to confidentiality and the obligation to preserve the confidentiality of information shared by others. Social workers inform participants in family, couples, or group counselling that social workers cannot guarantee that all participants will honour such agreements.

1.5.5 When social workers provide services to children, they outline for the child and the child's parents (where appropriate) their practices with respect to confidentiality and children. Social workers may wish to reserve the right to disclose some information provided by a young child to parents when such disclosure is in the best interest of the child. This should be declared prior to the first session with a child (see section 1.3.3 regarding consent and capacity).

1.5.6 Social workers take care to not discuss confidential information in public or semi-public areas such as hallways, waiting rooms, elevators, and restaurants.

1.5.7 Social workers take precautions to ensure and maintain the confidentiality of information transmitted to other parties through the use of computers, electronic mail, facsimile machines, telephone answering machines and other electronic technology. Social workers inform clients of the limits to confidentiality that may apply to these forms of communication.

1.5.8 Social workers protect the confidentiality of clients' written and electronic records. Social workers take reasonable steps to ensure that clients' records are stored in a secure location and that clients' records are not available to others who are not authorized to have access (see section 1.6 regarding protection of vulnerable members of society).

1.5.9 Social workers do not disclose identifying information when discussing clients for teaching or training purposes, unless the client has consented to such disclosure.

1.5.10 Social workers do not disclose identifying information when discussing clients with consultants unless the client has provided informed consent or if there is a compelling need for such disclosure. If the agency practices and policies involve routine consultations with a supervisor or professional team, social workers make clients aware of these practices as a limitation to confidentiality.

1.5.11 Social workers protect the confidentiality of deceased clients consistent with the preceding responsibilities.

1.5.12 Social workers take reasonable precautions to protect client confidentiality in the event of the social worker's termination of practice, incapacity, or death.

1.5.13 Social workers take appropriate steps to address a breach of confidentiality should it occur, with due care to the values and principles of the *Code*, the standards of their employer and relevant regulatory body.

1.6 Protection of Vulnerable Members of Society
(See sections 1.3 on informed consent; 1.5 on confidentiality.)

1.6.1 Social workers who have reason to believe a child is being harmed and is in need of protection are obligated, consistent with their provincial/ territorial legislation, to report their concerns to the proper authorities.

1.6.2 Social workers who have reason to believe that a client intends to harm another person are obligated to inform both the person who may be at risk (if possible) as well as the police.

1.6.3 Social workers who have reason to believe that a client intends to harm him/herself are expected to exercise professional judgement regarding their need to take action consistent with their provincial/territorial legislation, standards of practice and workplace policies. Social workers may in this instance take action to prevent client self-harm without the informed consent of the client. In deciding whether to break confidentiality, social workers are guided by the imminence of self-harm, the presence of a mental health condition and prevailing professional standards and practices.

1.6.4 Social workers who have reason to believe that an adult client is being abused take action consistent with their provincial/territorial legislation. Only a minority of jurisdictions in Canada have mandatory reporting of abuse of adults.

1.7 Maintenance and Handling of Client Records

Social workers maintain one written record of professional interventions and opinions, with due care to the obligations and standards of their employer and relevant regulatory body. Social workers document information impartially and accurately and with an appreciation that the record may be revealed to clients or disclosed during court proceedings. Social workers are encouraged to take care to

- report only essential and relevant details,
- refrain from using emotive or derogatory language,
- acknowledge the basis of professional opinions, and
- protect clients' privacy and that of others involved.

1.7.1 Social workers do not state a professional opinion unless it can be supported by their own assessment or by the documented assessment of another professional.

1.7.2 Where records are shared across professions or agencies, information is recorded only to the degree that it addresses clients' needs and meets the requirements of an employer or professional standards of practice.

1.7.3 Before using clients' records for any purpose beyond professional services, for example education, social workers obtain the informed consent of clients.

1.7.4 In some circumstances, access to client records may be officially authorized or required by statute. Where consent of clients is not required, social workers attempt to notify clients that such access has been granted, if such notification does not involve a risk to others.

1.7.5 Social workers ensure that clients have reasonable access to official social work records concerning them. However, if there are compelling professional, ethical or legal reasons for refusing access, social workers advise clients of their right to request a review of the decision through organizational or legal channels, e.g., *Access to Information Act* (1983).

1.7.6 Social workers take due care to protect the confidences of others when providing clients with access to records. This may involve masking third party information in the record.

1.7.7 If clients are not satisfied with their records, social workers advise them regarding complaint mechanisms.

1.7.8 Social workers protect clients' records, store them securely and retain them for any required statutory period.

1.7.9 Social workers transfer or dispose of clients' records in a manner that protects clients' confidentiality and is consistent with provincial/territorial statutes governing records and social work regulation. Social workers also ensure that mechanical or electronic records are properly transferred or disposed of.

1.8 Practices for Termination or Interruption of Services

1.8.1 Social workers renegotiate or terminate professional services when these services are no longer required or no longer meet the needs of clients.

1.8.2 Social workers respect the right of voluntary clients to discontinue service, engage another practitioner or seek a second opinion.

1.8.3 Whether the decision to renegotiate or terminate is that of the client or the social worker, social workers (where appropriate) initiate a discussion with the client to appreciate, and if possible, address any difficulties or misunderstandings that may have occurred. If the client desires other professional services, the social worker may assist in referral.

1.8.4 Social workers discuss client's needs, options and preferences before continuing or discontinuing services, or offering to seek transfer or referral.

1.8.5 Social workers at the earliest opportunity inform clients of any factor, condition or pressure that affects their ability to practice adequately and competently.

1.8.6 When obliged to interrupt or terminate a professional relationship, social workers advise clients regarding the discontinuation of service and if possible, ensure their referral to another professional.

2.0 Ethical Responsibilities in Professional Relationships

It is the responsibility of the social worker to establish the tenor of their professional relationship with clients and others, and to ensure that the relationship serves the needs of clients, and others to whom there is a professional duty, over the needs of the social worker. In establishing a professional relationship the social worker takes into account relevant contextual issues, such as age, culture and gender of the client, and ensures the dignity, individuality and rights of the person and vulnerable members of society are protected.

2.1 Appropriate Professional Boundaries

2.1.1 Social workers maintain appropriate professional boundaries through-out the course of the professional relationship and after the professional relationship.

2.2 No Exploitation for Personal or Professional Gain

2.2.1 Social workers do not exploit professional relationships for personal benefit, gain or gratification.

2.2.2 Social workers do not take unfair advantage of any professional relationship or exploit others to further their personal, religious, political or business interests.

2.3 Declare Conflicts of Interest

Social workers avoid conflicts of interest that interfere with the exercise of professional discretion and impartial judgement. Social workers inform clients when a real or potential conflict of interest arises, and take reasonable steps to resolve the issue in a manner that makes the clients' interests primary. In some cases, protecting clients' interests may require termination of the professional relationship with proper referral of the client to another professional.

2.3.1 When social workers provide services to two or more people who have a relationship with each other (e.g., couples, family members), social workers clarify with all parties which individuals will be considered clients and the nature of the professional relationship with other involved parties.

2.3.2 Social workers who anticipate a conflict of interest among the individuals receiving services, or who anticipate having to perform a difficult role, clarify with clients their role and responsibilities. (For example, when a social worker is asked to testify in a child custody dispute or divorce proceedings involving clients.)

2.3.3 Social workers consider carefully the potential for professional conflicts of interest where close personal relationships exist or where social, business or sexual relationships with colleagues are contemplated or exist.

2.4 Dual and Multiple Relationships

Dual or multiple relationships occur when social workers relate to clients in more than one relationship, whether professional, social or business. Dual or multiple relationships can occur simultaneously or consecutively. While having contact with clients in different life situations is not inherently harmful, it is the responsibility of the social worker to evaluate the nature of the various contacts to determine whether the social worker is in a position of power and/or authority that may unduly and/or negatively affect the decisions and actions of their client. (See section 3.2.3 regarding supervisees, and section 3.3.9 regarding students.)

2.4.1 Social workers take care to evaluate the nature of dual or multiple relationships to ensure that the needs and welfare of their clients are protected.

2.5 Avoid Physical Contact with Clients

2.5.1 Social workers avoid engaging in physical contact with clients when there is a possibility of harm to the client as a result of the contact. Social workers who engage in appropriate physical contact with clients are responsible for setting clear, appropriate and culturally sensitive boundaries to govern such physical contact.

2.6 No Romantic or Sexual Relationships with Clients

2.6.1 Social workers do not engage in romantic relationships, sexual activities or sexual contact with clients, even if such contact is sought by clients.

2.6.2 Social workers who have provided psychotherapy or in-depth counselling do not engage in romantic relationships, sexual activities or sexual contact with former clients. It is the responsibility of the social worker to evaluate the nature of the professional relationship they had with a client and to determine whether the social worker is in a position of power and/or authority that may unduly and/or negatively affect the decisions and actions of their former client.

2.6.3 Social workers do not engage in a romantic relationship, sexual activities or sexual contact with social work students whom they are supervising or teaching. (See Section 3.5 "Responsibilities to Students.")

2.7 No Sexual Harassment

Sexual harassment refers to unwelcome sexual comments or lewd statements, unwelcome sexual advances, unwelcome requests for sexual favours or other unwelcome conduct of a sexual nature in circumstances where a reasonable person could anticipate that the person harassed would be offended, humiliated or intimidated.

2.7.1 Social workers do not sexually harass any person.

3.0 Ethical Responsibilities to Colleagues

3.1 Respect

Social workers relate to both social work colleagues and colleagues from other disciplines with respect, integrity and courtesy and seek to understand differences in viewpoints and practice.

3.2 Collaboration and Consultation

When collaborating with other professionals, social workers utilize the expertise of other disciplines for the benefit of their clients. Social workers participate in and contribute to decisions that affect the well-being of clients by drawing on the knowledge, values and experiences of the social work profession.

3.2.1 Social workers co-operate with other disciplines to promote and expand ideas, knowledge, theory and skills, experience and opportunities that improve professional expertise and service provision.

3.2.2 Social workers seek the advice and counsel of colleagues whenever such consultation is in the best interests of clients.

3.2.3 Social workers keep themselves informed about colleagues' areas of expertise and competencies. Social workers only consult colleagues who have, in the judgement of the social worker, knowledge, expertise and competence related to the subject of the consultation.

3.2.4 Social workers take responsibility and credit, including authorship credit, only for work they have actually performed and to which they have contributed.

3.2.5 Social workers honestly acknowledge the work and the contributions made by others.

3.3 Management of Disputes

Social workers remain open to constructive comment on their practice or behaviour. Social workers base criticism of colleagues' practice or behaviour on defensible arguments and concern, and deal with differences in ways that uphold the principles of the *Code of Ethics*, the *Guidelines for Ethical Practice* and the honour of the social work profession.

3.3.1 Social workers who have ethical concerns about the actions of a colleague attempt to resolve the disagreement through appropriate channels established by their organization. If the disagreement cannot be resolved, social workers pursue other avenues to address their concerns consistent with client well-being, ethical principles and obligations outlined by their regulatory body.

3.4 Responsibilities in Supervision and Consultation

In addition to the general provisions of the *Code*, social workers in supervisory or consultation roles are guided by the following specific ethical responsibilities.

3.4.1 Social workers who have the necessary knowledge and skill to supervise or consult do so only within their areas of knowledge and competence.

3.4.2 Social workers do not engage in any dual or multiple relationships with supervisees when there is a risk of exploitation of, or potential harm to the supervisee. If questioned, it is the responsibility of the supervisor to demonstrate that any dual or multiple relationship is not exploitative or harmful to the supervisee. (See section 2.4 regarding dual and multiple relationships.)

3.4.3 Social workers evaluate supervisees' performance in a manner that is fair and respectful and consistent with the expectations of the place of employment.

3.5 Responsibilities to Students

In addition to the general provisions of the *Code*, social worker educators and field instructors who supervise students are guided by the following specific ethical responsibilities.

3.5.1 Social workers provide instruction only within their areas of knowledge and competence.

3.5.2 Social workers endeavour to provide instruction based on the most current information and knowledge available in the profession.

3.5.3 Social workers foster in social work students' knowledge and understanding of the social work profession, the *Code of Ethics* and other appropriate sources of ethical practices.

3.5.4 Social workers instruct students to inform clients of their student status.

3.5.5 Social workers inform students of their ethical responsibilities to agencies, supervisors and clients.

3.5.6 Social workers adhere to the principles of privacy and confidentiality in the supervisory relationship, acknowledging with students any limitations early in the professional relationship.

3.5.7 Social workers recognize that their role in supervising students is intended to be educational and work-focused. In the event that a student requests or requires therapy, the instructor refers the student to another competent practitioner.

3.5.8 Social workers evaluate a student's performance in a manner that is fair and respectful and consistent with the expectations of the student's educational institution.

3.5.9 Social workers do not engage in any dual or multiple relationships with students in which there is a risk of exploitation or potential harm to the student. Social work educators and field instructors are responsible for setting clear, appropriate and culturally sensitive boundaries. (See section 2.4 regarding dual and multiple relationships.)

4.0 Ethical Responsibilities to the Workplace

4.1 Professional Practice

4.1.1 Social workers acknowledge and strive to carry out the stated aims and objectives of their employing organization, agency or service contractor, consistent with the requirements of ethical practice.

4.1.2 Social workers work toward the best possible standards of service provision and are accountable for their practice.

4.1.3 Social workers use the organization's resources honestly and only for their intended purpose.

4.1.4 Social workers appropriately challenge and work to improve policies, procedures, practices and service provisions that

- are not in the best interests of clients;
- are inequitable;
- are in any way oppressive, disempowering or culturally inappropriate; and
- demonstrate discrimination.

4.1.5 When policies or procedures of employing bodies contravene professional standards, social workers endeavour to effect change through consultation using appropriate and established organizational channels.

4.1.6 Social workers take all reasonable steps to ensure that employers are aware of their professional ethical obligations and advocate for conditions and policies that reflect ethical professional practices.

4.1.7 Social workers take all reasonable steps to uphold their ethical values, principles and responsibilities even though employers' policies or official orders may not be compatible with its provisions.

4.2 Labour-Management Disputes

4.2.1 Social workers may engage in organized action, including the formation of and participation in labour unions, to improve services to clients and professional wages and working conditions.

4.2.2 The actions of social workers who are involved in labour-management disputes, job actions or labour strikes are guided by the profession's values and principles. Reasonable differences of opinion exist among social workers concerning their primary obligation as professionals during an actual or threatened labour strike or job action. Social workers carefully examine relevant issues and their possible impact on clients before deciding on a course of action.

4.3 Responsibilities of Managers

In addition to the general provisions of the *Code of Ethics* and *Guidelines for Ethical Practice*, social workers in management or similar administrative positions are guided by the following specific ethical responsibilities.

4.3.1 Social workers acquaint organizational administrators with the ethical responsibilities of social workers. Social workers encourage employers to eliminate workplace factors that prohibit or obstruct adherence to ethical practice.

4.3.2 Social workers strive to promote effective teamwork and communication and an efficient and accountable social work service.

4.3.3 Social workers strive to obtain and maintain adequate staff levels and acceptable working conditions.

4.3.4 Social workers strive to facilitate access to appropriate professional consultation or supervision for professional social work practice.

4.3.5 Social workers strive to facilitate access for staff under their direction to ongoing training and professional education, and advocate for adequate resources to meet staff development needs.

4.3.6 Social workers provide or arrange for appropriate debriefing and professional support for staff, especially when they experience difficult or traumatic circumstances.

5.0 Ethical Responsibilities in Private Practice

In addition to the general provisions of the *Code of Ethics* and *Guidelines for Ethical Practice*, social workers in private practice are guided by the following specific ethical responsibilities.

5.1 Insurance Requirements

5.1.1 Social workers maintain adequate malpractice, defamation and liability insurance.

5.2 Avoid and Declare Conflicts of Interest

(See also section 2.3 regarding conflicts of interest.)

5.2.1 Social workers do not solicit clients for their private practice from their colleagues or their place of work, unless there is a request for social workers to do so. (For example, in hard to serve areas, employers may need employees who also have a private practice to provide follow-up services).

5.2.2 Subject to 5.2.1, social workers may accept clients from their workplace when the workplace does not provide a similar service or in accordance with established workplace guidelines regarding such referrals.

5.3 Responsible Fee Practices

5.3.1 Social workers who enter into a fee for services contract with a client:

- Disclose at the outset of the relationship, the fee schedule for social work services including their expectations and practices with respect to cancellations and unpaid bills.
- Only charge a fee that was disclosed to and agreed upon by the client.
- Charge only for the reasonable hours of client services, research, consultation and administrative work on behalf of a given client.

- Avoid accepting goods or services from clients as payment for professional services. Bartering arrangements, particularly involving services, create the potential for conflicts of interest, exploitation and inappropriate boundaries in social workers' relationships with clients.

- Social workers may participate in bartering when it can be demonstrated that such arrangements are an accepted practice for professionals in the local community, considered to be essential for the provision of services, negotiated without coercion, and entered into for the client's benefit and with the client's informed consent. Social workers who accept goods or services from clients as payment for professional services assume the full burden of demonstrating that this arrangement will not be detrimental to the client and the profession.

5.3.2 Social workers may charge differential fees for services when such a difference in fee is for the benefit of the client and the fee is not discriminatory.

5.3.3 Social workers may charge a rate of interest on delinquent accounts as is allowed by law. When such interest is being charged, social workers state the rate of interest on all invoices or bills.

5.3.4 Social workers may pursue civil remedies to ensure payment for services to a client, where the social worker has advised the client of this possibility at the outset of the contract. (See section 1.5 regarding confidentiality.)

6.0 Ethical Responsibilities in Research

In addition to the general provisions of the *Code of Ethics* and *Guidelines for Ethical Practice*, social workers engaged in research are guided by the following ethical responsibilities.

6.1 Responsible Research Practices

6.1.1 Social workers educate themselves, their students and their colleagues about responsible research practices.

6.1.2 Social workers observe the conventions of ethical scholarly inquiry when engaged in study and research. Social workers utilize only appropriately qualified personnel (or provide adequate training) to carry out research, paying particular attention to qualifications required in conducting specialized techniques.

6.2 Minimize Risks

6.2.1 Social workers place the interests of research participants above the social worker's personal interests or the interests of the research project.

6.2.2 Social workers consider carefully the possible consequences for individuals and society before participating in, or engaging in, proposed research and also when publishing research results.

6.2.3 Social workers submit research proposals to an appropriate independent scientific and ethical review prior to implementation of the research.

6.2.4 Social workers strive to protect research participants from physical, mental or emotional discomfort, distress, harm or deprivation.

6.2.5 Social workers take appropriate steps to ensure that research participants have access to appropriate supportive services.

6.2.6 Social workers ensure that due care has been taken to protect the privacy and dignity of research participants.

6.3 Informed Consent, Anonymity and Confidentiality

Social workers obtain informed consent to take part in research from either participants or their legally authorized representatives. In addition, social workers offer children and others whose ability to provide consent is compromised for any reason, the opportunity to express their assent or objection to research procedures and give their views due regard.

6.3.1 Social workers ensure that consent is given voluntarily, without coercion or inferred disadvantage for refusal to participate. Participants are informed that they may withdraw from a study at any time without compromising any professional service being offered in the research project or future access to social work services.

6.3.2 Social workers ensure confidentiality of research participants' identity and discuss them only in limited circumstances for professional purposes. It is recommended that any identifying information obtained from or about participants during the research process is treated as confidential and the identity of participants separated from data that is stored, for example, through the use of identification numbers for surveys or similar questionnaires, and pseudonyms in transcripts of qualitative interviews.

6.3.3 Social workers ensure the anonymity of research participants is maintained in subsequent reports about the research.

6.3.4 Social workers store research material securely and for the required period as indicated by relevant research ethics guidelines.

6.4 Avoid Deception

6.4.1 Social workers generally avoid the use of deception in research because of its negative implications for the public trust in the profession.

6.4.2 Social workers only design or conduct research that involves deception or waiver of consent, such as certain forms of naturalistic observation and archival research, when third party review of the research has found it to be justified because of its anticipated scientific, educational, or practice value and when equally effective alternative procedures that do not involve deception or waiver of consent are not feasible.

6.5 Accuracy of Report of Research Findings

6.5.1 Social workers report research results accurately and objectively, acknowledging the contributions of others, and respecting copyright law. In research and scholarly endeavours, credit is taken only for work actually performed.

6.5.2 Where feasible, social workers inform research participants or their legally authorized representatives of research results that are relevant to them.

6.5.3 Where feasible, social workers bring research results that indicate or demonstrate social inequalities or injustices to the attention of the relevant bodies.

7.0 Ethical Responsibilities to the Profession

7.1 Maintain and Enhance Reputation of Profession

7.1.1 Social workers promote excellence in the social work profession. They engage in discussion about and constructive criticism of the profession, its theories, methods and practices.

7.1.2 Social workers uphold the dignity and integrity of the profession and inform their practice from a recognized social work knowledge base.

7.1.3 Social workers cite an educational degree only after it has been conferred by the educational institution.

7.1.4 Social workers do not claim formal social work education in an area of expertise or training solely by attending a lecture, demonstration, conference, workshop or similar teaching presentation.

7.1.5 Social workers uphold provincial and territorial regulations for continuing professional education, where such regulations exist.

7.1.6 Social workers do not make false, misleading or exaggerated claims of efficacy regarding past or anticipated achievements regarding their professional services.

7.1.7 Social workers strive to promote the profession of social work, its processes and outcomes and defend the profession against unjust criticism.

7.1.8 Social workers distinguish between actions and statements made as private citizens and actions and statements made as social workers, recognizing that social workers are obligated to ensure that no outside interest brings the profession into disrepute.

7.2 Address Unethical Practices of Colleagues

7.2.1 Social workers take appropriate action where a breach of professional practice and professional ethics occur, conducting themselves in a manner that is consistent with the *Code of Ethics* and *Guidelines for Ethical Practice,* and standards of their regulatory body.

7.2.2 Social workers who have direct knowledge of a social work colleague's incompetence or impairment in professional practice consult with colleagues about their concerns and when feasible assist colleagues in taking remedial action. Impairment may emanate, for example, from personal problems, psychosocial distress, substance abuse or mental health difficulties.

7.2.3 Social workers who believe that a colleague has not taken adequate steps to address their impairment to professional practice take action through appropriate channels established by employers, regulatory bodies, or other professional organizations.

7.2.4 Social workers do not intervene in the professional relationship of other social workers and clients unless requested to do so by a client and unless convinced that the best interests and well-being of clients requires such intervention.

7.3 Support Regulatory Practices (in jurisdictions where social work is regulated)

7.3.1 Social workers co-operate with investigations into matters of complaint against themselves or other social workers and the requirements of any associated disciplinary hearings.

7.3.2 Social workers may release confidential information as part of a disciplinary hearing of a social worker when so directed by a tribunal or disciplinary body, taking care to divulge the minimum information required.

7.3.3 Social workers report to the relevant professional body persons who misrepresent their qualifications as a social worker or their eligibility for regulation or membership in a professional association.

8.0 Ethical Responsibilities to Society

Social workers advocate for change in the best interests of clients and for the overall benefit of society, the environment and the global community. In performing their responsibilities to society, social workers frequently must balance individual rights to self-determination with protection of vulnerable members of society from harm. These dual ethical responsibilities are the hallmark of the social work profession and require well-developed and complex professional skills. When social workers' legal obligations require them to break confidentiality and limit client self-determination they do so with the minimum compulsion required by law and/or the circumstances (see Value 1).

8.1 Source of Information on Social Needs

8.1.1 Social workers identify and interpret the basis and nature of individual, group, community, national and international social problems with the intention of bringing about greater understanding and insight for policy makers and the public.

8.2 Participate in Social Action

8.2.1 Social workers strive to identify, document and advocate for the prevention and elimination of domination or exploitation of, and discrimination against, any person, group, or class on the basis of age, abilities, ethnic background, gender, language, marital status, national ancestry, political affiliation, race, religion, sexual orientation or socio-economic status.

8.2.2 Social workers endeavour to engage in social and/or political action that seeks to ensure that all people have fair access to the resources, services and opportunities they require to meet their basic human needs and to develop fully.

8.2.3 Social workers are aware of the impact of the political arena on practice and strive to advocate for changes in policy and legislation to improve social conditions in order to meet basic human needs and promote social justice.

8.2.4 Social workers endeavour to expand choice and opportunity for all people, with special regard for vulnerable, disadvantaged, oppressed and exploited people and groups.

8.2.5 Social workers strive to promote conditions that encourage respect for cultural and social diversity within Canada and globally. Social workers promote policies and practices that demonstrate respect for difference, support the expansion of cultural knowledge and resources, advocate for programs and institutions that demonstrate cultural competence and promote policies that safeguard the rights of and confirm equity and social justice for all people.

8.3 Encourage Public Participation

8.3.1 Social workers strive to facilitate informed participation by the public in shaping social policies and institutions.

8.4 Assist in Public Emergencies

8.4.1 Social workers provide professional services during public emergencies to the greatest extent possible.

8.5 Advocate for the Environment

8.5.1 Social workers endeavour to advocate for a clean and healthy environment and advocate for the development of environmental strategies consistent with social work principles and practices.

Glossary

Capacity

The ability to understand information relevant to a decision and to appreciate the reasonably foreseeable consequences of choosing to act or not to act. Capacity is specific to each decision and thus a person may be capable of deciding about a place of residence, for example, but not capable with respect to deciding about a treatment. Capacity can change over time (Etchells, Sharpe, Elliott, and Singer, 1996).

Recent references in law point to the concept of "a mature minor," which Rozovsky and Rozovsky (1990) define as ". . . one with capacity to understand the nature and consequences of medical treatment. Such a person has the power to consent to medical treatment and parental consent is not necessary" (p. 55). They quote the comments by The Honorable Justice Lambert in *Van Mol v. Ashmore*, which help clarify common law with respect to a minor's capacity to consent. He states:

> At common law, without reference to statute law, a young person, still a minor, may give, on his or her own behalf, a fully informed consent to medical treatment if he or she has sufficient maturity, intelligence and capacity of understanding what is involved in making informed choices about the proposed medical treatment. Once the capacity to consent has been achieved by the young person reaching sufficient maturity, intelligence and capability of understanding, the discussions about the nature of the treatment, its gravity, the material risks and any special and unusual risks, and the decisions about undergoing treatment, and about the form of the treatment, must all take place with and be made by the young person whose bodily integrity is to be invaded and whose life and health will be affected by the outcome.

Child

The *Convention on the Rights of the Child* passed by the United Nations in 1959 and ratified by Canada in 1990, defines a child as a person under the age of 18 years unless national law recognizes an earlier age of majority (Alberta Law

Reform Institute, 1991). The age of majority differs in provinces and territories in Canada. Under the *Criminal Code of Canada*, the age of consent is held to be over the age of 14 years; age in the context of the criminal code frequently refers to capacity to consent to sexual relations. All jurisdictions in Canada have legislation regarding child protection, which defines the age of a child for the purposes of protection. In Canada, in the absence of provincial or territorial legislation, courts are governed by common law. Social workers are encouraged to maintain current knowledge with respect to legislation on the age of a child, as well as capacity and consent in their jurisdiction.

Client

A person, family, group of persons, incorporated body, association or community on whose behalf a social worker provides or agrees to provide a service or to whom the social worker is legally obligated to provide a service. Examples of legal obligation to provide service include a legislated responsibility (such as in child welfare) or a valid court order. In the case of a valid court order, the judge/court is the client and the person(s) who is ordered by the court to participate in assessment is recognized as an involuntary client.

Conduct Unbecoming

Behaviour or conduct that does not meet social work standard of care requirements and is, therefore, subject to discipline. In reaching a decision in Matthews and Board of Directors of Physiotherapy (1986) 54 O.R. (2d) 375, Saunders J. makes three important statements regarding standards of practice, and by implication, professional codes of ethics:

1. Standards of practice are inherent characteristics of any profession.
2. Standards of practice may be written or unwritten.
3. Some conduct is clearly regarded as misconduct and need not be written down, whereas other conduct may be the subject of dispute within a profession.

(See "Standard of Practice.")

Confidentiality

A professional value that demands that professionally acquired information be kept private and not shared with third parties unless the client provides informed consent or a professional or legal obligation exists to share such information without client informed consent.

Discrimination

Treating people unfavourably or holding negative or prejudicial attitudes based on discernable differences or stereotypes (AASW, 1999).

Informed Consent

Voluntary agreement reached by a capable client based on information about foreseeable risks and benefits associated with the agreement (e.g., participation in counselling or agreement to disclose social work report to a third party).

Human Rights

The rights of an individual that are considered the basis for freedom and justice, and serve to protect people from discrimination and harassment. Social workers may refer to the *Canadian Charter of Rights and Freedoms* enacted as Schedule B to the *Canada Act* 1982 (U.K.) 1982, c. 11, which came into force on April 17, 1982, as well as the *Universal Declaration of Human Rights* (1948) proclaimed by the United Nations General Assembly December 10, 1948.

Malpractice and Negligence

Behaviour that is included in "conduct unbecoming" and relates to social work practice behaviour within the parameters of the professional relationship that falls below the standard of practice and results in, or aggravation of, injury to a client. It includes behaviour that results in assault, deceit, fraudulent misrepresentations, defamation of character, breach of contract, violation of human rights, malicious prosecution, false imprisonment or criminal conviction.

Self-Determination

A core social work value that refers to the right to self-direction and freedom of choice without interference from others. Self-determination is codified in practice through mechanisms of informed consent. Social workers may be obligated to limit self-determination when a client lacks capacity or in order to prevent harm (Regehr and Antle, 1997).

Social Worker

A person who is duly registered to practice social work in a province or territory; or where mandatory registration does not exist, a person with social work education from an institution recognized by the Canadian Association of Schools of Social Work (CASSW) or an institution from outside of Canada that has been approved by the CASW, who is practising social work and who voluntarily agrees to be subject to this *Code of Ethics*. **Note:** Social workers living in Quebec and British Columbia, whose social work education was obtained outside of Canada, follow a separate approval process within their respective provinces.

Standard of Practice

The standard of care ordinarily expected of a competent social worker. It means that the public is assured that a social worker has the training, the skill and the diligence to provide them with social work services. Social workers are urged to refer to standards of practice that have been set by their provincial or territorial regulatory body or relevant professional association (see "Conduct Unbecoming").

Voluntary

"In the context of consent, 'voluntariness' refers to a patient's right to make treatment decisions free of any undue influence, such as ability of others to exert control over a patient by force, coercion or manipulation. . . . The requirement for voluntariness does not imply that clinicians should refrain from persuading patients to accept advice. Persuasion involves appealing to the patient's reason in an attempt to convince him or her of the merits of a recommendation. In attempting to persuade the patient to follow a particular course of action, the clinician still leaves the patient free to accept or reject this advice." (Etchells, Sharpe, Dykeman, Meslin and Singer, 1996, p. 1083).

References

AASW. (1999). *AASW Code of Ethics.* Kingston: Australian Association of Social Workers (AASW).

Alberta Law Reform Institute. (1991). *Status of the Child: Revised Report* (Report No. 60). Edmonton, Alberta: Law Reform Institute.

BASW. (2002). *BASW: A Code of Ethics for Social Workers.* British Association of Social Workers (BASW).

Canadian Charter of Rights and Freedoms Enacted as Schedule B to the *Canada Act* 1982, c.11 (1982). [http://laws.justice.gc.ca/en/charter/]

CASW. (1994). *Social Work Code of Ethics.* Ottawa: Canadian Association of Social Workers (CASW).

Criminal Code, R.S., c. C-34, s.1. (1985). [http://laws.justice.gc.ca/en/C-46/40670.html]

Etchells, E.; G. Sharpe; C. Elliott and P. Singer. (1996). Bioethics for clinicians: 3: Capacity. *Canadian Medical Association Journal*, 155, 657-661.

Etchells, E.; G. Sharpe; M. J. Dykeman; Meslin, and P. Singer. (1996). Bioethics for clinicians: 4: Voluntariness. *Canadian Medical Association Journal*, 155, 1083-1086.

IFSW. (1994). *The Ethics of Social Work: Principles and Standards.* Geneva, Switzerland: International Federation of Social Workers (IFSW).

———. (2004). *Ethics in Social Work: Statement of Principles.* Geneva, Switzerland: International Federation of Social Workers (IFSW).

Lens, V. (2000). Protecting the confidentiality of the therapeutic relationship: Jaffe v. Redmond. *Social Work*, 45(3), 273-276.

Matthews and Board of Directors of Physiotherapy (1986) 54 O.R. (2d) 375.

NASW. (1999). *Code of Ethics*. Washington: National Association of Social Workers (NASW).

Regehr, C. and B. J. Antle. (1997). Coercive influences: Informed consent and court-mandated social work practice. *Social Work*, 42(3), 300-306.

Rozovsky, L. E. and F. A. Rozovsky. (1990). *The Canadian Law of Consent To Treatment*. Toronto: Butterworths.

United Nations. (1948). *Universal Declaration of Human Rights*. New York: United Nations. [http://www.unhchr.ch/udhr/]

United Nations Centre for Human Rights. (1992). Teaching and learning about human rights: A manual for schools of social work and the social work profession (Developed in co-operation with International Federation of Social Workers and International Association of Schools of Social Workers). New York: United Nations.

Index

383 Parkdale Avenue, Suite 402
Ottawa, Ontario, Canada K1Y 4R4
Telephone: (613) 729-6668
Fax: (613) 729-9608
Email: casw@casw-acts.ca
Web Site: www.casw-acts.ca

Appendix D

Biopsychosocial Form
Monmouth University

Instructor's Guide for An Empowering, Strengths-Based Psychosocial Assessment and Intervention Planning Outline for Children and Families in the Global Environment

by Rosemary Barbera, LaSalle University

When you are reviewing the Monmouth University Psychosocial with students in your classes, please use this guide to further elaborate with them in certain areas that might not be so self-explanatory. Let them know that this format comes from the perspectives that form the foundation for our program—strengths-based empowerment social work that advances social justice and human rights. This format may be different than what they are accustomed to, and that is for a reason.

> Be sure to explain why we are not using the medical model, but that in many agencies in the field it is used. Also discuss why we use the term "Intervention" and not "Treatment."

> Encourage students to use person-centered language—do not reduce people to their diagnoses or situations. Likewise, encourage them to write from the strengths perspective.

> Give them various examples about the types of questions you might use to obtain certain information. Maybe even do this in a role-play format in class.

Explain to them the difference between Family of Creation, Family of Experience, and Family of Choice.

Be clear that we are not asking for student opinions. They are to work collaboratively with people to gather information and to use the professional skills of observation that they are developing.

They should think about their role as the person gathering information in this process. How might they influence the process? How might they be perceived by others?

They should think in advance how they will ask these questions to special populations: LGBTQI persons; adoptees; undocumented immigrants; military personnel and their families; prisoners; children; people seeking asylum; immigrants; people with varying abilities—including people with traumatic brain injury; elderly.

You also may want to give them an example of a psychosocial from the past that was done well.

When you review with them the section that asks them to reflect on possible human rights violations, use this list to give them examples of some forms of abuse.

Article 16

"Men and women of full age, without any limitation due to race, nationality or religion, have the right to marry and to found a family. They are entitled to equal rights as to marriage, during marriage and at its dissolution."

The denial of marriage equality for Lesbian and Gay persons creates unequal intervention under the law and undue financial hardships due to inequality in access to spousal benefits and issues with inheritance taxes. Additionally the denial of marriage equality creates issues regarding access to partners when hospitalized and decision-making powers regarding medical intervention.

Article 23: The right to jobs at a living wage and just conditions of work

"Everyone has the right to work, to free choice of employment, to just and favorable conditions of work and to protection against unemployment . . . Everyone who works has the right to just and favorable remuneration ensuring for himself and his family an existence worthy of human dignity, and supplemented, if necessary, by other means of social protection . . . Everyone has the right to form and to join trade unions."

Your government is supposed to ensure that you can have a job of your choice that is safe, pays enough to live on, and does not infringe on your civil rights, including your right to be part of a union to protect your rights as a worker.

Examples of violations include problems in these areas:

Fair wages

- Minimum wage jobs that deny workers a living wage and health care.
- Workfare policies that force recipients to work for their checks at sub-minimum wage.

Safe and just working condition

- Workfare jobs without safety and health protection.
- Conditions and wages for sweatshop workers, farm workers, and other exploited workers.
- Being forced into a job that is a threat to one's physical health, well-being, or dignity.
- Injuries and deaths resulting from unsafe or unhealthy working conditions.

The right to organize

- Being fired or demoted for trying to form a union.
- Policies that pit the employed against the unemployed.

Free choice of employment

- Work requirements in the TANF plan that force recipients to take any job offered them.
- Prison labor in which prisoners are forced to work for unjust wages.
- Having to take unsafe jobs or jobs with nonlivable wages because the government will not provide you with enough other income to survive.
- Forced overtime or working more than forty hours to make enough to survive (see also Article 24).

Article 25: (1) The right to well-being of a person and his/her family, including food, clothing, housing, health care and necessary social services

"Everyone has the right to a standard of living adequate for the health and well-being of himself and of his family, including food, clothing, housing and medical care and necessary social services, and the right to security in the event of unemployment, sickness, disability, widowhood, old age or other lack of livelihood in circumstances beyond his control. Motherhood and childhood are entitled to special protection."

The government has to ensure that every resident has enough money to provide all the basics for living. If you live below a recognized standard of income and other resources, your human rights are being violated—regardless of your source of income.

Examples of violations include problems in these areas:

Housing

- Being evicted for inability to pay rent or arbitrary decision of landlord.
- Diseases, family break-up, violence, etc., in homeless shelters.
- Injuries, death, or suicide resulting from being forced to live on the streets, in cars, or in other dangerous circumstances.
- Police brutality and imprisonment for being homeless.

Housing and utilities

- House fires resulting from faulty wiring, crowding, use of kerosene because of gas being shut off, lack of smoke alarms, children left alone, unsafe conditions in the house, etc.
- Injuries, death, or homelessness caused by unsafe or structurally unsound housing situations, or fires.
- Injury or death resulting from lack of heat or proper ventilation.
- Injury, death, or homelessness from gas, water, or electricity being shut off.
- Denial of civil rights to, and unfair intervention of, public housing residents.

Health and nutrition

- Injuries and death related to lack of proper medical care or being cut off of medical care.
- Malnutrition or hunger.
- Lack of proper clothing or other protection against the weather.
- Emotional or physical injury/illness related to lack of decent food, clothing, housing, medical care, and other basic necessities.
- Illnesses and deaths related to living in a polluted environment (i.e., asthma, lead poisoning, proximity to toxic waste or polluted air, etc.).

Emotional stress

- Women and children being forced to stay with an abuser because of lack of economic options.
- Suicide resulting from being cut off of public assistance, desperation caused by poverty, or lack of mental health care.
- Child abuse resulting from parental stress due to economic circumstances.
- Denial of mental health care.

Abuses against children

- Harm done to children from lack of decent, safe childcare.
- Mothers having to leave children alone to work or because of inability to pay for childcare.
- Childhood accidents caused by lack of childcare or a decent play area or supervision at school or by hazards in the house or school caused by landlord or city neglect.
- Children having to work to support the family.

The right to security in the event of unemployment

You must be given assistance by the government whenever, for whatever reason, you are not getting enough income for yourself or your family to get by. In fact welfare and disability payments (and often social security) that do not pay at least more than the poverty level are violations of your rights even if you can access them. No state has welfare paymernts at the federal poverty level (frequently disability and social security payments are not) and if this is your source of income, your economic rights are being violated.

- Welfare policies or practices that deny aid based on immigrant status, family background, paternity, or time on welfare
- Welfare reform that takes away guarantee of assistance in time of unemployment, or that calls for unnecessary, inhumane, or humiliating requirements for getting assistance.
- Loss of benefits because of the welfare department's mistake, lack of communication, arbitrary decision of a caseworker, or recipient's lack of knowledge of rights.
- Being forced to sign an impossible and invasive contract to get benefits.

Article 25: (2) Protection of mothers and children, regardless of birth status

Any way in which you as a woman are denied access to needed resources, especially when you are working to raise and/or support children, is a violation.

Examples of specific violations include the following:

- Denial of aid because paternity cannot be proven, because of birth status of child or age of parents.
- Welfare cuts that target single mothers and children.
- Women being forced to work in jobs that do not support their families and that endanger their health, safety, and well-being and that of their children.

- Women and children being forced to identify their abusers to get welfare.
- Women and children having to stay with abusers because they can't get welfare or don't have money to leave.
- Women having to leave their children alone or in unsafe conditions to get a job.

Article 26: Right to education

"Everyone has the right to education."

You and your children have the right to all levels of education of your choice as long as you or they have the skills to be admitted regardless of availability of facilities or income.

Examples of violations include the following:

- Welfare recipients being forced to leave school, job training, language classes, or GED training to go to work, because of lack of child care or because of arbitrary decision of caseworker.
- Children having to leave school to work to support family or to care for siblings.
- Children missing school or being unable to learn because of homelessness or malnutrition or because of other circumstances listed above.
- University costs and financial aid cuts burdening students with great debt or making higher education inaccessible for financial reasons.
- LGBT, elderly, people with disabilities (including traumatic brain injury), military, prisoners, undocumented immigrants. Giving lots of open-ended specific questions.

Finally, think about your role as a social worker in this assessment and how that may affect how the questions are understood or perceived.

An Empowering, Strengths-Based Psychosocial Assessment and Intervention Planning Outline for Children and Families in the Global Environment

By Nora Smith

Edited by Rosemary Barbera, LaSalle University, 2013

1. **Identifying Information**
2. **Reason for Referral/Presenting Concern**
   A. Referral Source
   B. Summary of the Presenting Concern
   C. Summary of Strengths and Resources (Actual and Potential)
   D. Impact of the Presenting Issues Challenges
3. **Person(s) in Client Status and Family Description and Functioning**
4. **Relevant History**
   A. Family of Origin History/Family of Choice History
   B. Relevant Developmental History
   C. Family of Creation History
   D. Educational and Occupational History
   E. Religious (Spiritual) Development
   F. Social Relationships
   G. Dating/Marital/Sexual Relations
   H. Medical/Psychological Health
   I. Legal
   J. Environmental Conditions
   K. Human Rights Issues That May Impact the Situation
5. **Collaborative Assessment between Worker and Person in Client Status (See Appendix)**
6. **Intervention Plan (See Appendix for Template)**

An intervention plan may also be referred to in your agency as a "treatment plan." The term intervention is preferable for a variety of reasons. Treatment is reflective of a medical model of understanding personal difficulties that is not consistent with the social work person in environment perspective. A medical model of understanding typically views the presenting concern as occurring within the individual; a person in environment perspective reflects on presenting concerns as a function of interrelated forces in an individual's environment. The term intervention also speaks to reflecting on intervening in the structural forces that may be helping or hindering the individual in being able to take meaningful steps at resolving their current challenge.

Please see the details below to guide your writing within each area.

1. Identifying Information

This section should include such information as age, sex, gender, race, religion, relationship status, occupation, living situation, sexual orientation, children, etc. Information should be factual, based on information from the Person(s) in Client Status, collateral contacts, and case records.

2. Reason for Referral/Presenting Concern

This section should identify the referral source and give a summary of the reason for the referral. This should include the 'Person(s) in Client Status' description of the concern or services needed including the duration of the concern and its consequences for the persons involved. Past intervention history by the individual, the family, or an agency or related to the presenting concern should also be summarized.

In addition, comment on any of the following areas that have been **impacted** by the presenting concern as reported by the person in client status as well as the referral source (if different). You should also include a discussion of how various systems have impacted the person in client status/organization:

- family situation
- physical and economic environment
- educational/occupational history
- physical well-being/health
- relevant cultural, racial, religious, sexual orientation, and cohort factors
- current social/sexual/emotional relationships
- legal involvement
- How has the person in client status/organization used internal and external resources to face challenges/concerns in the past?

3. Person(s)/Family in Client Status Description and Observations

Understand that at times the family, not an individual person, is in client status. Think about how you will broaden the questions and topic areas to be inclusive of the family as the unit.

In this section be sure to cover different family forms—family of creation, family of experience (e.g., through adoption), and family of choice, for example.

This section should contain data **observed** by the worker. That said, this section is not to contain opinions. It is to be as objective as possible. It is important, however, to note how these observations might be influenced by the worker's personal experiences and biases. Keep in mind also that the circumstances of the person may impact the following areas in a variety of ways. For example, does the individual come right to the appointment from working a long shift? Could that have led to a tired-looking appearance? What is the person's economic means? Could that impact dress or appearance? What experiences has the individual had prior with social workers/social services that may impact their receptiveness to services (defensiveness, etc.).

Ideally, this information should be collected from the first few interviews with the person; some practice settings though may require this assessment occur after just one interview, typically an intake. If that is the case, note in this section that the information was collected from one in-person meeting.

In this section, include pertinent and objective information about:

- The Person(s) in Client Status' physical appearance (dress, grooming, striking features);
- Communication styles and abilities or challenges;
- Thought processes (memory, intelligence, clarity of thought, mental status, etc.);
- Expressive overt behaviors (mannerisms, speech patterns, etc.);
- Reports from professionals or family (medical, psychological, legal); and
- Mental status exam (if appropriate).

4. Relevant History

This section should discuss past history as it relates to the presenting issue. While this section should be as factual as possible, it is the place to present how the specifics of the Person(s) in Client Status' culture, race, religion, or sexual orientation, for example, affect resolution of the presenting concern(s). How might perceptions affect the situation (see above)? Additionally, keep in mind that what the social worker may think is not accurate may have significant impact on a person/organization. Some things, like institutionalized discrimination, may not be directly at play, but certainly may indirectly affect the situation and a person/organization's experience of the situation.

Include applicable information about each of the following major areas or about related areas relevant to the person in client status/organization (you are not limited by the outline below):

A. Family of Creation/Family of Choice/Family of Experience History: Family composition; birth order; where and with whom reared; relationship with parents or guardian; relationships with siblings; abuse or other trauma; significant family events (births, deaths, divorce, separations, moves, etc.) and their effect on the Person(s) in Client Status. Is the Family of Origin History different from the Family of Experience History? For example, was the person raised by/with original (birth) family members or with individuals not related by birth? If Family of Birth and Family of Experience differ, what is the relationship with/knowledge of birth family members?

B. Relevant Developmental History: Were there any medical problems/conditions at birth or problems around the birth process; developmental milestones including mobility (crawling, walking, coordination); speech; toilet training; eating or sleeping problems; developmental delays or gifted areas; positive experiences such as relationships. This section is especially important for Persons in Client Status who are children. It is critical to identify non-Western expectations and practices for child rearing and development for clients from diverse backgrounds as applicable. When noting successes and struggles with developmental milestones, bear in mind that traditional theories often negate the complexity and cultural meaning ascribed to the developmental process. Note here also the nature of stresses and experiences the Person(s) in Client Status has encountered throughout his/her life in relation to the ability to handle them.

C. Family of Creation/Experience/Choice Interrelationships: Interacting roles within the family (e.g., who makes the decisions, handles the money, disciplines the children, does the marketing); typical family issues (e.g., disagreements, disappointments, rituals, celebrations), social networks or family of choice, which is particularly relevant for LGBT persons.

D. Educational and Occupational History: Level of education attained; school performance; learning problems, difficulties; areas of achievement; peer relationships. Skills and training; type of employment; employment history; adequacy of wage earning ability; quality of work performance; relationship with authority figures and coworkers.

E. Religious and/or Spiritual Development: Importance of religion in upbringing; affinity for religious and/or spiritual thought or activity; involvement in religious activities; positive or negative experiences.

F. Social Relationships: Size and quality of social network; ability to sustain friendships; pertinent social role losses or gains; social role performance within the client's cultural context. Historical patterns of familial and social relationships.

G. Intimate Relationships: Type and quality of relationships; relevant sexual history; ability to sustain intimate (sexual and nonsexual) contact; significant losses; traumas; conflicts in intimate relationships; way of dealing with losses or conflicts. Currently, where do problems exist and where does the client manage successfully? Positive relationships and/or positive elements of relationships?

H. Health: including drug, alcohol, or tobacco use or misuse; medications; accidents; disabilities; emotional difficulties including mental illness; psychological reports; hospitalizations; impact on functioning; use of previous counseling help; break down; medical/psychological/substance abuse.

I. Legal: Juvenile or adult contact with legal authorities; type of problem(s}; jail or prison sentence; effects of rehabilitation or lack of access to truly rehabilitative services within and without the criminal justice system; effects of the prison system.

J. Environmental Conditions: Urban or rural; length of time in the current living environment; living arrangement history; economic and class structure of the neighborhood in relation to that of the client; description of the home.

K. Human Rights Issues: In this section note how any of the following human rights issues may have been part of the person in client status' life experience and how they may impact the presenting concern. Bear in mind the below should occur as a discussion with the person in client status and should focus on their perceptions of how the below issues may have impacted their experience and presenting concern. The wording in italics is information you can share with the individual as examples of how these issues are human rights versus personal needs.

Article 16.

"Men and women of full age, without any limitation due to race, nationality or religion, have the right to marry and to found a family. They are entitled to equal rights as to marriage, during marriage and at its dissolution."

The denial of marriage equality for lesbian and gay persons creates unequal intervention under the law and undue financial hardships due to inequality in access to spousal benefits and issues with inheritance taxes. Additionally the denial of marriage equality creates issues regarding access to partners when hospitalized and decision-making powers regarding medical intervention.

Article 23: The right to jobs at a living wage and just conditions of work

"Everyone has the right to work, to free choice of employment, to just and favorable conditions of work and to protection against unemployment . . . Everyone who works has the right to just and favorable remuneration ensuring for himself and his family an existence worthy of human dignity, and supplemented, if necessary, by other means of social protection . . . Everyone has the right to form and to join trade unions."

Your government is supposed to ensure that you can have a job of your choice that is safe, pays enough to live on, and does not infringe on your civil rights, including your right to be part of a union to protect your rights as a worker.

Article 25: (1) The right to well-being of a person and his/her family, including food, clothing, housing, health care, and necessary social services

"Everyone has the right to a standard of living adequate for the health and well-being of himself and of his family, including food, clothing, housing and medical care and necessary social services, and the right to security in the event of unemployment, sickness, disability, widowhood, old age or other lack of livelihood in circumstances beyond his control. Motherhood and childhood are entitled to special protection."

The government has to ensure that every resident has enough money to provide all the basics for living. If you live below a recognized standard of income and other resources, your human rights are being violated—regardless of your source of income.

You must be given assistance by the government whenever for whatever reason you are not getting enough income for yourself or your family to get by. In fact welfare and disability payments (and often social security) that do not pay at least more than the poverty level are violations of your rights even if you can access them. No state has welfare payments at the federal poverty levels (frequently disability and social security payments are not) and if this is your source of income, your economic rights are being violated.

Article 25 (2) Protection of mothers and children, regardless of birth status.

Any way in which you as a woman are denied access to needed resources, especially when you are working to raise and/or support children, is a violation.

Article 26: Right to education

"Everyone has the right to education . . ."

You and your children have the right to all levels of education of your choice as long as you or they have the skills to be admitted regardless of availability of facilities or income.

5. Collaborative Assessment between Worker and Person in Client Status

This section should contain the thoughts and opinion of the consulting social worker in conjunction with the perspectives, views, and understanding as articulated by the Person in Client Status. It is based on initial observations and information gathering efforts that have occurred in discussion with the person in client status; however, it takes the observations and information to a new level. Here, the worker and the person in client status integrate his or her view with an understanding of the person in client status situation, its underlying causes and/or contributing factors, and the prognosis for change.

As appropriate, the following factors should be included in this section.

Social emotional functioning—ability to express feelings, ability to form relationships, predominant mood or emotional pattern (e.g., optimism, pessimism, anxiety, temperament, characteristic traits, overall role performance and social competence, motivation and commitment to intervention)

Psychological factors—reality testing, impulse control, judgment, insight, memory or recall, coping style and problem-solving ability, characteristic defense mechanisms, notable problems. If applicable, include a formal diagnosis (e.g., DSM-V, International Classification of Diseases, etc.)

Environmental issues and constraints or supports from the family, agency, community that affect the situation and its resolution. What does the environment offer for improved functioning (family, friends, church, school, work, clubs, groups, politics, leisure-time activities).

Issues related to cultural or other diversity that offer constraints or supports from the family, agency, community that affect the situation and its resolution.

- Strengths and areas for change in relation to Needs/Demands/Constraints in which the person functions
- Capacities and skills
- Meaningful access to opportunities to achieve personal capabilities
- Activity patterns

- Ways of communicating
- Perceptions of him/herself and others
- How energy is invested
- What disturbs or satisfies him or her
- Capacity for empathy and affection
- Affects and moods
- Control vs. impulsivity
- Spontaneity vs. inhibition
- Handling of sexuality and aggressiveness; dependency needs, self-esteem and anxiety
- Attitudes toward authority, peers and others
- Nature of defenses
- Method and ability to solve issue/challenge and build on strengths and capacities
- The impact of structural constraints on the presenting concern

Conclude the assessment with a statement about the person in client status' motivation for help, the agency's ability to provide help, resources in addition to the agency that may be necessary to resolve the presenting concern (including relevant organizations that may impact the larger structural concerns) and anticipated outcome of services to be provided.

6. Intervention Plan

This section should map out a realistic intervention strategy to address the situation and the assessment of the factors that underlie it. The development of this plan must be guided by the understanding and perspectives of the person in client status. Below you will find a model to organize this plan. This plan should include:

- Concern(s) chosen for intervention
- Goals and objectives
- How worker will connect the person to organizations/movements working for change in areas that impact her/his life.
- How the person in client status, with the worker's and a social organization's help, will achieve these goals
- The worker's role in the interventions

- The anticipated time frame (e.g., frequency of meetings, duration of the intervention)
- Potential factors that may affect goal achievement (including motivation; willingness to engage in change activities; personal and cultural resources; and/or personal abilities or limitations; agency resources or limitations; community resources of limitations). Whose motivation? Here we have to think about noncompliant social workers, as Finn and Jacobson say.
- Method(s) by which goal achievement will be evaluated.

Intervention plan

Area(s) of Concern	Goal	Objectives	Responsibilities: Who?	Time Frame	Evaluation Procedure
		Anticipated Strengths:			
		Anticipated Obstacles:			
		Anticipated Strengths:			
		Anticipated Obstacles:			

You may also wish to state whether further exploration is needed, whether you plan to refer the person in client status/organization to another agency or source of help instead of or in addition to your agency's help.

Appendix E
Process Recording for Individuals and/or Families
Monmouth University

Process recordings offer you the opportunity to revisit interviews you have completed and analyze them in retrospect. They are opportunities to examine your interactions with persons in client status, get feedback from your supervisor and instructor, and address any feelings (*yours*) that may have surfaced during the interview. Therefore, *you are addressing and examining both the content and the process of the interaction with others.*

Format:

1. Cover page should include your name and the date of the interview.

   a. Setting—agency context; describe place (office, classroom, playground, home etc.)

   b. Background of person in client status (be sure to change any identifying characteristics to maintain the anonymity of the person). You want to include the general age of the person(s), gender, race, and any other information that you think useful, without disclosing their identity! How well do you know this person, etc.

   c. Purpose of interview—You are seeing the person in client status for some professional reason.

2. Re-create up to fifteen minutes of the interview. You should do this as soon after the actual interview as possible and be as precise in terms of the verbal and nonverbal communication as possible.

Content/Dialogue	Skills Used	Workers Awareness	Analysis through a Theoretical Lens	Supervisor's Comments
Include all verbal and nonverbal interaction—including interruptions or other unplanned events as well as beginnings and endings. Include other people if relevant. This should be dialogue; i.e., Worker: Good morning Ms. Person: Hello	Identification of the skills you are using	Focus on your feelings—not your thoughts or intellectual fancy—what are you feeling? Are you nervous? Relaxed? Disgusted? Upset? Happy? Relieved? Angry? This is your unspoken thoughts and reactions to person and interview as it takes place. Be honest!!! feel_____ because_____	What theoretical orientation guided your work? Give an example. How did you apply the theory or how did you attempt to apply the theory? You should also identify relevant social work values and/or ethical principles.	

3. Summarize parts not included above.

4. <u>Evaluation and impressions (1.5–2 pages minimum).</u>

   a. What was your overall impression of the interview?

   b. Were goals/objectives accomplished?

   c. What knowledge and skills did you make use of? Include issues such as: use of values, professional ethics, diversity, strengths, attending skills, active listening, use of questions, clarifying, summarizing, observing and reflecting feelings, pitfalls or barriers to communication. You need not have used all these skills but where COULD they have been applied in retrospect? Expand on issues identified in analysis section that identify the skill(s) that was applied.

   d. What would you have done differently and where?

5. <u>Other</u>

   a. Remember, the focus is on the worker, not the person, so it's more important to remember what you said than what the other person said.

   b. You may summarize parts in dialogue not important in looking at worker's skills.

   c. Perfect practice is NOT expected. We learn from our mistakes—so we can make more sophisticated mistakes!

   d. Proofread your paper. Professional grammar and spelling are expected.

Appendix F
UN Declaration of Human Rights

PREAMBLE

Whereas recognition of the inherent dignity and of the equal and inalienable rights of all members of the human family is the foundation of freedom, justice and peace in the world,

Whereas disregard and contempt for human rights have resulted in barbarous acts which have outraged the conscience of mankind, and the advent of a world in which human beings shall enjoy freedom of speech and belief and freedom from fear and want has been proclaimed as the highest aspiration of the common people,

Whereas it is essential, if man is not to be compelled to have recourse, as a last resort, to rebellion against tyranny and oppression, that human rights should be protected by the rule of law,

Whereas it is essential to promote the development of friendly relations between nations,

Whereas the peoples of the United Nations have in the Charter reaffirmed their faith in fundamental human rights, in the dignity and worth of the human person and in the equal rights of men and women and have determined to promote social progress and better standards of life in larger freedom,

Whereas Member States have pledged themselves to achieve, in co-operation with the United Nations, the promotion of universal respect for and observance of human rights and fundamental freedoms,

Whereas a common understanding of these rights and freedoms is of the greatest importance for the full realization of this pledge,

Now, Therefore THE GENERAL ASSEMBLY proclaims THIS UNIVERSAL DECLARATION OF HUMAN RIGHTS as a common standard of achievement for all peoples and all nations, to the end that every individual and every organ of society, keeping this Declaration constantly in mind, shall strive by teaching and education to promote respect for these rights and freedoms and by progressive measures, national and international, to secure their universal and effective recognition and observance, both among the peoples of Member States themselves and among the peoples of territories under their jurisdiction.

Article 1.

- All human beings are born free and equal in dignity and rights. They are endowed with reason and conscience and should act towards one another in a spirit of brotherhood.

Article 2.

- Everyone is entitled to all the rights and freedoms set forth in this Declaration, without distinction of any kind, such as race, colour, sex, language, religion, political or other opinion, national or social origin, property, birth or other status. Furthermore, no distinction shall be made on the basis of the political, jurisdictional or international status of the country or territory to which a person belongs, whether it be independent, trust, non-self-governing or under any other limitation of sovereignty.

Article 3.

- Everyone has the right to life, liberty and security of person.

Article 4.

- No one shall be held in slavery or servitude; slavery and the slave trade shall be prohibited in all their forms.

Article 5.

- No one shall be subjected to torture or to cruel, inhuman or degrading treatment or punishment.

Article 6.

- Everyone has the right to recognition everywhere as a person before the law.

Article 7.

- All are equal before the law and are entitled without any discrimination to equal protection of the law. All are entitled to equal protection against any discrimination in violation of this Declaration and against any incitement to such discrimination.

Article 8.

- Everyone has the right to an effective remedy by the competent national tribunals for acts violating the fundamental rights granted him by the constitution or by law.

Article 9.

- No one shall be subjected to arbitrary arrest, detention or exile.

Article 10.

- Everyone is entitled in full equality to a fair and public hearing by an independent and impartial tribunal, in the determination of his rights and obligations and of any criminal charge against him.

Article 11.

- (1) Everyone charged with a penal offence has the right to be presumed innocent until proved guilty according to law in a public trial at which he has had all the guarantees necessary for his defence.
- (2) No one shall be held guilty of any penal offence on account of any act or omission which did not constitute a penal offence, under national or international law, at the time when it was committed. Nor shall a heavier penalty be imposed than the one that was applicable at the time the penal offence was committed.

Article 12.

- No one shall be subjected to arbitrary interference with his privacy, family, home or correspondence, nor to attacks upon his honour and reputation. Everyone has the right to the protection of the law against such interference or attacks.

Article 13.

- (1) Everyone has the right to freedom of movement and residence within the borders of each state.
- (2) Everyone has the right to leave any country, including his own, and to return to his country.

Article 14.

- (1) Everyone has the right to seek and to enjoy in other countries asylum from persecution.
- (2) This right may not be invoked in the case of prosecutions genuinely arising from non-political crimes or from acts contrary to the purposes and principles ofthe United Nations.

Article 15.

- (1) Everyone has the right to a nationality.
- (2) No one shall be arbitrarily deprived of his nationality nor denied the right to change his nationality.

Article 16.

- (1) Men and women of full age, without any limitation due to race, nationality or religion, have the right to marry and to found a family. They are entitled to equal rights as to marriage, during marriage and at its dissolution.
- (2) Marriage shall be entered into only with the free and full consent ofthe intending spouses.
- (3) The family is the natural and fundamental group unit of society and is entitled to protection by society and the State.

Article 17.

- (1) Everyone has the right to own property alone as well as in association with others.
- (2) No one shall be arbitrarily deprived of his property.

Article 18.

- Everyone has the right to freedom of thought, conscience and religion; this right includes freedom to change his religion or belief, and freedom, either alone or in community with others and in public or private, to manifest his religion or belief in teaching, practice, worship and observance.

Article 19.

- Everyone has the right to freedom of opinion and expression; this right includes freedom to hold opinions without interference and to seek, receive and impart information and ideas through any media and regardless of frontiers.

Article 20.

- (1) Everyone has the right to freedom of peaceful assembly and association.
- (2) No one may be compelled to belong to an association.

Article 21.

- (1) Everyone has the right to take part in the government of his country, directly or through freely chosen representatives.
- (2) Everyone has the right of equal access to public service in his country.
- (3) The will of the people shall be the basis of the authority of government; this will shall be expressed in periodic and genuine elections which shall be by universal and equal suffrage and shall be held by secret vote or by equivalent free voting procedures.

Article 22.

- Everyone, as a member of society, has the right to social security and is entitled to realization, through national effort and international co-operation and in accordance with the organization and resources of each State, of the economic, social and cultural rights indispensable for his dignity and the free development of his personality.

Article 23.

- (1) Everyone has the right to work, to free choice of employment, to just and favourable conditions of work and to protection against unemployment.
- (2) Everyone, without any discrimination, has the right to equal pay for equal work.
- (3) Everyone who works has the right to just and favourable remuneration ensuring for himself and his family an existence worthy of human dignity, and supplemented, if necessary, by other means of social protection.
- (4) Everyone has the right to form and to join trade unions for the pro-tection of his interests.

Article 24.

- Everyone has the right to rest and leisure, including reasonable limitation of working hours and periodic holidays with pay.

Article 25.

- (1) Everyone has the right to a standard of living adequate for the health and well-being of himself and of his family, including food, clothing, housing and medical care and necessary social services, and the right to security in the event of unemployment, sickness, disability, widowhood, old age or other lack of livelihood in circumstances beyond his control.
- (2) Motherhood and childhood are entitled to special care and assistance. All children, whether born in or out of wedlock, shall enjoy the same social protection.

Article 26.

- (1) Everyone has the right to education. Education shall be free, at least in the elementary and fundamental stages. Elementary education shall be compulsory. Technical and professional education shall be made generally available and higher education shall be equally accessible to all on the basis of merit.

- (2) Education shall be directed to the full development of the human personality and to the strengthening of respect for human rights and fundamental freedoms. It shall promote understanding, tolerance and friendship among all nations, racial or religious groups, and shall further the activities of the United Nations for the maintenance of peace.
- (3) Parents have a prior right to choose the kind of education that shall be given to their children.

Article 27.

- (1) Everyone has the right freely to participate in the cultural life of the community, to enjoy the arts and to share in scientific advancement and its benefits.
- (2) Everyone has the right to the protection of the moral and material interests resulting from any scientific, literary or artistic production of which he is the author.

Article 28.

- Everyone is entitled to a social and international order in which the rights and freedoms set forth in this Declaration can be fully realized.

Article 29.

- (1) Everyone has duties to the community in which alone the free and full development of his personality is possible.
- (2) In the exercise of his rights and freedoms, everyone shall be subject only to such limitations as are determined by law solely for the purpose of securing due recognition and respect for the rights and freedoms of others and of meeting the just requirements of morality, public order and the general welfare in a democratic society.
- (3) These rights and freedoms may in no case be exercised contrary to the purposes and principles of the United Nations.

Article 30.

- Nothing in this Declaration may be interpreted as implying for any State, group or person any right to engage in any activity or to perform any act aimed at the destruction of any of the rights and freedoms set forth herein.

Appendix G
Safety and Health Checklist for Home Visits

Social workers go to homes of the people they are working with for a few different purposes.

1. School social workers often go to the home when a child is first being considered for special education services. This home visit is meant to obtain particular information regarding the child's home life including birth and developmental milestones, the dynamics in the home, and the initial family assessment.

2. Adoption social workers go to family homes several times for the home study, checking safety and health concerns that may get in the way of a successful placement. Home studies continue after placement of the child until the adoption is finalized. Social workers' responsibilities also include looking through the house for safety and health concerns, pointing the issues out to the new parents so they have opportunity to correct the situation before the child arrives.

3. Social workers who work for in-home therapy programs or wrap-around services schedule home visits for the purpose of working on issues identified during the family's initial assessments or from the referral source. On this visit while social workers must be keenly observant and point out any safety or health issue, their main focus is to engage the family in treatment to improve the initial reason for the referral.

4. Social workers who work for child protection have the most difficult job. They are there to investigate a report of abuse or neglect. Their job is to tactfully, thoroughly, and supportively examine the house for safety and health issues while interviewing all the family members in the house regarding the report.

The following are the guidelines of what to look for in general:

✔ Insects and rodents—There must be no visible evidence of insect or rodent infestation.

✔ Utilities—Hot and cold running water must be available as well as electricity. At minimum one working toilet and one bath/shower is available.

✔ Garbage—Garbage should be kept covered .

✔ <u>Fire safety</u>—Houses should have carbon monoxide and smoke detectors as well as one fire extinguisher.

✔ <u>Appliances</u>—house needs a working refrigerator and stove.

✔ <u>Dangerous implements/substances</u>—Firearms and other weapons need to be stored in a locked area out of the reach of children. Poisons, drugs, and dangerous cleaning supplies likewise are labeled and stored out of the reach of children.

✔ <u>Alcoholic beverages</u>—are stored in an area inaccessible to children.

✔ <u>Tobacco and paraphernalia</u>—keep them safe in areas that cannot catch fire like near stoves or grills. Don't smoke in bed for fear of falling asleep while smoking.

✔ <u>Medicine</u>—but especially prescription medication—is stored in areas inaccessible to children.

✔ <u>Climate control</u>—Windows ought to allow for adequate ventilation. Doors and windows used for ventilation must have screening. The temperature in the living areas ought not to jeopardize the health of occupants.

✔ <u>Paint</u>—Paint must not be flaking, peeling, chipped.

✔ The house must be generally clean, in good repair, and reasonably free of clutter that would present a hazard.

✔ The land, including the outdoor play area, must be free of standing surface water.

✔ All cleaning supplies, insecticides, fuel, etc., that are flammable and/or poisonous and dangerous need to be stored in areas not accessible to children under the age of ten or with special needs and kept at least three feet away from boilers, heaters, etc.

✔ Houses caring for toddlers have childproof locks and other safety devices on cupboards, drawers, and electrical outlets, and gates for stairs and rooms that are not childproof.

✔ When basements and attics are used for bedroom occupancy, state standards and local laws are to be followed:

- look for two exits, one of which is a working window or door leading directly outside;

- walls, ceiling, and floors must be finished;

- a window has to open in for ventilation; and

- room should meet regulated room size.

Appendix H

The Genogram Format for Mapping Family Systems

PDF E-Book

By Monica McGoldrick

The genogram has been established as a practical framework for mapping and understanding family patterns. The word "genogram" is just a fancy term for a family tree that maps out who you belong to and some basic patterns of these belonging relationships. It is a language that has been established over the past 50 years to depict for clinicians some of the basic demographic, functioning, and relationship issues in families. Genograms include biological and legal members of a family but also pets, friends, and other kinship relationships.

Genograms map out the basic biological and legal structure of the family—who was married to whom, the names of their children, and so on. Just as important, they can show key facts about individuals and the relationships of family members. For example, one can note the highest school grade completed, a serious childhood illness, or an overly close or distant relationship. The facts symbolized on the genogram also offer clues about the family's secrets and mythology, since families tend to obscure what is painful or embarrassing in their history.

A genogram includes multiple types of family information: the basic facts: who is in the family, the dates of their births, marriages, moves, illness, deaths; information regarding the primary characteristics and level of functioning of different family members: education, occupation, psychological and physical health, out standing attributes, talents, successes and failures; relationship patterns in the family: closeness, conflict, or cut off. Once the primary family information is indicated on the genogram, it is possible to examine it from the multiple perspectives of all family members. One genogram might emphasize the relationship patterns in a family, another might highlight the artistic patterns, another the patterns of illness, and so forth. A genogram is generally drawn from the point of view of a key person or nuclear family, going back in time at least two generations and forward to the children and grandchildren of the key person or people. Other genograms may be drawn to show in detail various branches of the family or aspects of their functioning and relationship.

This standardized Genogram format is becoming a common language for tracking family history and relationships. Despite the widespread use of genograms by family therapists, family physicians, and other health care providers, prior to the first edition of *Genograms: Assessment & Intervention* in 1985, there was no generally agreed-upon format for a genogram. Even among clinicians with similar theoretical orientations, there was only a loose consensus about what specific information to seek, how to record it, and what it all meant. The standardized genogram format offered here was worked out in the early 1980's by a committee of leading proponents of genograms from family therapy and family medicine, including such key people as Dr. Murray Bowen, Dr. Jack Froom, and Dr. Jack Medalie. They became part of a committee organized by the North American Primary Care Research Group to define the most practical genogram symbols and agree on a standardized format. Since the format was originally published in 1985, there have been a number of modifications recommended by different groups around the world. We see this format as a work in progress, Expanded use of genograms will undoubtedly extend the format further. For example, computers have led us to begin development of standard color coding for names, location, occupation, illnesses, etc. The symbols will surely be further modified in the future as they have been modified over the years.

Genograms record information about family members and their relationships over at least three generations. They display family information graphically in a way that provides a quick gestalt of complex family patterns; as such they are a rich source of hypotheses about how clinical problems evolve in the context of the family over time.

Once you master this format you will want to learn the interpretive principles upon which genograms are based (see *Genograms: Assessment and Intervention*, W. W. Norton, 2008), and possibilities for software, which can record genogram information and store it for retrieval for research purposes. In our view the symbols make genograms the best shorthand language for mapping and summarizing family information and describing family patterns.

Genograms allow you to map the family structure clearly and to note and update the map of family patterns of relationships and functioning as they emerge in a clinical session. For a clinical record, the genogram provides an efficient summary, allowing a person unfamiliar with a case to grasp quickly a huge amount of information about a family and to scan for potential problems and resources. While notes written in a chart or questionnaire may become lost in the mass of information, genograms are immediately recognizable and can be expanded and corrected at each clinical visit as one learns more about a family. They can be created for any moment in the family's history—showing the ages and relationships of that moment to better understand family patterns as they evolve through time.

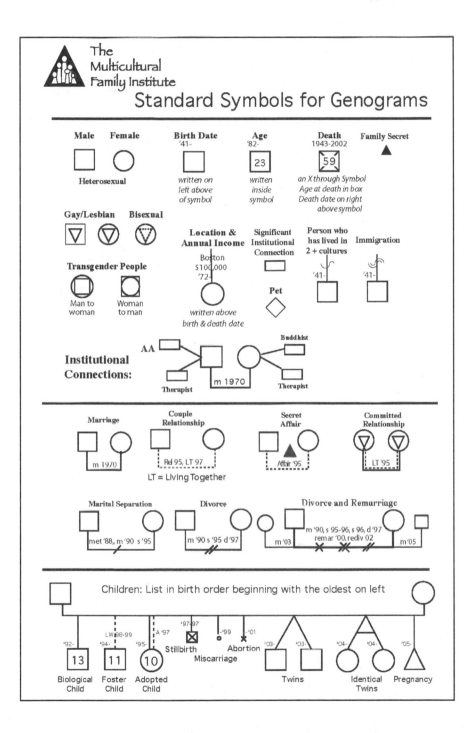

Symbols Denoting Addiction, and Physical or Mental Illness

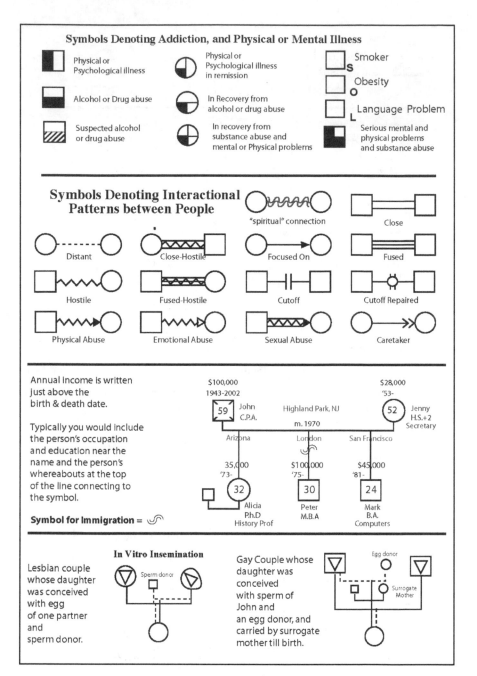

Physical or Psychological illness

Physical or Psychological illness in remission

Smoker

Alcohol or Drug abuse

In Recovery from alcohol or drug abuse

Obesity

Suspected alcohol or drug abuse

In recovery from substance abuse and mental or Physical problems

Language Problem

Serious mental and physical problems and substance abuse

Symbols Denoting Interactional Patterns between People

"spiritual" connection

Close

Distant

Close-Hostile

Focused On

Fused

Hostile

Fused-Hostile

Cutoff

Cutoff Repaired

Physical Abuse

Emotional Abuse

Sexual Abuse

Caretaker

Annual income is written just above the birth & death date.

Typically you would include the person's occupation and education near the name and the person's whereabouts at the top of the line connecting to the symbol.

Symbol for Immigration =

$100,000
1943-2002

59 John C.P.A.

Highland Park, NJ
m. 1970

$28,000
'53-

52 Jenny H.S.+2 Secretary

Arizona

London

San Francisco

35,000
'73-

32

Alicia
Ph.D
History Prof

$100,000
'75-

30

Peter
M.B.A

$45,000
'81-

24

Mark
B.A.
Computers

In Vitro Insemination

Lesbian couple whose daughter was conceived with egg of one partner and sperm donor.

Sperm donor

Gay Couple whose daughter was conceived with sperm of John and an egg donor, and carried by surrogate mother till birth.

Egg donor

Surrogate Mother

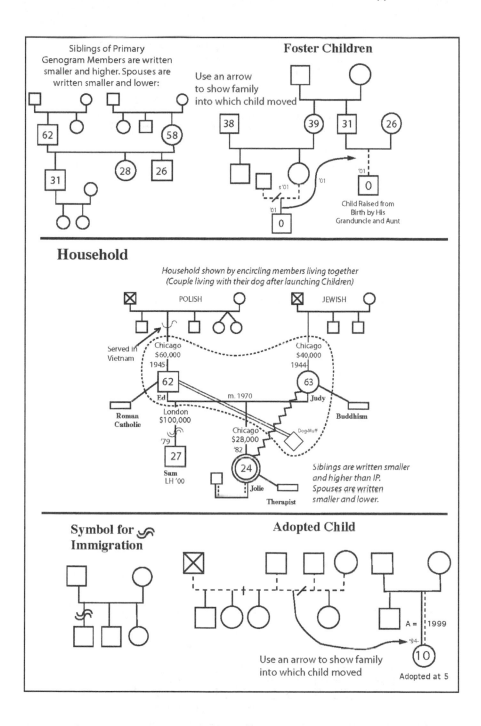

Siblings of Primary Genogram Members are written smaller and higher. Spouses are written smaller and lower:

Foster Children

Use an arrow to show family into which child moved

Child Raised from Birth by His Granduncle and Aunt

Household

Household shown by encircling members living together
(Couple living with their dog after launching Children)

POLISH

JEWISH

Served in Vietnam

Chicago
$60,000
1945

Chicago
$40,000
1944

Ed

m. 1970

Judy

Roman Catholic

London
$100,000

Buddhism

Chicago
$28,000

Dog-Muff

Sam
LH '00

Jolie

Therapist

Siblings are written smaller and higher than IP. Spouses are written smaller and lower.

Symbol for Immigration

Adopted Child

A = 1999

Use an arrow to show family into which child moved

Adopted at 5

1 Husband, His Current Wife and his Ex-Wives (who are shown lower and smaller). Husband's wives may go on left to be closest to him. Indicators "1st," "2nd" etc. make clear the order of his marriages.

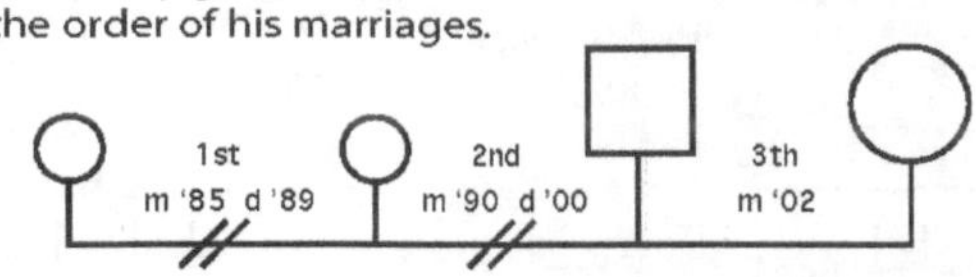

1st m '85 d '89 2nd m '90 d '00 3th m '02

2 Wife, Her Current Husband and her Ex-Husbands (who are shown lower and smaller). Wife's previous relationships are shown on left to keep children in birth order, since they remained in her custody.

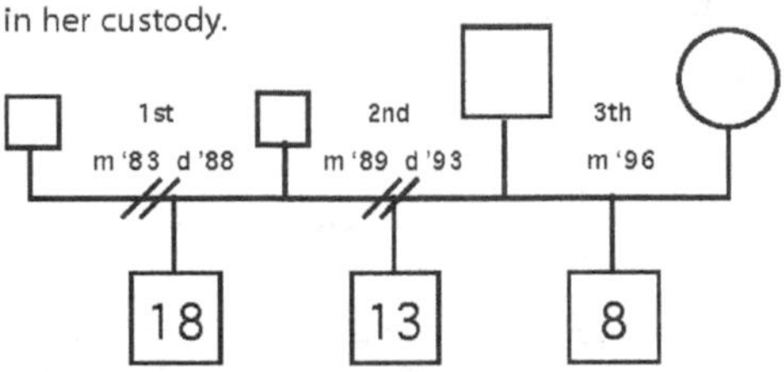

1st m '83 d '88 2nd m '89 d '93 3th m '96

18 13 8

3 Couple with 3 year old, showing their previous spouses (smaller) and those spouses' new partners (even smaller)

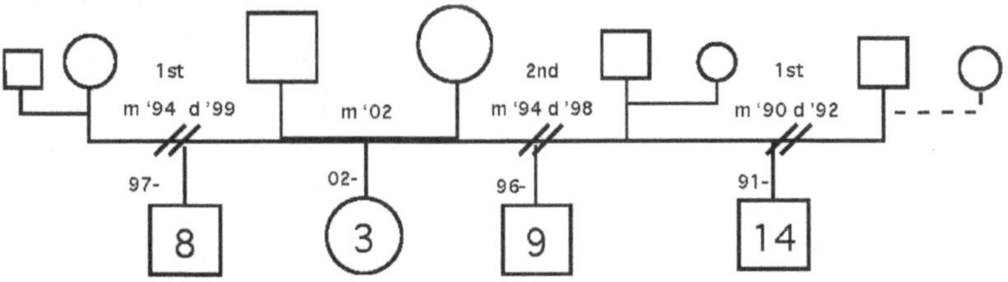

1st m '94 d '99 m '02 2nd m '94 d '98 1st m '90 d '92

97- 02- 96- 91-

8 3 9 14

4 Couple living with their joint child and her child from a previous relationship. The other spouses of the partners are shown smaller and lower on either side of the present household, indicated by a dotted line.

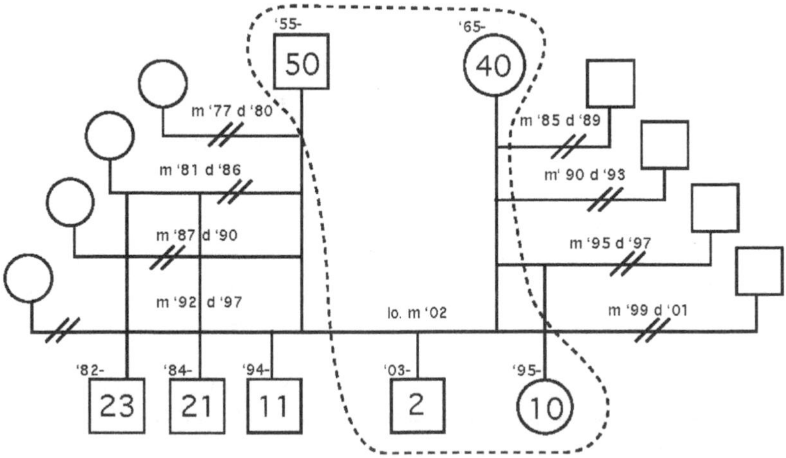

'55- 50 '65- 40

m '77 d '80 m '85 d '89

m '81 d '86 m' 90 d '93

m '87 d '90 m '95 d '97

m '92 d '97 lo. m '02 m '99 d '01

'82- '84- '94- '03- '95-

23 21 11 2 10

Genograms make it easier for us to keep in mind the complexity of a family's context, including family history, patterns, and events that may have ongoing significance for patient care. Just as our spoken language potentiates and organizes our thought processes, genograms, which map relationships and patterns of family functioning, help clinicians think systemically about how events and relationships in their clients' lives are related to patterns of health and illness.

Gathering genogram information should be an integral part of any comprehensive, clinical assessment, if only to know who is in the family and what are the facts of their current situation and history. The genogram is primarily an interpretive tool that enables the clinician to generate tentative hypotheses for further evaluation in a family assessment. It cannot be used in a cookbook fashion to make clinical predictions. But it can sensitize the clinician to systemic issues, which are relevant to current dysfunction and to sources of resilience.

Scanning the breadth of the current family context allows the clinician to assess the connectedness of the immediate members of the family to each other, as well as to the broader system—the extended family, friends, community, society and culture, and to evaluate the family's strengths and vulnerabilities in relation to the overall situation. Consequently, we include on the genogram the immediate and extended family members, as well as significant non-blood "kin" who have ever lived with or played a major role in the family's life. We also note relevant events (moves, life cycle changes) and problems (illness, dysfunction). Current behavior and problems of family members can be traced on the genogram from multiple perspectives. The index person (the "I.P." or person with the problem or symptom) may be viewed in the context of various subsystems, such as siblings, triangles, and reciprocal relationships, or in relation to the broader community, social institutions (schools, courts, etc.), and socio-cultural context.

Genograms "let the calendar speak" by suggesting possible connections between family events over time. Patterns of previous illness and earlier shifts in family relationships brought about through loss and other critical life changes, which alter in family structure and other patterns can easily be noted on the genogram.

Computerized genograms will soon enable us to explore specific family patterns and symptom constellations, which provide a framework for hypothesizing about what may be currently influencing a crisis in a particular family. In conjunction with genograms, we usually include a family chronology, which depicts the family history in chronological order. A computerized program for gathering and mapping genogram information with a database will in the future make it a lot easier for the clinician to track family history, because a chronology will be able to show events for any particular moment in the family's history.

Genograms need to show not just the biological and legal members of a family, but also the network of friends and community essential for understanding the family. This includes current relationships, but also the relationships that came before and live in the person's heart, giving hope and inspiration in times of distress. It is also important to show the context around the biological and legal family in order to understand a family in context. Such people include those who live in one's heart, some long dead, and some in daily life, who could offer a loan, help your husband or children out, or give you strength and courage, if you are in a crisis. It is this kinship network, not just the biological relatives, and not just those who are alive now, who would be relevant to know about if you want to understand clients or access their resources. Such genograms are important to illustrate in greater depth the context around the immediate family.

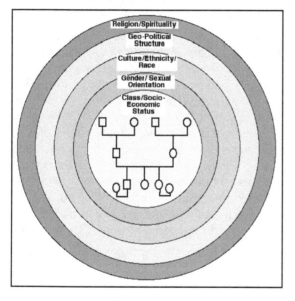

Family history always evolves in the context of larger societal structures: cultural, political, religious, spiritual, socio-economic class, gender, racial and ethnic structures, which organize each member of a society into a particular social location.

It is important always to think of the genogram in its broader context. At times we actually define the resources and institutions of the community to highlight families' access or lack of access to community resources (which can be noted around the genogram).

Many have been attempting to expand genograms to take these larger social structures into account in understanding genogram patterns.

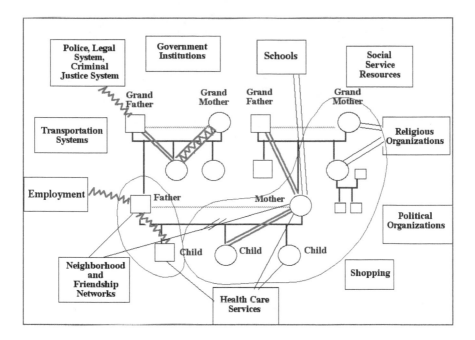

We look forward to the continued evolution of genograms to enable us to better illustrate the larger cultural levels along with the specific individual and kinship dimensions of family patterns.

References

Barker, R. L. (2013). *The social work dictionary* (6th ed.). Washington, DC: NASW Press.

Conference of Intellectuals from Africa and and Diaspora (CIAD) (1981, June). *African Charter on Human and Peoples' Rights*. Accessed at http://www.hrcr.org/docs/Banjul/afrhr.html.

CRE (2015). Conflict Resolution Education Connection http://www.creducation.org/resources/nonverbal_communication/proxemics.html

Dewane, C. (2006). Use of self: A primer revisited. *Clinical Social Work Journal, 34*(3), 543–558.

Eroles, C. (1997). *Los derechos humanos: Compromiso ético del trabajo social* [*Human rights: An ethical imperative for social work*]. Buenos Aires: Espacio Editorial.

Goldstein, S. R., & Bebe, L. (2010). National Association of Social Workers. In R. Edwards (Ed.), *Encyclopedia of social work* (19th ed., vol. 2, pp. 1747–1764). Washington, DC: NASW Press.

Honey, P., & Mumford, A. (2000). *The learning styles helper's guide*. London, UK: Peter Honey Publications Ltd.

Kadushin, A., & Harkness, D. (2014) Supervision in Social Work (5th ed.). New York NY: Columbia University Press.

Kolb, D. A. (1983). *Experiential learning: Experience as the source of learning and development*. Upper Saddle River, NJ: Prentice Hall.

Luft, J. (1970). *Group process: An introduction to group dynamics* (2nd ed.). New York: Harper and Row.

Malott, K. M, Paone, T. R., Schaefle, S., & Gao, J. (in press). Is it racist? Addressing racial microaggressions in counselor education. *Journal for Creativity in Mental Health*.

Maslow, A. (1970). *Motivation and personality* (2nd ed.). New York: NY: Harper and Row.

McGoldrich, M. (2012). Genogram how-to. The Multicultural Family Institute. Accessed at http://multiculturalfamily.org/publications/genogram-life-stories/genogram-how-to-pdf/.

Myers-Briggs, I. (1995). *Gifts differing: Understanding personality type*. Mountain View, CA: Davies Black.

National Association of Social Workers. (2013). *Guidelines for social worker safety in the workplace*. Accessed at https://www.socialworkers.org/practice/nasw standards/safetystandards2013.pdf.

North Carolina Division of Social Services. (1998). A look at safety in social work. *Children's Services Practice Notes, 3*(2). Accessed at http://www.practicenotes .org/vol3_no2.htm.

Sánchez, M. D. (1989). Trabajo social en derechos humanos: Reencuentro con la profesión [Social Work in human rights. A reunión with the profesión]. In Colectivo de Trabajo Social (Ed.), *Trabajo social y derechos humanos: Compromiso con la dignidad—la experiencia chilena* [*Social work and human rights: A commitment with dignity—the Chilean experience*] (pp. 17–30). Buenos Aires: Editorial Humanitas.

Snow, K. (2008). To ensure inclusion, freedom, and respect for all, it's time to embrace people first language. Disability Is Natural. Accessed at http://www .disabilityisnatural.com/images/PDF/pfl09.pdf.

United Nations. (1997). International Covenant on Civil and Political Rights. Accessed at http://www.hrweb.org/legal/cpr.html.

US Department of Labor. (2004). *Guidelines for preventing workplace violence for health care and social service workers*. OSHA 3148-01R. Washington, DC: Author.

Winston, C., & LeCroy, E. S. (2004). Public perception of social work: Is it what we think it is? *Social Work, 49*, 164–174.

Wodarski, J. S., Rapp-Paglicci, L. A., Dulmus, C. N., & Jongsma, A. E. (2000). *The social work and human services treatment planner*. New York: Wiley.

Index